Habits of the
High-Tech Heart

Habits of the High-Tech Heart

Living Virtuously in the Information Age

Quentin J. Schultze

Foreword by Jean Bethke Elshtain

 Baker Academic

A Division of Baker Book House Co
Grand Rapids, Michigan 49516

Published by Baker Academic
a division of Baker Book House Company
P.O. Box 6287, Grand Rapids, MI 49516-6287

Printed in the United States of America

Library of Congress Cataloging-in-Publication Data

Schultze, Quentin J. (Quentin James), 1952–
    Habits of the high-tech heart : living virtuously in the information age / Quentin J. Schultze.
        p.   cm.
    Includes bibliographical references and index.
    ISBN 0-8010-2322-X (cloth)
    1. Technology—Religious aspects—Christianity. 2. Computers—Religious aspects—Christianity. 3. Religion and science. I. Title.
    BR115.T42.S34 2002
    241′.65—dc21   2002016392

Unless otherwise indicated, Scripture quotations are from the HOLY BIBLE, NEW INTERNATIONAL VERSION®. NIV®. Copyright © 1973, 1978, 1984 by International Bible Society. Used by permission of Zondervan Publishing House. All rights reserved.

Scripture quotations identified *The Message* are from THE MESSAGE. Copyright © by Eugene H. Peterson 1993, 1994, 1995. Used by permission of NavPress Publishing Group.

For information about Baker Academic, visit our web site:
www.bakeracademic.com

To
Stephen and Bethany

Contents

Foreword

■ We live in parlous times. Before the terrorist attacks of September 11, 2001, we were told repeatedly that a glorious new age of technological advance and discovery lay before us. I recall vividly participating in a discussion on the *Lehrer News Hour* on public television with a gentleman who had made his millions in a dot-com start-up company. When I raised the matter of a growing gap between those who are full-fledged members of the cyber-revolution and those who are being left behind—as people are always left behind when new technologies take hold—his expression was one of bemusement and disdain. Clearly, I was a fuddy-duddy who wanted to stand in the way of unstoppable progress. Utopian rhetoric flowed like punch at a junior prom: The new technology would, within a short period of time, cure cancer, solve traffic jams, and usher in an era of world peace. The list seemed a bit odd, especially the world peace part. But, not to worry, the cyber-age enthusiast continued, for the elements were already there. People in the global village would be bound together by consumer products. Everybody wants brand names, and this loyalty to and enthusiasm for brand names would bind people together in a way that would trump such atavistic urges as nationalism.

Needless to say, I had the sensation of having fallen down Alice in Wonderland's rabbit hole and entered an eerie world absent of any solid human markers. The combination of libertarian individualism and the binding power of consumerism presupposes as a human subject a person who is the sum total of his or her voluntaristic choices. In this vision, we are not bound to one another in substantive and constitutive ways in families, churches, or polities. Quentin Schultze, in this lively, scholarly polemic—and polemic is not, for me, a dirty word—shows just how vacuous the techno-triumphalist worldview can be. Indeed, he notes, quoting David F. Noble, that we are in a world dominated by "the religion of technology." Technology has transmogrified from a tool we use to serve human needs and make possible human flourishing to "triumphalistic propaganda," in Schultze's words. The result, he argues compellingly, is that the "moral fabric of our lives" has begun to unravel. We have lost, or are in danger of losing, our moorings. These moorings derive from our creatureliness, from the fact that we move through the world in bodies. We begin as helpless and dependent infants. Most of us end our days dependent once more as our bodies weaken and finally fail us. We are both natals and mortals. But the religion of technology denies this, either implicitly by paying no mind to the human condition, or explicitly by talking of "immortalization." Immortalization, part of the religion of technology, holds that we are very close to finding ways to live forever. Living forever means that one's DNA goes on . . . and on . . . and on in a body of some sort.

Schultze understands that the deep question—Who are we?—turns on the ways in which we evaluate what we have become with reference to certain ethical commitments. Cyberculture disconnects us from human communities in a particular temporal location—sharing an actual physical space—even as it connects us in thin ways to strangers. These thin connections can be helpful if information is being shared, or human rights abuses reported, or medical technology being made available. But when the word *community* is used to describe what goes on in chat rooms, we realize, if we think about the matter at all, that the understanding of community is euphemistic in such a context. Real community means to be in relationship in the flesh or for that to be a possibility *in situ*. The advantage of cyber-community is that you can just log off if you don't want to deal with a member of your community anymore. Human relations take on a quality of temporariness and proceed on strictly cost-benefit lines.

Often it is said that our ethics has yet to catch up with our technologies and with new developments in many important areas, especially cybernetics and biological and genetic engineering. That isn't the problem at all. The problem is that we are not using the ethics we have, for we have largely abandoned those great traditions, including religious traditions, that once formed us by maintaining "transcendentally framed and morally directed ways of life," argues Schultze. Cultivating gratitude, responsibility, care, mutual accountability, and patience and alerting us to "our tomfoolery" has been the great task of our religious and moral traditions. There is no substitute—no counter tradition that does the same thing. In the world Schultze limns, "self-reported preferences" of sovereign subjects predominate. We do not want to be subject to anyone about anything. Citing Paul Virilio, Schultze calls this "techno-fundamentalism." The PR proclaims freedom and open-mindedness. The reality is an ideological straightjacket that manages to fend off challenges and grind everything down into manageable bits suited to a speeded-up and thinned-out culture.

Of course, Schultze will be taxed with alarmism and overstating his case. Nearly everyone who moves beyond boosterism in this area is thus charged. But he means to shake us out of our lethargy; to recall us to something richer and deeper; to nurture a living dialogue that includes the remembered voices of the past, as urged on us by G. K. Chesterton. Responsible stewardship demands nothing less, and it is responsible stewardship alone that will determine whether the future is one in which we are all wired as millions of isolates or whether we are connected as creatures of the flesh who can be lifted up in spirit and nurtured in hope only through community. The "primordial questions" will not be gainsayed. Echoing Vàclav Havel, Schultze bids us ask ourselves, "Who are we? Why were we created? What is good and worthy of our attention? How shall we then live?" We are creatures whose very natures cluster around the modal point of such questions. The asking of them honors our Creator. Hopefully, the way we answer does too.

JEAN BETHKE ELSHTAIN

Preface

▪ The older I get, the more pleasure I find in simple things, such as walks with my wife and mealtime conversations with friends. But the hurried pace of contemporary life seems to work against my ability to nurture such pleasures. My Calvinistic outlook might exacerbate this problem; it drives me to work harder and accomplish more, while my human instincts increasingly tell me to slow down and enjoy the gift of life. I feel torn between progress and delight—as if the two are necessarily incompatible.

This book is partly a personal journey to find my way in an era when many human beings seem, like me, to have wandered off the trail that leads to what Socrates called the "good life." I enjoy the Internet and other communication and information technologies, but I must admit that they do not satisfy my need for moral coherence and spiritual direction. If anything, such machines seem to divert my attention from the central concerns of life—such as love, gratitude, and responsibility—to relatively trivial pursuits with little enduring value. Moreover, as I talk with colleagues, students, relatives, and neighbors, I find that they generally feel a similar tyranny of the informationally urgent. My own uneasiness about the information age seems to reflect a widespread disquiet about the technologizing of everyday life.

I am sure that some readers of this book will label me a modern-day Luddite, since such stereotyping is the easiest way of dismissing anyone who expresses concerns about the information age. But I hope that the careful reader will recognize instead that I am trying to reclaim a sense of moral proportion amidst informational overindulgence. My goal is not so much to discard database and messaging technologies as much as to adapt them to venerable ways of life anchored in age-old virtues. Our search for the good life invariably will lead us to be critical of some of our communication habits and informational practices. History shows that every technological advance also delivers us to new moral quandaries. If we do not address such moral dilemmas, we will lose our capacity to act responsibly. We will wrongly let instrumental practices unravel the moral fabric of our lives. The habits of our hearts will become high-tech instead of virtuous.

My argument rests on the observations of many people who have preceded me on the journey. Readers will see how indebted I am to the writings of wise people from this and other ages: Alexis de Tocqueville, Václav Havel, Eugene H. Peterson, James W. Carey, James M. Houston, Jacques Ellul, and many others. At times I wonder if I am saying anything new. Then again, the past often is the finest source of insight.

For the journey that ensues in this book, I owe a debt of gratitude to the Louisville Institute and its supporting institution, the Lilly Endowment. The Institute sponsored two "conversations" with groups of scholars whose insights helped me formulate some of the ideas in this book. Moreover, a grant from the Institute made it possible for me to give the manuscript the attention it needed during the fall of 2001. David Wood, former associate director of the Institute, was particularly supportive.

Robert N. Hosack and Melinda Van Engen of Baker Book House were joys to work with even as deadlines loomed. I thank both of them for their good advice and gracious help.

My journey in these pages was possible also because of the kindness of many friends and colleagues who were willing to listen to my ideas, encourage me, and save me from my own foolishness. I especially wish to thank David Lyon, Richard Mouw, John Verbrugge, Neal Plantinga, Cliff Christians, Helen Sterk, Mark Fackler, and Randy Bytwerk for their charitable reviews of all or parts of the manuscript.

Four former students at Calvin College were among the best critics of the manuscript: Nathan Bierma, Sara Jane Toering, Lise Evans, and Stacey Wieland. They prove that Calvin's undergraduates are scholars in their own right. Stacey's research abilities, organizational acumen, and editorial insights helped me significantly. I extend to her special appreciation.

As always, my family has been a tremendous source of love and encouragement. Barbara is a friend beyond normal goodness; she proves Tocqueville's argument in *Democracy in America* that women are particularly attuned to the habits of the heart. Our children, Bethany and Stephen, journeyed into adulthood as this book took final shape. They demonstrated to Barbara and me that by grace virtue can blossom across the generations even in a high-tech age. For that we are both eternally grateful. I dedicate this book to these offspring in the hope that they will remember, long after their parents have departed this life, that the past holds the wisdom that can inform the future.

Identifying
Our Techno-Moral Crisis

Danny Hillis, a renowned designer of computer architecture, in the late 1990s sensed a problem with high-tech life:

> In some sense, we've
> run out of our story, which
> we were operating on, which
> was the story of power taking over nature—it's not
> that we've finished that, but we've gotten ahead of ourselves, and
> we don't know what
> the next story is after that.[1]

His solution was remarkably low-tech—a monumental mechanical clock that would continue ticking from January 1, 2001, through the year 12,000. He hoped that by taking the clock seriously, people in Silicon Valley and beyond would stop thinking so much about short-term interests and would focus instead on long-term human needs.[2] In spite of Hillis's high-tech expertise, his planned clock was mechanical, not digital. By calling our attention to an older tool, he hoped to interest us in the future of humanity. Maybe people would create a better story of real progress for coming generations.

Hillis's criticism of Silicon Valley's short-term horizon is a far cry from the optimism of today. We prefer a more sanguine tale of technological innovation and social progress. We desire to believe in a promising high-tech future, not an old-fashioned mechanical past. So we listen hopefully to futurists such as Nat Goldhaber, who tells us that the "Internet largely has released us from the tyranny of space and time."[3] We can already exchange information "at enormous speed and almost infinite scale," trumpets George Gilder. "When anyone can transmit any amount of information, any picture, any experience, any opportunity

15

to anyone or everyone," he rhapsodizes, the "resulting information becomes a transfiguration. The powers it offers bring us back to the paradigms of paradise and its perils, prophets and their nemeses: infinite abundance and demonic scarcities."[4] Amen!?

This kind of utopian rhetoric about the cyber-revolution seductively reformulates age-old human dreams to build heaven on earth. For centuries people have equated the work of engineers, explorers, and inventors with the actions of God—a recurring theme that David F. Noble dubs the "religion of technology."[5] People have long dreamed of communication technologies that will grant humans greater freedom, more power, and everlasting peace. Still enchanted by such rhetoric, we continue to label even incremental innovations as "revolutionary."[6]

A few people criticize the utopian rhetoric, citing concerns about information overload, technological anxiety, cultural upheaval, and moral decline.[7] Sven Birkerts in *The Gutenberg Elegies* says that we now face an "argument between technology and soul." He wonders, "Do people understand there might be consequences, possibly dire, to our embrace of these technologies, and that the myth of the Faustian bargain has not become irrelevant just because we studied it in school?"[8] Most of the cyber-elite (sometimes called the *digerati*) too quickly dismiss such legitimate concerns about our high-tech future.

The idea that we are witnessing the emergence of a beneficent information society is triumphalistic propaganda. The information-oriented convergence of telecommunications and computers is grounded in old-style industrial capitalism and shaped by the foibles of human nature. Although we are witnessing an explosion in the number of people who work with computerized information rather than with physical products, information technology's infrastructure rests on little more than dynamic market economies. Although cyber-technologies may appear to function in a wholly revolutionary manner, they have quickly become another means of expanding industrial capitalism and consumerism around the world.

This book addresses some of the deepest reservations that we should have about the impact of information technologies on the moral fabric of our lives. I use the term "information technology" to refer to all computer-based technologies that enable people to collect, store, access, and exchange information of any kind, including personal messages communicated via the Internet. Admittedly, cyber-technologies can help us accomplish a wide range of tasks in our personal lives as well as in business, science, education, and government. There is much worth celebrating, from the joys of emailing friends to the Web sites that publish up-to-date information about medical treatments. Nevertheless, our tendency to adopt every new information technology uncritically—without discerning the options, setting appropriate limits, and establishing humane practices—is simply irresponsible. North Americans are largely unreflective, voracious consumers of cyber-novelty and informational trivia. We have naively convinced ourselves that cyber-innovations will automatically improve society and make us better people, regardless of how we use them. The benefits of information technologies depend on how responsibly we understand, develop, and employ them in the service of venerable notions of the meaning and purpose of life.

Two writers have particularly shaped my thoughts on the crucial need for moral vision in technological societies: nineteenth-century Frenchman Alexis de Tocqueville and contemporary Czech Republic president and playwright Václav Havel. Both have articulated moral responsibility as a prerequisite to democratic life. Unless we cultivate virtuous character with as much energy and enthusiasm as we pursue cyber-technologies, our technological mindedness and habits will further unravel the moral fabric of society. Moreover, our concept of virtuous character must be tied to a coherent notion of the "good life" rather than merely the efficient, effective, or successful life. In their own ways, Tocqueville and Havel have addressed age-old concerns about virtue that we need to revisit in the information age.

When Tocqueville visited the United States in the 1830s, he wondered how a representative form of political governance could survive among purely self-interested individuals. Tocqueville discovered that Americans' individual self-interests are leavened morally by "habits of the heart."[9] In his view, these social mores emerge from Americans' commitments to each other and to the general public good. He concluded that voluntary religious associations, in particular, cultivate moral sentiments that soften self-interest, with an overarching commitment to the common good.[10]

Without such habits of the heart today, we will face growing moral confusion in the midst of our informational wealth. A former Internet company CEO says, "Nobody knows what's going on. The technology people don't know. The content people don't know. The money people don't know. Whatever we agree on today will be disputed tomorrow. Whoever is leading today . . . will be adrift or transformed some number of months from now. Whoever screws with you will get screwed with, too. It's a kind of anarchy. A strangely level playing field. The Wild West."[11] J. Budziszewski appropriately calls this kind of thinking "the religion of radical selfism."[12]

Havel similarly reflected on the responsibilities that accompany democratic freedoms in technological societies. Imprisoned in 1979 in his native land by the Soviet-controlled regime, Havel authored a series of philosophical letters to his wife. Later published as *Letters to Olga*, these writings address the crucial significance of personal and collective responsibility in maintaining democratic freedoms amidst increasingly technological and bureaucratic social institutions. Havel recognized that the enemies of democracy today include not just oppressive political regimes but also an uncritical faith in technology.

Our uses of information technologies should be guided primarily by moral responsibilities, not by empty rhetoric about "a computer in every classroom" or "digital democracy." Perhaps the most important question should be whether our cyber-practices are making us better persons and our society more civil and democratic. Given what is now occurring in cyberspace—dishonesty, incivility, immorality, and foolishness of all kinds—such progress is more hope than reality.

Although information technologies increase our capacity for acquiring and disseminating information, the resulting informational practices actually foster individualism and self-interest over community and responsibility. Information technologies are not just tools but also value-laden techniques that we rely on increasingly to organize and understand nearly every aspect of our lives. As Jacques Ellul argues, this technological-mindedness is essentially a faith in *la technique,* the means of efficiency and control.[13] The cover of *Business Week* shouts in large type, "The Infotech 100: Efficiency Rules! Who's Got It. Who's Selling It."[14] Today, we increasingly assume that doing things quickly and effectively is more important than doing them carefully, thoughtfully, and ethically. As a result, much of our daily communication slips into *junk messaging*—the informational equivalent of junk food. While we gain access to more information and speedier means of messaging, we also weaken the kinds of shared practices, such as neighborliness and hospitality, that we need to maintain our moral bearings. Our manner of informational living deflates our moral character.

Today, the markets for computerized information are creating what I call *cyberculture:* the technique-laden values, practices, and beliefs of people who spend a great deal of time in cyberspace and who perceive themselves as informationally well connected. Cyberculture fosters information-intensive, technique-oriented habits—from emailing to online researching—that rely on the speed and pervasiveness of information technologies. As cyberculture extends to nonprofessional computer users, it socializes them in technological values. Although the vast majority of people in the world lack access to computers, let alone to the Internet, information-rich elites and experts assume on behalf of others that efficiency and control are inherently good values that will necessarily improve society, enrich private lives, and empower individuals. They assume that a faith in technique is good, progressive, and beneficial for all.

In the cyber-age, we become so enamored with our technical skill at manipulating information that we can lose track of noninstrumental virtues such as moderation, discernment, and humility. We transform the means of technique into the ends of our ever greater efficiency and control. We also naively believe that for most personal and social needs there must be largely technological solutions, such as Web filtering software designed to protect children from cyber-pornographers. Hillis, who also founded the company Thinking Machines and advises the Disney Corporation, says, "So far we have used computers to do things we used to do before, like text editing." He insists that we are just beginning "to change the *kinds* of things we do because of computers." This "real revolution will be much more interesting. It's going to be a mass market; it's going to be a lot about entertainment; it's going to be a lot about education; it's going to be a lot about kids, because kids are the only ones flexible enough to understand this whole new medium." Hillis concludes that for children the new computer world is "not even a force of change; it's a part of their world, like cars."[15] Hillis's rhetoric, like that of many cyber-gurus, creates the impression that computers will fundamentally improve our lives.

We can discover our growing technological-mindedness in the mechanistic language we employ to understand who we are, how we should act, and what kinds of persons we should be. We replace humane, morally informed words such as "wisdom," "person," and "justice" with technical terms such as "information," "user," and "access." At the sentencing of his mother for killing his father, a son told his mother before the court, "Delete. Delete. Consider yourself deleted from our lives."[16] Half of the new words added to the 2001 edition of the *Random House Webster's College Dictionary* came from technology.[17] Our informational jargon implicitly values individuals, organizations, and even entire societies in terms of their ability to distribute messages, control audiences, and reap profits. In the process, our technological-mindedness can supplant noninstrumental practices such as friendship and neighborliness. Unless we focus as much on the quality of our character as we do on technological innovation, potentially good informational techniques will ultimately reduce our capacity to love one another.

We ought to face the fact that our cyber-innovations today are running far ahead of our moral sensibilities. As masters of technique, we imagine quick, efficient solutions to all individual and social problems. We assume that all we need is more technology, such as access to larger databases and greater messaging capacity. But if we examine the degree of immorality and incivility online, we cannot help but see the folly of our cyber-hopes. Hailed by some as "the largest functioning anarchy in the history of the world," the Internet seems to serve for many people

as a "place" to be foolish.[18] "All the celebrated technological achievements of progress," warned Aleksandr I. Solzhenitsyn, "do not redeem
the twentieth century's moral poverty."[19] As the century passed, cyberspace proved Solzhenitsyn's point.

The context for moral decline has included the "militarization" of
cyber-technologies, a reduction in governmental regulation of communication technologies, a remarkable expansion in economic freedom
and property rights, and the resulting increase in global trade and private investment.[20] Capital markets and technological innovations have
advanced synergistically, with little respect for religious or other cultural traditions.[21] Instead of intentionally embedding cyber-technology
within existing cultures, we let cyber-technology shape our ways of life.[22]
Open markets are now spreading information technology so quickly that
cultures have little time to assess it critically, let alone to adopt or reject
it wisely. Information technology—including both computing and
telecommunications—is already the largest industry in the United
States.[23] When Time-Warner merged with AOL, the writing was on the
wall: Cyberspace became the domain of corporate empires that are not
particularly interested in serving cultures as much as capturing larger
markets. Meanwhile, governments are trying unsuccessfully to regulate
new technologies that are changing faster than bureaucratic legislators
can possibly keep up with. The hectic pace of high-tech innovation often
results in de facto public policies that do little more than legitimate the
evolving technological status quo.[24] Amidst all of these changes we
should remind ourselves that the actions of people in cyberspace are
best regulated by "extra-market values," which Tocqueville called "habits
of the heart."[25]

In short, we are sharpening our informational practices while dulling
the habits of our hearts. Although better government regulation is in
order in some cases, information technologies are not particularly reg-
ulatable because they extend across different jurisdictions. Just as critical as public regulation of information technologies today is more virtuous use—both by individuals and communities. Cyberculture's underlying
libertinism, which celebrates technique and promotes strident individualism, affords little respect for moral order. Langdon Winner calls this
"cyberlibertarianism" a "collection of ideas that links enthusiasm for electronically mediated forms of living with radical, right wing libertarian
ideas about the proper definition of freedom, social life, economics, and
politics in the years to come."[26] The Internet, in particular, has become
a portal to evil where many people learn that incivility is fun, crudeness
is a game, and the individual alone should be the only arbiter of truth
and justice. As cyberspace detaches information and messaging from

moral responsibility, it becomes an open market with few overarching habits of the heart to leaven libertinism.

Of course, dismantling all information technologies is not a realistic or even a good solution. Wholesale destruction is both impractical and rash—a quick-fix technique with no lasting value. Instead, we have to give as much attention to the habits of our hearts as we do to our cyber-endeavors. We need to understand information technologies in the light of the virtues nurtured historically within religious traditions. Revealed religions, such as the Hebrew and Christian traditions, are rich sources of moral wisdom that can virtuously shape our informational practices.

Unfortunately, today we listen to the messages of the day and barely turn an ear to voices of moral wisdom. As members of the information society, we are so concerned with divining the near future that we lose some of our historical grounding in moral ways of understanding. We even forget that religious traditions, in spite of their own moral lapses, can cultivate virtuous thought and action. Developing cyberspace without also nurturing virtuous character is a recipe for cultural and social chaos, as we are now discovering in the immoral muck on the Internet. In a sense, we need to look back and listen carefully before we can wisely step forward and act responsibly. If we do not take virtue seriously, the information explosion will become a plague of *misinformation*—endless volleys of nonsense, folly, and rumor masquerading as knowledge, wisdom, and even truth.

In a speech he gave at the 1992 World Economic Forum in Switzerland, Havel said, "We have to abandon the arrogant belief that the world is merely a puzzle to be solved, a machine with instructions for use waiting to be discovered, a body of information to be fed into a computer in the hope that sooner or later it will spit out a universal solution." Instead, he continued, "we have to release from the sphere of private whim and rejuvenate such forces as a natural, unique, and unrepeatable experience of the world, an elementary sense of justice, the ability to see things as others do, a sense of transcendental responsibility, archetypal wisdom, good taste, courage, compassion, and faith in the importance of particular measures that do not aspire to be a universal, thus an objective or technical, key to salvation."[27] To that I am willing to say amen.

Finding a virtuous path through the information age begins when we *discern* our present moral condition. Chapter 1 critiques the quasi-religious philosophy of *informationism:* a "faith" in the collection and dissemination of information as a route to social progress and personal happiness. Informationism derails any quest for moral wisdom by emphasizing the *is* over the *ought, observation* over *intimacy*, and *measurement* over *meaning*. If the information society is to be a source of human progress, we must be able to discriminate between information and wisdom, and between instrumental skill and virtue. We think we are getting smarter as we cleverly compile information into expanding databases, while we are actually knowing the world ever more superficially. Real knowing requires intimate knowledge, whereas informationism engenders what I call *promiscuous knowing*. Online day traders, for instance, buy and sell equities based on market momentum and the faddishness of economic sectors, not on a knowledge of companies and the economy.

Chapter 2 argues for *moderation* in the growing tide of incoherent and trivial information that renders our lives morally superficial. The quest for "unlimited bandwidth"—faster and faster information delivery systems—is not so much a means to virtue as a route to greater noise and distraction. Expanding the scope and increasing the speed of digital messaging will not themselves equip us with moral bearings. Even if everyone on earth had a personal Web site and all citizens were granted unlimited email rights, we would probably not communicate with each other any more charitably, carefully, and respectfully. Our desire for more and more information technology is an unvirtuous lust for messaging power—a kind of *bandwidth envy*.

Chapter 3 considers the importance of *wisdom* for revitalizing our habits of the heart. Moral wisdom, in particular, helps us to act rightly, with prudence and good judgment, rather than merely efficiently and effectively. We gain such wisdom primarily by listening to and communicating with *religious traditions*, which maintain transcendentally framed and morally directed ways of life. In the information age, however, everyone wants to chatter; few of us sincerely aspire to become good listeners. If we listen to the Hebrew and Christian traditions, we hear primarily two messages that point us to virtuous living: *gratitude* for creation and *responsibility* to care for this inheritance. These traditions locate us in a meaningful cosmic story, or "metanarrative," that transcends informational noise and technological change. They also foster virtue by nurturing the wisdom of *shared memory, caring practices,* and *mutual accountability*.

Chapter 4 discusses the importance of *humility* in our informational endeavors. Without humility, we foolishly put too much hope in the power of technique to solve practically every human problem. Havel warns that pride "will lead the world to hell."[28] We ought to accept humbly our responsibility for the world. Humility helps us to maintain a healthy skepticism about experts who foolishly claim that information technology will eliminate the gap between the way things are in the world and the way they should be. Humility naturally leads us to laugh at ourselves and at the entire human race as foolish people who somehow survive their own cyber-folly. Humor, in particular, can *give us a proper sense of proportion, reveal our tomfoolery,* and *cultivate much-needed patience.* Cyberculture without humor is cold, calculating, and crude. Just ask Dilbert.

Chapter 5 suggests that cyber-communication desperately needs greater *authenticity.* The Internet has become another means for individuals and organizations to communicate disingenuously, as if they have no mutual obligations and shared responsibilities. In the information society, people selfishly fabricate both online and offline personas. The same freedom makes it easier for hucksters and spin artists to contort our perceptions of reality. Cyberspace ushers in a new wave of professional *symbol brokers* who now have additional messaging technologies for creating public personas and persuading audiences. In a digital world, we desperately need to live authentically—to say what we mean and to mean what we say—and to hold our public and private institutions accountable for doing the same. Authenticity depends on *truthfulness, empathy,* and *integrity.*

Chapter 6 argues that cyberculture needs a *cosmic diversity* that includes shared moral concerns, not just technical expertise or celebrity status. Cyberculture claims to be cosmopolitan and open-minded, when it is really parochial and easily co-opted by special interests. The rise of information technologies deepens our reliance on media celebrities— such as news pundits and talk show hosts—and even creates new ones, including touted Internet columnists, celebrated technology book authors, and heralded convention speakers. Moreover, cyberculture elevates the social status and authority of information workers who are proficient with information technologies. In order to be truly diverse, cyberculture must open its doors to the margins of high-tech society, where noninstrumental habits of the heart still thrive. Otherwise technocrats and their bankers and promoters will eventually manage the information society with cold efficiency.

Chapter 7 maintains that each of the six habits of the heart discussed in earlier chapters—discernment, moderation, wisdom, humility, authenticity, and diversity—require *organic community life.* In spite of all the rhetoric about cyberspace creating new and better communities, online communities are typically little more than interest groups, demographic colonies, or what historian Daniel J. Boorstin calls "consumption communities."[29] Real community is marked by lay participation over expert control, geographic proximity instead of disembodied messaging, open dialogue rather than one-way messaging, neighborliness above bureaucratic authority, and cross-generational continuity instead of intra-generational myopia. More than anything else, community is the chief means by which we undertake the public responsibilities that emanate from shared habits of the heart. Communities should be places where we seek the common good even while respecting our individual and tribal differences.

The concluding chapter suggests six callings for people who seek to live by habits of the heart in the information age. After *admitting the "lightness" of our digital being*—its cosmic and moral shallowness—we should *distrust the prevailing techno-magic* that promises us inflated benefits from our use of cyber-technologies. We also need continually to *de-technologize our religious traditions* by ridding them of excessive technique and renewing their virtue-nurturing practices. Gratefully recognizing our inheritance of the created world, we should *responsibly serve* God and our neighbors. *Inviting friendship* is one of the most natural ways of building moral relationships with others. Finally, we should *sojourn with heart* through life, using information technologies as virtuously as possible.

To be virtuous people in a high-tech world is to be neither moralists nor pragmatists but rather *sojourners* who humbly seek goodness in an eternal adventure that began before we were born and will continue after we die. As sojourners, we realize that this world is not our final destination but only one leg of a journey whose outcome we can neither fully control nor completely envision. We also admit that we must do all we humanly can to avoid folly along the way. Hillis traveled this path when he recognized the moral poverty in our short-term thinking and inflated tales of cyber-progress. He cared for his neighbor and thereby accepted obligations that are deeply historical and inherently moral and that reverberate to the heart of our humanness. When we take this sojourn together, we renew the habits of the heart for future generations.

chapter one

Discerning
Our Informationism

■ In 1978, Aleksandr I. Solzhenitsyn delivered the 327th commencement address at Harvard University. Titled "A World Split Apart," his speech focused on the growing moral vacuum in Western civilization. In spite of our "abundance of information, or maybe partly because of it," he said, "the West has great difficulty in finding its bearings amid contemporary events." The rising racket of information repeatedly breaks our concentration. We claim to be truth seekers, he argued, but instead we follow simplistic "formulas." We wrongly assume that the overall condition of the world is improving because of our wealth of technology and information. We forget that "truth seldom is sweet; it is almost invariably bitter."[1]

Although we celebrate the arrival of the information society, we have not fully faced its implications. Along with information come misinformation and disinformation. Rumor and hearsay abound. Opinions fly through digital networks. Deceitful persons and institutions spread half-truths. While we understandably revel in the apparent power of information technologies to collect and disseminate information, we also ought to question the quality of such information. Does it help us to grasp the condition of our personal lives and social institutions? Is it trivial or significant, helpful or harmful, relevant or meaningless? How can we discern the real value of the growing caches of database information culled by specialists, collated and analyzed via computers, and distributed through high-speed networks?

The plethora of available information makes us ever more dependent on experts who supposedly can interpret it for us. We need help, so we

25

turn to popular guides for "dummies" and "idiots." Bookstores are selling millions of books designed to give laypersons a modicum of insight into professions, technical skills, avocations, history, and even religion and sexuality. Two publishers have released over one thousand titles for dummies and idiots. Such volumes are popular, suggests the author of *Philosophy for Dummies*, because people "have less access to the experts, who are locked up on college campuses."[2] Maybe so, but perhaps we are so overwhelmed by information and so underwhelmed by our own knowledge that we all feel like insecure dummies. "We all have bits of the 'idiot' in us," says the author of *The Complete Idiot's Guide to Self Esteem*.[3] To overcome our insecurities, we reach for information produced by apparent non-dummies. Adrift in a sea of information, yet hoping to arrive safely on the shore of success, we paddle around using the techniques outlined in self-help books.

Living in the age of cyberspace, we have faith in the processes of collecting and distributing information. Words such as "data," "knowledge," and "information" connote social progress and personal enlightenment. We revere technologies such as computers and the World Wide Web that will supposedly transform data into information and information into knowledge. Mary E. Boone argues that the computer "may enable the next big leap in the evolution of human intellect" and "dramatically extend the memory of our species and our ability to work with ideas." She calls computers "supplements of the mind."[4] Everywhere we look, in news reports and public television documentaries, experts are extolling the benefits of information technologies for social progress.

We are succumbing to *informationism:* a non-discerning, vacuous faith in the collection and dissemination of information as a route to social progress and personal happiness.[5] We are particularly hopeful that more efficient and powerful messaging systems will improve the quality of our lives. As presently constituted, however, information technologies limit our abilities to perceive our moral condition and dampen our capacity to be virtuous people. In a society steeped in informationism, disciplined human activities that require time, patience, and perseverance are anathema. Self-help solutions, themselves usually technological practices, replace moral disciplines. Instrumental habits—practices that might be efficient and effective but are not necessarily good—eclipse virtuous practices. Acting like machines rather than humans, we do what is immediately convenient and efficacious, not necessarily what is right and good. The exigencies of technique tend to override our ability to employ other means and to seek truly good ends. As a quasi-religion, informationism preaches the *is* over the *ought*, *observation* over *intimacy*, and *measurement* over *meaning*.

The first section of this chapter explores informationism's emphasis on the *is* over the *ought*. Informationism places the highest value on contemporary culture, current events, and immediate action. In cyberculture, we are increasingly obsessed with documenting the present rather than understanding the human condition, particularly our moral situation. Uninterested in the hard work of nurturing virtuous character, we hope for technological solutions to our moral problems. We more or less accept our informational world the way it is and then proceed to make it even more that way.

The second section examines how our informational practices position us as *impersonal observers* of the world rather than *intimate participants* in the world. The glut of information at our disposal creates the illusion that we understand our predicament. We become promiscuous knowers, flitting from one bit of information to another, with no fidelity to an overarching worldview. In search of informational knowing, humans have long objectified knowledge and collected it in libraries, and now in databases. Ironically, as we gain more access to such objectified information, we lose our own capacity to know. We depend more and more on supposed experts to give us knowledge, while distrusting our own intimate connections to the world around us. Although we selfishly gain more knowledge *about* the world, we lose the more intimate knowledge *of* the world.[6] We become informational voyeurs of life rather than responsible participants in the knowing of our own cultures and communities. "Surfing" is an apt word for our condition because it connotes living on the surface of reality.

The third section discusses our high-tech penchant for *measurement* over *meaning*. Information technologies foster statistical ways of perceiving and systematic modes of imagining. Under their influence, we see the world in terms of cybernetic systems composed of measurable causes and effects. The resulting cyber-worldview is a closed system that elevates the value of control over moral responsibility. Manipulating information to cause particular "outcomes" becomes more important than being virtuous persons or contributing to a good society.

This chapter concludes with a brief critique of this quasi-religious informationism. Information technologies themselves will never enable us to become more responsible persons or communities. People are more than atoms in cyber-systems. Culture is more than a formal organization. And human action is intrinsically a matter of making moral as well as informational decisions. The more we imagine our lives and our societies as informational systems, the more likely it is that we will manipulate and control human beings as mere cogs in digital networks. Informationism lacks both the *means* to acquire moral wisdom and the good *ends* that should frame our desires. It is a morally bankrupt faith in our own ability to engineer the Promised Land.

Wallowing in the *Is* While Forgetting the *Ought*

During the height of the so-called New Economy craze in 1999, as media pundits declared greater efficiency and prosperity fueled by high-tech innovation, the *Wall Street Journal Interactive Edition* examined the charitable giving practices of Internet companies.[7] Given all the money being made in the stock market, one would have expected flurries of new philanthropy. Reporters discovered instead that high-tech firms were among the least likely to participate in philanthropic causes, and Internet companies were the worst of all. Amazon.com, with a market capitalization of $28 billion, contributed little to charitable causes. Yahoo! boasted a market capitalization of roughly $47 billion but indicated on its Web site that the company "does not provide cash grants or financial sponsorships."[8] Although those kinds of organizations were not interested in giving away money, their workers enjoyed spending it; nightlife thrived in high-tech areas.[9] One observer suggested that the young owners of Internet companies did not yet understand the value of investing in charities.[10] "You have a lot of young people making a lot of money who care more about themselves than helping others," explained one Internet CEO.[11] Maybe so, but such an explanation misses the broader ethos of cyberculture. High-tech endeavors are usually organized around short-term goals and immediate practical needs, such as achieving incremental product upgrades or securing the next round of investment capital. Cyberculture is so focused on the here and now that it implicitly rejects the human need for a long-term vision, let alone a moral compass. In this milieu, charitable causes simply are irrelevant.[12]

Lacking any clear "oughts," today's informationism is a religion of quick decisions and instant deletes. Acting like processors of information, we become info-religionists who carelessly transmit, receive, and discard torrents of messages with little reflection. As the list of new email messages comes up on our screens, we begin deleting the junk mail and typing telegraphic responses to worthy recipients. We live in the digital world of the now, instant everything. We seek immediate solutions to even moral crises, as if Web sites and email petitions can change the world. We fill our lives with temporary satisfactions, such as surfing the Web, watching DVDs, or chatting on a cell phone while driving a vehicle. Modern technologies provide us with a myriad of ways to "delete" the moral life by focusing only on immediate, instrumental activities.

Preoccupied with the present, informationism focuses on "what is" instead of "what ought to be." Cyberculture, for instance, obsessively documents current events, from business transactions and consumer profiles to personal schedules and news reports. Probably no culture has ever been more enchanted with its ability to collect and publish contemporaneous information, from the foods that Hollywood celebrities prefer to the sexual practices of politicians. Cyberculture also chases after the latest technological products, models, and upgrades—the endless whirlwind of test products and "beta" technologies that promise us immediate progress.

Ethics, the realm of moral obligations and standards of right conduct, enters cyberculture primarily through moralistic campaigns that faddishly capture the public imagination via news reports. We focus briefly on such things as ensuring credit card security for online purchases, protecting the privacy of children while they surf the Web, shielding private medical records from corporate databases, or improving the civility in online chat rooms. Terms such as "infogap," "technological poverty," and "digital divide" come and go in the news, championed by one or another consumer group or self-appointed watchdog association. High school shootings momentarily prompt the nation to examine the impact of violent video games on young people, but before long we are back to business as usual, producing promotional Web sites for violent movies based on the same video games.

Like ethical chameleons, we adapt our moral practices to the latest technologies rather than summoning our technologies to follow a long-term moral vision.[13] Our desire to become skillful technologists increasingly dictates our moral decisions. We rarely think about what it means to be good and wise people; instead, we focus on whether we are technically connected. We assume that by adopting novel technologies we can solve the moral problems created by earlier ones. Supposedly, encryption will ensure privacy. Web site "blocking" software at public libraries will protect children from access to adult materials online. Our romance with information technology leads us to assume that moral issues are best solved technologically.

This emphasis on the technological now is a recipe for cultural chaos as well as a license for self-interest. One-time Internet company CEO Michael Wolff describes the boom time of the World Wide Web as a frenzied era of moral confusion and nearly unbridled selfishness.[14] Caught in the escalating game of buying and selling unproven companies, many inventors, investors, and executives hoped eventually to make it big on public stock offerings. The frenzy of the moment overtook any reasonable standards of conduct. Billions of dollars changed hands, thanks to the machinery of Wall Street, the bravado of venture capitalists, the spreadsheets of creative accountants, and the elliptical tales of self-promotional CEOs. As Wolff recalls, dot-com wannabes were playing with abstract data and overblown financial predictions.[15] Hindsight now shows that dot-com mania swamped any long-term sense of moral responsibility.

Journalistic reporting is the primary mode of "knowing" in informationism. Information technologies are particularly efficient at collecting and disseminating current fads. Cyberspace makes it enormously easy and inexpensive to make and distribute endless copies of up-to-date documents. It also leads to dynamic online content that changes by the day, hour, and even minute. Cyberspace turns us all into reporters who daily compose telegraphic messages online for friends, relatives, and anonymous others. Instant messaging becomes a means of reporting to friends the minutiae of our lives.[16] Theodore Roszak argues that information itself has "taken on the quality of that impalpable, invisible, but plaudit-winning silk from which the emperor's ethereal gown was supposedly spun."[17] One result is a "Breaking News Syndrome" in which people become nervous and exhausted while chasing after the latest reports about current events.[18]

Informational reporting includes endless high-tech prognostications that entertain us in the present more than they illuminate the future. Late-breaking news stories about technological innovations sound like popular science fiction.[19] A flight magazine predicts that "shrinking technology promises mobile professionals the world at their fingertips."[20] It quotes experts who say that by 2010, 40 percent of teens will own always-on, wearable communications and computing technology. Dick Tracy meets Star Wars. Such pie-in-the-sky predictions are entertaining reports, not realistic assessments of our future. Furthermore, they offer no real solutions to our moral dilemmas of today or tomorrow. Will a fingertip-controlled world or a wearable computer bring us more peace and justice? Will they foster virtue at home and work?

Being up-to-date technologically symbolizes to us the likelihood of our future success. We assume that we must be plugged in, networked, subscribed, paged, and emailed. So we open the technological floodgates to the latest forms of instant communication. Even if we fail to master information technology, the sheer ownership of it becomes a self-help mechanism for improving our social status. Many people buy the latest equipment before its value is proven; they love being on the cutting edge before their friends are. But what is the real value of greater processing speed, a larger monitor, or expensive software with so many bells and whistles that we will rarely use, let alone master? Informationism thrives when our rhapsodies about the latest technologies give us the illusion of being informationally up-to-date, socially elevated, and professionally successful.

Yet in the wear and tear of consuming daily information, we find that it is increasingly difficult to know exactly whom to believe and which messages to value. As we follow the buzz of the latest popular culture, we have little time to think about the kinds of individuals that we are becoming, let alone the types of persons that we should be. James M. Houston writes, "We are living in a time of verbal explosion. We are deluged by words, in bulletins, in data collecting, in advertisements, in books, in the promises and slogans of politics, in the mishmash of news." But most of what we find in such chaotic messaging is "talk but not deeds, information but not insight, promises but not fulfillment, words not events."[21] Lacking an overarching sense of the meaning and purpose of life, informationism cannot meet our need for discernment. In David Gross's words, modern "life becomes increasingly vacuous, as entire populations become unable to discern what is valuable from what is valueless."[22] Locked into the informational "is," itself a simplistic version of current reality, we find it progressively more difficult to imagine any means to the "oughts" of virtuous character. Only the impressive jargon of technique—of greater informational efficiency and control—seems to offer hope. A moral endeavor such as philanthropic giving disappears from our informational radar.

Feigning Intimacy by Observing

Lorie Anderson and her husband had an idea for a Web site finely tuned to the needs of individuals in the information society: a host of multiple-choice "selectors" that would help people make quick decisions about even the most significant aspects of their lives.[23] The resulting Web venture, SelectSmart.com, makes decisions for people by analyzing their self-reported preferences. Selector Centers provide multiple-choice instruments for people to choose everything from a pet to a belief system. Need a faith? Fill in the multiple-choice answers to twenty religion-related questions and find out which religion suits you the best.[24] According to this technique for identifying the real-world analogue to one's personal faith, an individual does not need intimate knowledge of any belief system to have religious beliefs. Religion is merely a personal preference, like breakfast cereal or clothing.

As such superficial religiosity suggests, informationism emphasizes *observation* over *intimacy*. In spite of our optimism about information technologies, they do not always deepen our relationships with others. The more time and energy we spend using information technologies,

the less likely we are to know intimately the world around us. Information technologies foster secondhand knowledge *about* rather than more
intimate knowledge *of*. Informationism produces what Lewis Mumford
calls "cold intelligence," a kind of knowing disengaged from the deeper
drama of life.[25] We ride through life like tourists, enthralled with the
means of transportation but largely indifferent to the individuals and
cultures that we visit along the way.[26]

Intimacy is firsthand knowledge of the inmost character of someone
or something. All human knowing requires some degree of intimacy. In
education, for example, teachers should know the students they serve,
not just know information about them. In an information society, we
tend to relate impersonally to the world through technology rather than
personally through direct experience. We become non-intimate *observers*
of life—what Jerzy Kosinski once called "videots."[27] We might prefer
watching televised sports to seeing them in person, or even watching
others play sports instead of participating in them. "We live on the surface of 'things,'" writes Houston, where "our lives are easily described
but rarely understood, busy going nowhere in particular. We live at the
edges of other people's lives, too busy to listen." We are like astronauts,
he says, "each in our own spacesuit, orbiting the earth."[28] Our comprehension of reality is "descriptive and speculative, and no longer partici-
patory knowledge in which the observer was personally involved."[29] Surfing the Web becomes one of the most relevant metaphors for conducting
our everyday lives.

As the pool of information grows, our actual knowing declines. Knowledge exists "out there" in cyberspace, not in our minds and hearts. The
Web, for example, is an enormous flea market of informational odds
and ends. Billions of pages exist in cyberspace, but no one can know
even a small percentage of them intimately. Nor is there an overarching Web librarian who knows the Web's "catalogue" well. We rely on
nonhuman search engines to find relevant—rather than good or truthful—information on the Web. Moreover, once we locate relevant information we will probably be unfamiliar with its source, the original
knower of the information. Surfing the Web is more like sampling bits
of information than gaining wisdom or even acquiring knowledge.

Informationism stresses the instrumental value of accessing information over the intrinsic good in knowing well. Under the spell of this
quasi-religion's technical power, we celebrate the sheer ability to search
databases for information that we need to satisfy our curiosities or to
solve an immediate problem, such as repairing a malfunctioning printer
or eliminating a patch of crabgrass from our lawn. We assume an instrumental rather than a moral purpose for accessing relevant information.
After all, we want to repair the printer, not worry about the ethics of

printing copyrighted information. We are immediately concerned about killing the crabgrass, not protecting the environment. We scarcely imagine that our knowing should also make us intimate with truth and goodness. Information technology becomes a means of manipulating the world to get what we want.

Today, such informational knowing influences all our domestic, vocational, and religious practices. In education, for instance, students often lack any personal commitment to what they are learning. They feel as though they are merely memorizing someone else's information and learning about others' data or skills, not developing their own knowledge. They want either to tell the teacher what the experts say or to present their "personal opinion." They do not want to articulate and defend knowledgeable conclusions based on reasonable evidence. They see school-oriented knowing as an instrumental means of getting grades and earning degrees, not as a means of becoming a wise person and contributing to a good society. Similar patterns of objectified knowing and informational dis-intimacy occur in churches, where sermons are abstracted lectures about religious information. Religious bookstores today sell an amazing array of spiritualized self-help literature designed to solve believers' immediate problems rather than to show them how to nurture faith over a lifetime. Concepts such as "religious tradition" and "spiritual discipline" evaporate in informationism. Whether in a classroom or a congregation, to "know" is to leverage information to accomplish instrumental goals. We forget that improved knowing is also a matter of being a wiser person in a better society.

If we do not attain intimacy with the world beyond our own psyches, we will feel little obligation to anything other than ourselves. Intimacy naturally leads us to empathize with others and thereby to consider their needs as well as our own. Good philanthropy, for instance, requires the giver to take an interest in recipients' lives, not just to send them a check. Similarly, a good computer programmer is one who can empathize with the people who will use a program, not just with her or his own expert use of software. Gaining intimacy with others gives a knower a means to break out of the limitations of self-interest and disinterest. Intimacy helps to nurture what Alexis de Tocqueville calls "self-interest well understood"—a self-interest softened by shared social mores. Selfishness, wrote Tocqueville, is a "vice of the heart" premised on "a passionate and exaggerated love of self." It "dries up" public virtues. The remedy for selfishness, according to Tocqueville, is "drawing" out of ourselves and entering into the "destiny" of others.[30] The habits of the heart depend on such empathetic intimacy.

Intimacy can lead us to what Tocqueville calls a "constant habit of benevolence."[31] As Mark Slouka suggests, cyberculture often exists in an "ethical vacuum" and displays an "utter lack of compassion for the world and its problems."[32] The *digerati*, too, are not inclined to advocate responsibility as much as personal freedom. Lacking the habit of benevolence, they are more concerned with instrumental logic and pragmatic design—with making systems work—than with moral obligations and the common good. Such libertinism results from technologically distancing themselves from others—like constructing interstate highways that segment neighborhoods and isolate social classes in major cities. We assume in our public imaginations that new communication technologies will forge voluntary associations among mutually benevolent persons. Instead, we discover that our overdependence on informational knowing makes our relationships superficial, transitory, and ultimately selfish.

Reading online about the needs of the world, for instance, is never the same as personally knowing people in need. Real knowledge is direct and more or less intimate: I know my wife and children, for instance, since I think about them often, pray for them regularly, and interact with them repeatedly in person as well as through mediated technologies.[33] If our understanding of people and life is overly mediated by informational technologies, we will lack such deep intimacy. Knowing about nature from reading online information, studying books, and viewing documents, for example, is not as intimate as communing with nature. Similarly, consuming political news and voting is not the equivalent of participating politically in our communities. Knowledge *about* is merely the accumulation of mediated information, whereas knowledge *of* includes intimate understanding, seasoned judgment, and active participation.

Our mediated involvement in cyberspace can render us mere observers of our own neighborhoods, schools, and communities of worship. Imagine a religious person who believes in the inerrancy of the Bible but who does not relate personally to God. Imagine, too, that he or she studies the church's sacred texts but is not actively involved in a congregation. Finally, consider this believer as an ardent student of biblical information who does not practice the spiritual disciplines described in the textual information. Like such a non-intimate religionist, informationists believe impersonally in people, information, and institutions that they may never know firsthand. Hooked on informational knowing, they discount the value of intimacy.

Informationism seeks instant knowledge with instrumental payoffs. For example, some Americans "try" a religion for a few months to see if it "works" for their immediate needs—as if they are taking a showroom car for a spin or using a free thirty-day trial membership at a fitness club. Richard Cimino and Don Lattin argue that this "shopping for faith" is part of the "consumerization" of religion—a trend that they say often leads to "looser-fitting" and "impersonal" religious institutions.[34] In religion and every other area of life, mediated technologies feign personal knowledge of us to create an air of intimacy. A few doctors actually offer online diagnoses without examining patients in person.[35] Database-driven Web sites create pseudo-intimacy by remembering our names, storing our preferences, and predicting what we want. They track "members" through usernames and passwords that enable site managers to create "personal profiles." Such techniques might sell more products, but they will not make anyone more intimate with anyone else.

Informationism encourages *informational promiscuity:* impersonal relationships based on feigned intimacies and lacking moral integrity. Day traders, who buy and sell equities by the minute, maintain no intimate knowledge of or loyalty to the companies whose stocks they trade.[36] By the end of the year 2000, the most active day traders alone represented 81 percent of online trading volume.[37] Hard-core day traders continued to increase their trading volume compared with other traders, representing a growing percentage of the overall market activity.[38] Moreover, online traders in general trade more often than offline traders. In other words, promiscuity increases with the use of information technologies.[39] Zigzagging in and out of the markets, they might not even care about the ethics of the companies involved; a corporation known for producing faulty products can be just as "good" a stock play as a business with a social conscience. The objective data—the share prices, the percentage gained and lost, the ticking of the market clocks, and the commission rates—give day traders a false sense of intimacy with the world. Mayer Offman, dubbed the "rabbi of day trading," says that it is "not a major thought-out process," just an "instantaneous reaction."[40] Day traders live an endless stream of one-day stands with different equities.

The use of information technologies to track mass markets engenders even greater promiscuity. In the information age, corporate shareholders are an increasingly endangered species, replaced by "shareflippers" who want to get in and out of the market quickly. "Responsibility to shareholders is rapidly becoming an irrelevant concept in our country," writes Jim Collins.[41] The CEO of eBay, Margaret C. Whitman, even suggests that many Silicon Valley companies were "founded by mercenaries, and they were not built to last. They were built to flip."[42] This lack of institutional intimacy transforms the market for Internet-related equities into "a popularity contest, based on consumer moods and filled with millions of networked investors bluffing the financial markets like a poker game."[43] Such a self-referential market operates as a "psychological feedback loop" inflated by "irrational exuberance."[44] In other words, information technologies can sustain impersonal markets devoid of intimate relations among the parties involved. Ironically, these high-tech markets coalesce around vague moods and sentiments rather than information per se. Moreover, professional media propagandists, such as financial pundits and investment analysts, try to create the illusion of their own, intimate knowledge of the markets. Relying on their advice, we become intimate with their propaganda rather than with the actual participants in the markets.

Feigned intimacy extends throughout digital societies, all the way to the executives of corporations. Peter Drucker says that he finds "more and more executives less and less well informed . . . if only because they believe that the data on the computer printouts are ipso facto information."[45] He recommends that CEOs take the place of a company salesperson for several weeks every six months.[46] Unless we intentionally cultivate intimacy in a cyber-world, we will find it evaporating from our lives as we pursue instrumental practices. Even the act of surfing the Web tends to be informationally promiscuous, since it requires no personal knowledge of the people or organizations whose sites are visited. The growing artifices of information technology create the potential for layers of digital promiscuity that encourage selfishness and stifle moral responsibility at all levels of society.

The explosive growth of pornography online illustrates cyberculture's capacity for pseudo-intimacy. Like the VCR and satellite television before it, the Web became a commercially viable medium partly because of males' desire to access erotic materials from the privacy of their homes. In spite of occasional news reports about the resulting broken marriages and sexual addictions, online sexual promiscuity became a profitable business predicated on people's inability to be satisfactorily intimate with real persons.[47] Publishers now offer self-help books on effective techniques for maximizing online sexual encounters, fostering cyber-relationships, and overcoming gender differences in cyberspace.[48]

From business to sex, informationism emphasizes amoral observation over virtuous intimacy. As observers in this digital arena, we are apt to see the world merely as a video game meant to be played for our own short-term pleasure—and if we find cheat codes, we will not hesitate to use them. Speed and success are more important than intimacy and discernment. If instead we become intimate participants in culture, we will see the world as an ecology in which we must reside responsibly. John Lukacs suggests that true knowledge is "participant." It "consists of the relationship of the knower and the known."[49] Intimacy requires us to live harmoniously with others whom we both know and respect. Forging such intimacy can take generations. Informationists treat life itself as a mere pastime, like filling out a multiple-choice test on the Web to find out which religion best suits their fancy.

Measuring Life without Meaning

Political pundits and techno-gurus speculated in the 1990s about cyberspace's potential impact on the fabric of democratic institutions. American political consultants and lobbyists forecasted "geometric changes in everything from fund raising to voting to grassroots campaigns." One consultant even predicted that the November 2000 election would "blow away clueless politicians and apparatchiks."[50] Supposedly, the Internet would renew democracy by returning political participation to citizens. The medium would extirpate the evil influences of soft-money donations to political action committees, educate voters with grassroots information untarnished by mainstream media, and grant politicians an inexpensive forum to communicate their messages directly to electorates.[51] Cyberspace would even offset the influence of political TV commercials, sound-bite reporting, and media-staged debates.

Critics of cyber-democracy are not nearly so sanguine. Paul Virilio, for example, argues that the "libertarian propaganda" about "automatic democracy" assumes that the "absence of deliberation would be compensated by a 'social automatism' similar to that found in opinion polls or the measurement of TV audience ratings." He worries that this would lead to a "reflex democracy, without collective reflexion, in which conditioning would have greater importance than 'electoral campaigning.'"[52]

Probably the most widely touted test of cyber-democracy occurred in Arizona, where the state Democratic Party and election officials conducted the nation's first binding online election.[53] The real-life cyber-experiment gave Democrats an opportunity to vote online for a few days preceding the traditional paper-ballot election. In only one day of online balloting, the total number of Democratic primary voters surpassed the number who had cast their votes in the traditional manner four years earlier. By the time Internet polling concluded at midnight the day preceding the traditional election day, 35,765 voters had cast Democratic ballots online. Some critics worried that the cyber-election would favor more educated and affluent voters who generally have Internet access.[54] But one grassroots African-American organization determined that roughly 85 percent of its urban constituency had access to the medium.[55] Moreover, the group's get-out-the-vote initiative boosted African-American voting by nearly 1,000 percent in some districts. All in all, Arizona's cyber-experiment appeared to be a rousing democratic achievement that discounted Virilio's dire concern about reflex democracy.

Statistical achievements, however, are not always incisive. Reporters assessed the experiment quantitatively, giving audiences the false impression that real democratic gains had been made. Although the voting data looked grand, what did they really mean? Were the voters better informed? Were campaign advertisements during the online balloting more civil and less deceptive? Did the technology enhance the quality of political life in Arizona by getting more citizens involved in the political affairs of their communities? What did we really gain through cyber-voting? All we can say for certain is that more people voted in what is typically a low-turnout primary, probably because of all the media attention. Nevertheless, journalists equated the numbers with political progress.

As the Arizona experiment with cyber-voting illustrates, informationism upholds *measurement* over *meaning* as a more valid way of comprehending reality.[56] Unwilling to accept the validity of meaningful experience, it strives for the objectivity of data. Informationism thereby transforms us into "number crunchers" and "bean counters" who equate data with meaning. The era of cyberculture is also an age of statistical measurement, prediction, and control. Calculating market shares, voting percentages, and other measurements pleases informationists. To borrow language from Jean Bethke Elshtain, informationism's "facts are reduced to brute data and our descriptions can no longer serve as a source of moral or ethical information."[57]

Numbers alone never tell any story. In fact, measuring progress without moral discernment can be a recipe for instrumental successes that are ethical disasters. During World War II, the Nazis used powerful, IBM-designed data-processing devices to keep track of prisoners in extermination camps.[58] They mastered the tabulation of inhumane efficiency and control, creating a cutting-edge system for "controlling inventory" and calculating the "best" murder systems. Our capacity in a high-tech world to gather and process voluminous amounts of statistical information is a dangerously two-edged sword. Without responsible frames of reference, we turn information technologies into cold machines that destroy our capacity to think wisely, feel empathetically, and act virtuously. Our statistical imaginations tell us that we are progressing, while we fall into moral chaos.

Americans love to measure problems and calculate social progress. In the 1900s, Americans became "the most energetic measurers of social life that ever lived," according to Theodore Caplow and his colleagues. In addition to calculating everything that had been counted before, Americans pioneered the measurement of crime, love, food, fun, religion, and work.[59] Daniel Boorstin suggests that Americans live in "statistical communities" that define culture in quantitative terms, from economic data to demographic trends and social norms.[60] When we adopt informationism, we see the world increasingly through the lenses of measurable norms, means, causes, and effects. "The digital age is causing a paradigm shift like you'll never see again," proclaims futurist Barry Asmus. "Everything gets better as it gets smaller. Everything gets cooler as it gets faster. Everything gets cheaper as it becomes more valuable."[61] We rhapsodize about size, speed, and cost. Email increases workers' productivity by nine thousand dollars annually, claims Ferris Research.[62] The media announce such remarkable data as sure signs of human progress. And we believe them! Today, we are not as interested in moral assessment—questions of proper proportion, the right scale, or appropriate duration—as we are in sheer numbers. We trust data more than goodness and rightness.

Informational experts treat their subjects as abstract, independent, and self-sufficient. Things that cannot be measured easily, such as virtue, are relatively unimportant to impatient experts. This is why managers, for example, speak a language of technique rather than virtue. They refer to employees as "resources" and assess workers' "bandwidth"—their available time and talent. Accounting experts define persons as "expenses," not as "assets," although some firms are trying to correct this situation by categorizing workers as "intellectual capital."[63] Accountants and chief information officers (CIOs) calculate the "bottom line." Drucker argues that most CIOs are really only "data officers," not information officers.[64] *Business Week*'s special issue on the "twenty-first century economy" proclaimed that the "optimists have it right" because "the numbers" suggest that the revolutionary new economy is "for real."[65] Tell that to the many information workers who lost their jobs only a few months later.

In the 1980s, MBA programs across the country integrated computer modeling and spreadsheet analysis into their curricula. As a result, much business education was transformed from teaching students historical lessons and semi-intuitive strategies to providing them with techniques for making statistical projections of the probabilities of future financial scenarios. By the late 1990s, software companies were producing PC-based "MBA-ware" that supposedly enabled individuals to automate complex statistical forecasting methods on their home computers. Some people dubbed this software "a consultant in a box" or simply "MBA-in-a-box."[66] Meanwhile, the role of top leadership in large American business was "shifting away from that of the dominant decision-maker to that of manager of the information system."[67] Former CEO Max DePree says, "Managers who have no beliefs but only understand methodology and quantification are modern-day eunuchs. . . . They can never be truly intimate."[68] Data-processing technologies are ennobling a new class of statistical kings while dethroning veterans of the older methods of experience, common sense, and even wisdom.

The penchant for measuring information is not all bad, since decision makers ought to be aware of important facts in a given case. Collecting and analyzing data are important ways of knowing. Yet something troubling is taking place when bean counters rise to priestly status in modern organizations. As we use information technologies to model reality, we implicitly embrace a *systemic* concept of human culture. We imagine cultures not as organic ways of life but as computer-like networks—closed systems that persons can objectively observe, measure, manipulate, and eventually control. Our attempts to quantify and analyze human endeavors implicitly assume that human beings act within naturalistic systems of causes and effects, like chemicals interacting in test tubes. In the 1940s, mathematician Norbert Weiner called the study of systemic models of reality *cybernetics* (from the Greek *kubernetes*, or "governor").[69] He equated persons and culture with machines, mathematical models, and cause-effect processes.[70] Although we are distinctively human, cybernetic models depict us as mere networks. When we become informationists, we conform our image of ourselves and society to a systemic metaphor, all the while venerating the data we collect about such systems.

Weiner's faith in the power of measurement and control is at the heart of the gospel of informationism. In *The Human Use of Human Beings*, he envisions persons as information-processing machines, akin to electronic signaling circuits and ultimately just as regular and predictable. "When I give an order to a machine," he writes, "the situation is not essentially different from that which arises when I give an order to a person."[71] Weiner adds, "To live effectively, is to live with adequate information. Thus, communication and control belong to the essence of man's inner life, even as they belong to his life in society."[72] Weiner writes that it is "best to avoid all question-begging epithets such as 'life,' 'soul,' 'vitalism,' and the like" because humans resemble machines.[73] According to this kind of cybernetic vision, human communication is a machine-like system for sending and receiving messages. By carefully measuring the flow of information, human beings supposedly will gain the power to regulate each other's thoughts and behaviors.

During the same period in which Weiner created his cybernetic ideas, Claude Shannon developed an "information theory" that further advanced experts' hopes to measure and control human messaging.[74] Shannon's theory took abstract quantification to the extreme by disconnecting messages from meaning and context.[75] In Shannon's view, human communication is nothing more than measurable signals—like the bits and bytes in a computer "packet" today.[76] Even random electrical impulses such as lightning crashes are deemed information. According to this view, contexts and shared meanings are irrelevant. Purpose, desire, obligation, virtue, and imagination are meaningless noise. Even storytelling and conversation evaporate into bits of signaling. The cybernetic vision assumes that the meaning of messages matters less than their instantaneous delivery.[77] Shannon's theory foreshadowed the informationism of today.

Cybernetic models of communication eventually became moral licenses for experts to manipulate others. Not surprisingly, during the birth of cybernetic theory in the 1940s, social scientists even conjured up forms of behaviorism that used simplistic stimulus-response theories to predict and control human behavior. Psychologist B. F. Skinner's *Walden Two*, published in 1948, describes a fictional utopia where experts are trying to engineer a perfect human community by scientifically controlling the social environment. Skinner's social engineers are the new "inculcators of wisdom" through the development of a "science of behavior as powerful as the science of the atom."[78] Skeptic Clifford Stoll writes, "Skinner's methods fit well with today's computers. Students peck at their keyboards for dollops of sound and animation; administrators get instant reports; parents hear how their kids now enjoy school. This is supposed to make learning fun, not to mention efficient."[79]

Informationism fosters the spread of cybernetic control into all areas of life. This philosophy's mechanistic schematic of effective communication becomes a de facto template for instrumental messaging. Information processing and communication are the two crucial activities in all human attempts to control everything from interpersonal to international relations.[80] Now information technologies are also means of technical influence. Online advertisements attempt to gain people's attention and divert them to other pages. Advertisers use "spam" (unsolicited email advertising) to coax potential customers to reply to sales pitches. So-called push technologies try to gain greater control over Web users by streaming "content"—such as Web-based broadcast channels—to their computer desktops. Regardless of the various ends—such as greater market share or a stronger political base—the cybernetic means are remarkably similar. In this sense, informationism is a highly evangelistic faith that preaches a gospel of cybernetic control.

These kinds of efforts at reducing human culture to measurable quantities limit our capacity for moral knowing. When we seek measurement over meaning, we adopt the language of probability rather than virtue, essentially making mathematics the preeminent route to all knowledge, and probabilities the means of discerning the value of human actions.

Like Descartes and other rationalists, informationists wrongly believe that humans can "know" without the biases of intimacy. The fact is that no matter how well we measure anything, we bring beliefs to the task, even the prejudice of what is worth measuring and what is not. The gospel of cybernetic control seduces us to join the "inner ring" of people who know how to make things happen and get results; it entreats us, to borrow C. S. Lewis's language, to taste the "delicious sense of secret intimacy" among its evangelists.[81] But it lacks any moral center, any higher sense of obligation beyond what the experts proclaim.[82]

Moral practices require far more than such informational knowledge. If we limit morality to what is measurable, we reduce it to risk management. Peter L. Bernstein argues in *Against the Gods* that the mastery of risk is the foundation of modern life, in which we all seek to play the probabilities.[83] Information technologies become risk-reducing systems rather than virtue-nurturing practices. Edward Yourdon says in *Rise and Resurrection of the American Programmer* that "formal risk management" is probably the most important business practice in computer programming.[84] For all the successes that we can score with quantitative analyses, we still face the danger of succumbing to one narrow, instrumental, quantitative way of thinking and means of discerning worth. Such "digital thinking" can "easily lead to all-or-nothing positions, extremism, stereotypes and oversimplification."[85]

Our belief in the power of cybernetic systems to improve our world ultimately rests on the faith that our use of information technologies will make us better human beings. Computer programs that enable machines to beat humans at games of chance and skill are indeed impressive. But moral questions about human life are beyond the interpretive scope of information technologies. The meaning of moral wisdom, in particular, cannot be captured through the binary capacity of machine logic. If we play God with such technologies, we also inhibit our own ability to make moral sense of our condition. As Lukacs says, the human mind consists not principally of facts but of words. "The words are not the packaging of the facts; the words are the facts themselves. We think in words."[86] Individual persons are inherently more complex and interpretive than computers could ever be—more than any machine could ever fathom. Human beings are capable of far more than processing data. They can be moral knowers and responsible agents in a world of seemingly infinite significance. Machines will never understand the intimate meaning of existence, the moral nature of human life, the joy of relationships, and the goodness of responsible action. We are not designed as mere informational beings but as moral creatures who can pursue virtue. If everyone votes, but no one votes wisely, we are no better off.

Conclusion

The goal in computer programming, writes Ellen Ullman, eventually "becomes the creation of a system itself. Any ethics or morals or second thoughts, any questions or muddles or exceptions, all dissolve into a junky Nike-mind: just do it." After all, she concludes, a computer program is not just "talk." A program "runs." "Whatever you might say, whatever the consequences, all you have are words and what I have is this, this thing I've built, this operational system. Talk all you want, but this thing here: it works."[87] Information technologies indeed can work. When we use them, it seems as though we do not have to concern ourselves with oughts, intimacies, and meanings. The machines work just as well when we do not direct them to function morally. We simply have to accept the "tunnel vision" of information while ignoring the "fuzzy stuff that lies around the edges—context, background, history, common knowledge, social resources" and the like.[88] "What happens," asks philosopher Peter Kreeft, "when we realize that objective reality includes not just brute facts but also goods, not only *is's* but also *oughts*, not only the fact that society *does* do such-and-such, but also the fact that society *ought* to do so-and-so?"[89]

No matter how many information technologies we devise, we cannot fashion them humanely unless we direct them toward coherent moral purposes. What is the telos to which our technologies should be aimed? How do information technologies relate to the aspects of life that we cherish and hope to maintain for future generations? We could debate these kinds of issues endlessly, but today we do not discuss them enough. We celebrate our cyber-savvy and informational abundance, but we are increasingly confused about what we truly ought to be doing with our information and machines. "Abundant data," writes Clifford G. Christians, "far from permitting people to make judgments and form responsible opinions, actually keep them busy with an instrumentalist paradigm that precludes moral obligation."[90] We are morally lost in an increasingly informational society, unsure where to turn except to yet more technological innovation. We congratulate ourselves for our informational accomplishments, but the real benefits or drawbacks of such innovations, in distinctly moral terms, elude us.

If human life is not intrinsically meaningful, we are all machines with no moral compass and no responsibilities. By the end of the twenty-first century, predicts Ray Kurzweil in *The Age of Spiritual Machines*, there will no longer be a "clear distinction between human and machine."[91] George Dyson argues in *Darwin among the Machines* that information networks are taking on a life of their own, independent of human cul-

ture. He predicts that eventually a new type of intelligence will automatically emerge out of the unpredictable interconnections of growing
numbers of complex networks.[92] Some technologists even imagine
information systems becoming so human-like that they gain "some of
the resilience and safeguards of living organisms."[93] If these kinds of
observers are correct, we will also have lost any sense of moral responsibility. Rich aspects of our humanness—such as motives, meanings,
sentiments, and obligations—cannot be understood purely through database designs and statistical renderings. Imagine how impoverished the
judicial system would be if court proceedings were merely informational
presentations with no human attention to the meaning of testimony or
the means of gathering evidence—as if computers themselves could
directly administer justice. Machines will never be able to be virtuous;
such a capacity is reserved for human beings.

The truth is that informationism divides human knowledge into bits
of information devoid of moral meaning. We justify cyber-technologies
in terms of our greater ability to collect and analyze information for the
purposes of prediction and control. Numbers speak. Data impress. Measurements connote certainty. We even accept isolated technological facts
as yardsticks for social progress, such as the number of television channels, the percentage of the population wired to the Internet, and the
bandwidth of our digital connections. All such technological expansion
symbolizes a greater human ability to socially engineer progress. We
love information, and we cannot get enough of it. "Personal computers"
(note how we anthropomorphize even computers) seem to offer a way
for us to escape our epistemological and moral limitations as human
beings. Technical knowledge, we assume, will satisfy "a need for mastery and control denied outlets elsewhere."[94]

The networked computing machine probably defines our age, just as
the printing press defined the Enlightenment. The metaphor of the
informed person in our age is the lone individual sitting at a computer,
surfing through cyberspace, buying and selling stocks online, zipping
in and out of chat rooms, exchanging instant messages, downloading
the latest sports trivia, and feeling the invigorating high of such digital
travel. Does this capture who we should want to be? Were we created
merely to be cyber-surfers? Virilio says that we face a "techno-fundamentalism" in which "information itself has become an absolute power
with totalitarian features."[95] Informationism carries the cybernetic seeds
of such secular-rational totalitarianism. The only alternative, Václav
Havel suggests, is "living in the truth," which requires one to take the
"moral act" of regaining "control over one's own sense of responsibility."[96] In other words, we must discern our condition as truthfully as

possible so that we might also act as responsibly as we can even amidst the uncertainties of the future.

Informationism preaches a secular-rational "faith" that silences moral discernment in the name of efficiency and control. But such faith is simply not enough to gain moral bearings. Although we now know more things and possess more technological methods, we are still plagued by what Jacques Ellul calls "inaccurate information and hazy facts."[97] Moreover, informationism betrays us by pretending to be the best, self-sufficient means to human progress. It evangelizes us to become observers of a world that we know less and less intimately and about which we are morally alienated. It cannot nurture good societies and raise virtuous persons.[98] As a religion, informationism is insufficient, for it cannot even save us from our own foolishness. "The only ethic in cyberspace," jokes one Silicon Valley executive, "is what you can get away with."[99] Surely we can do better.

chapter two

Moderating
Our Informational Desires

■ The encyclopedist and philosopher Denis Diderot predicted in the eighteenth century that a "time will come when it will be almost as difficult to learn anything from books as from the direct study of the whole of the universe." The printing press, he continued, "never rests" and will soon fill "huge buildings with books." Eventually the "world of learning—our world—will drown in books," he concluded.[1] So much for the literary age!

Diderot recognized that information technologies—even books—are ways of knowing that enable people to store, organize, and present information. Libraries' decisions about which books to acquire significantly affect future patrons' abilities to know what others have said in philosophy, literature, business, and the like. Perhaps Diderot worried that the plethora of newly published books eventually would make it more difficult for people to know others' ideas and sentiments. Academic libraries would turn into stockpiles of fragmented information rather than places of integrated knowing. Readers would be faced with unmanageable quantities of novel and specialized information devoid of any meaningful coherence. In recent decades, for instance, the publication of social-scientific research was not "matched by an equal application of talent and energy to rendering the resulting knowledge intelligible and accessible to a broader public."[2] In spite of all the psychological research and publication in the last century, it would be difficult to make the case that people are better off psychologically.

The shift in society from library stacks to computer databases, from circulation rooms to computer networks, and from paper pages to electronic screens has transformed both the *amounts* and the *kinds* of information available. The corpus of online information is exploding so quickly that even the "spiders" that automatically index Web pages for search engines cannot keep up with the growth.[3] At the same time, all kinds of previously unpublished information are now appearing in cyberspace, from personal journals and message boards to college course syllabi and restaurant menus. Most college students begin their term paper research online, if only to search a library catalogue.

This chapter addresses how our immoderate informational desires affect our knowing, especially our moral knowing. Informationism drives us to create greater and greater quantities of information, but it simultaneously dismisses the importance of moral good, as if our use of information does not need any moral frame of reference. Consequently, we are drowning in a deepening sea of fragmented, trivial, and incoherent information. Our insatiable desire for information results in moral confusion, not virtue.

The first section of this chapter considers the impact of "information overload" on the moral fabric of culture. Information technologies are biased against the discovery of coherent moral wisdom and in favor of the spread of fragmented information. The dissemination of information can become an incessant noise that repeatedly diverts our attention from greater matters. Like slot machine players in a casino, we lose track of the rhythms of the natural world. Unless we learn moderation, our lives will be a mishmash of messages and information that is ever more tenuously connected to concrete obligations, cultures, and traditions. More and more people have the power to exchange messages and access databases, but fewer people seem to know what life means or how to live it well. Coping with the pace of messaging is enough trouble for the day. In the information age, who has time and energy to cobble together a moral vision?

The second section critiques the bandwidth envy of those cyber-philes who believe that society will necessarily be better served by faster messaging. Increasing the ease and reducing the cost of messaging does not normally improve the quality of our communication. Instead of knowing well, we spend more time merely *messaging*—quickly sending and receiving email missives, downloading and uploading digital files, and surfing through cyberspace. When we message too much, we begin to lose intimacy with others, the natural world, the Creator, and even ourselves. Faster messaging can be an *instrumental* good—such as getting stock market quotes more quickly—but it is far less likely to be a *moral* good. Morally conducive forms of knowing, such as conversing and contemplating, are slow, thoughtful, and personal. Greater digital bandwidth engenders instantaneous, unreflective, and impersonal messaging. Restricting bandwidth is a moral task of setting limits to avoid the gluttony of excess messaging and the chaos of moral incoherence.

The third section examines how unmoderated informational messaging can hinder our communication. Newer communication technologies paradoxically are making it more difficult for us to know each other well and to know anything for certain. We are especially losing any sense of moral purpose in our messaging. An overdependence on messaging reduces human communication to an instrumental means of satisfying our own immediate desires.

As the conclusion of this chapter suggests, much of the rhetoric of cyberspace is predicated on an insatiable desire for more information and more powerful messaging technologies. We seem to be increasingly ill at ease in recognizing that more is not always better. Although we can easily see the value of moderation in eating and drinking, we do not recognize the same virtue when it comes to informational pursuits. We naively give users of cyber-technologies special protection from charges of avarice or greed. As a result, we practice what the Greeks called *pleonexia:* a deep-seated desire for something to the point of greed.[4]

Confronting Database Babel

In a short story titled "The Library of Babel," Jorge Luis Borges considers the real value of humankind's expanding collections of information. He pictures the universe metaphorically as a library composed of an "indefinite, perhaps an infinite, number of hexagonal galleries, with enormous ventilation shafts in the middle, encircled by very low railings." Shelf after shelf is loaded with volumes of printed materials. Through the entrance area passes a spiral staircase that "plunges down into the abyss and rises up to the heights." There seems to be no limit to the expanding array of catalogued information.[5]

This library, Borges writes, exists *ab aeterno* (from eternity). "Man, the imperfect librarian, may be the work of chance or of malevolent demiurges," but the universe itself "can only be the work of God." In spite of all their information, the inhabitants of Borges's universe live in literary and psychic disarray. One group of librarians is superstitious, trying to divine meaning from books as some people discover meaning in dreams or in "the chaotic lines of one's hands." Others believe that the library contains "everything which can be expressed in all languages." The always exhausted "official searchers"—*inquisitors*—look for infamous words but really do not expect to find anything; they lack faith. In contrast, one "blasphemous sect" suggests that everyone give up searching the volumes and instead try to compose, "by means of an improbable stroke of luck, the canonical books." Pilgrims hope to find the one "god-book" that will decipher all the rest, while the "impious" say that "absurdities are the norm in the library and that anything reasonable . . . is an almost miraculous exception." Borges concludes that although the human species is probably "on the road to extinction," the library "will last on forever: illuminated, solitary, infinite, perfectly immovable, filled with precious volumes, incorruptible, secret."[6]

Borges's vision of the post-Babel universe, in which we suffer from a grand confusion of irreconcilable information, is both enchanting and depressing. The idea of one master library filled with everything ever published is intriguing to anyone with a smidgeon of curiosity. Imagine all the treasures—and nonsense—of human literary activity represented within a truly comprehensive collection. What would we do with such a bibliographic treasure? Borges suggests that we would merely carry on as humans always do: disagreeing with each other over how to interpret texts, hunting for revelations, deluding ourselves, and forming cults of tribal wisdom. The sheer scope, complexity, and mystery of the universe, according to Borges, confines us all to a Babel-like existence in which we can neither fully know nor completely agree. Nevertheless, we go on with our lives, hopeful that one day perhaps we will figure out how to find some coherence in the expanding morass of humanly conceived texts.

Borges's library metaphor captures the state of the information age.[7] The scope of collecting, storing, and distributing information has increased dramatically in recent decades, thanks largely to digital networks and computer databases. We forget how slowly humans gathered information in earlier centuries. Even for several hundred years after Gutenberg's invention, only a fraction of the world's inhabitants could read, and even fewer had access to books.[8] Scribes continued to reproduce religious manuscripts for elites, but most information was communicated orally, from individual to individual and from generation to generation. People spent more time remembering the past—in ritual, song, and story—than they did trying to create new information. Not until the late eighteenth century did most Americans begin reading numerous books quickly rather than carefully rereading a few of them, such as the Bible.[9]

Electronic and digital media greatly escalated the dissemination of information. By the 1950s, television delivered to most Americans in one year more dramatic fiction than an eighteenth-century American was likely to see on the stage in a lifetime. A weekday edition of the *New York Times* today probably contains more printed information than a typical person was likely to read in a lifetime in seventeenth-century England.[10] One information service, Lexis Nexis, encompasses more than 13,050 different databases with over 3.2 billion documents and adds another 900,000 news stories daily and 6.6 million documents weekly.[11] No one really knows how to quantify the "information supply" in modern society, but some pundits claim that roughly every five years digital technologies double the total amount of stored information.[12] If these kinds of estimates are accurate, we cannot help but wonder about the implications for contemporary life. Each of us is like most of the patrons in Borges's mythical library, overwhelmed by the magnitude of information.[13]

Technophiles celebrate this supercharged messaging as if it were necessarily a good thing. Some optimists cite Moore's Law, which says that "computer power" doubles every eighteen months, presumably enabling us to collect, distribute, and analyze more information in less time.[14] Others cite Metcalfe's Law, which posits that the "value" of the Internet increases at the rate of the square of the number of people using it.[15] These kinds of "laws" are triumphalistic symbols that some eager information-ists employ rhetorically to convince us that greater messaging speed and quantity are signs of social progress. Such slogans do not explain our condition so much as exhort us to greater faith in information technology. As theologian Eugene H. Peterson argues, we are "hell-bent ploughing full speed ahead and damn the torpedoes. We are so sure that a little more knowledge will make us more effective, that a breakthrough in technology will usher in a new level of competence. . . . For us to not do something when it is possible to do anything at all, escapes our imagination."[16]

Some techno-gurus even equate the escalating surfeit of informa-tional messaging with spiritual renewal and human salvation. "The Inter-net is not merely a radiance of connections," futurist George Gilder preaches, but also a "mesh of constant invention." Our informational "telecosm" will "make human communication universal, instantaneous, unlimited in capacity, and at the margins free." His predictions are not mere futurism, Gilder boasts, because the science behind the emerging telecosm is already history. "Futurists falter because they belittle the power of religious paradigms, deeming them either too literal or too fantastic. Yet futures are apprehended only in the prophetic mode of the inspired historian." When anyone can transmit any amount of infor-mation anywhere, he claims, the "resulting transformation becomes transfiguration." Our "universal resonance," the "velocity of light," is both "the abundance and scarcity of the new world economy, the cre-ative interplay of limit and infinite, the flesh and the divine."[17] In Gilder's scenario, high-speed messaging and information abundance are utterly sublime if not salvific.

Whereas skeptics such as Borges question the enduring value of humanly created knowledge, technophiles such as Gilder venerate information tech-

nologies. They see godlike power in our capacity to transmit vast quantities of information almost instantaneously from one computer to many
others. In his 1989 book, *Microcosm: The Quantum Revolution in Economics and Technology,* Gilder proclaimed the "overthrow of matter."[18] By
2000, he was declaring that those who can "waste" bandwidth will inherit
the future.[19] He rhetorically transforms the problems of information overload and incoherence into signs of impending human triumph—the veri-
table winds if not the tongues of fire of Pentecost. In Gilder's view, wide-
open, unfettered communication makes the markets for information
function more efficiently and therefore sublimely. The Internet, in particular, represents a capitalistic "triumph of intelligence over time and
chaos."[20] Capitalism, he continues, "teaches every venturer the rules of resonance, the laws of right and light. . . . It ruthlessly filters out the ego trips
and feckless tries and self-indulgences and investments of disguised consumption, and products that exploit and diminish their customers."[21]
According to technophiles such as Gilder, digital messaging advances innovation, improves competition, and ultimately serves human beings. The
new telecosm of nearly unlimited information will save us from the sins
of inefficiency, slothfulness, and ignorance. In other words, we do not have
to concern ourselves with the habits of our hearts, because the market is
a sufficiently moral arbiter of information and progress.

This type of triumphalistic rhetoric focuses too much on the sheer
volume and speed of our messaging, while ignoring the quality of the
information, the character of the messengers, and the resulting confusion that can make actual communication ever more difficult. The value
of a library, for instance, is not simply how many volumes it stores or
how many patrons it attracts, but even more so how well it enables us
to be better and wiser persons. We once thought of public libraries as
places where people could learn to become better citizens. Our concept
of informational databases, on the other hand, does not carry such moral
weight. Gilderites encourage us to imagine databases as sources of
knowledge and agents of progress, but Borges's vision of the Babel-like
library should bring us back to reality. The informational database "is
its own endless library" characterized by infinity, redundancy, and elu-
siveness.[22] The database offers us no moral integrity or even intellectual
coherence, only more information that is delivered ever more speedily.
For all of their utility, lightning-fast databases cannot make us virtuous
people or engender a good society. Gilder's triumphalistic vision of the
future is less likely than Borges's chaotic vision—unless we figure out
how to moderate wisely our desire for the entire digital project.

The moral value of information depends on distinctly human facul-
ties, such as insight, discernment, and judgment. These kinds of interpretive abilities cannot be derived from the secular-rational logic of dig-

ital networks and database systems. No matter how great our messaging skill, it alone will never enable us to consider information wisely and use it for worthy purposes. On the contrary, advances in messaging power without a corresponding renewal of our moral abilities create greater confusion and discontinuity in our personal and communal lives. We might eventually "face the prospect of drowning in trivia as the generations succeed each other."[23] Even the best search engines and the fastest microprocessors cannot save us from such incoherence, since informational incoherence is more of an interpretive problem than a technological one. "The best search engine," says the CEO of one Web search engine company, "is the one between your ears."[24] In short, we need moral wisdom—the capacity to recognize what is intrinsically good and right, what is worth knowing and remembering, and how to use it wisely, if at all. Without such insight, we will discover that greater quantities of information become more of a curse than a blessing.

Today, we face a situation in which the dynamics of digital information further destabilize human messaging. Much information does not stay in focus long enough for us to make sense of it or to assess its moral implications. As technologies change and markets shift, technicians build and purge databases without concerns about consistency and integrity. The Web, for example, acts like a grand self-deconstructor, effortlessly combining and recombining ideas, data, history, and images in an ongoing shuffle, with no connection to its "referent subject."[25] Since much database information is proprietary, we should assume that the organizations that own it will use it to advance their own interests—including keeping some of it out of the public domain or purging it completely from databases when it no longer has instrumental value or could be used against its owners. Paper shredders are hot commodities in information societies, since hard-copy destruction has to keep up with digital erasure. Unlike public libraries, most databases are privately owned and therefore can be permanently discarded when they lose their instrumental value. In Jeremy Rifkin's terminology, consumers and librarians are shifting from owning copies of information merely to accessing them.[26] In a digital world, we turn on and off digital information with the fits of the markets, the self-interested actions of organizations, and the innovations in storage and retrieval technologies.

Nevertheless, some informationists still promise technological solutions to our moral problems. They predict a time in the future when we will once and for all be able to access all desired information—as if the basic human need is more information and faster search engines. Instead of considering the wisdom of the past, they turn to technological prophecy. Of course, the predicted Eden never arrives, because the expanding scope of available information always surpasses people's ability to make good and worthwhile sense of it.[27] The technologies that are supposedly going to transcend Babel invariably unleash new information cascades that are even harder to tame. Databases produce more databases. Technological "solutions" eventually compound the problem. As Ivan Illich suggests, "The pooling of stores of information, the building up of a knowledge stock . . . is the ultimate attempt to solve a crisis by escalation."[28]

Ultimately, we place too much trust in informational rather than moral ways of knowing. We wrongly equate knowledge with the mere identification, classification, and dissemination of storable information. As a result, we fill libraries and now databases with studies, reports, and findings—information of all kinds. We organize this information in almanacs, encyclopedias, and compendia and now through online directories and Boolean filters. We convince ourselves that information technologies are routes to wisdom, even as we find it more difficult to define knowledge, let alone to discern wisdom. All the while, we lose the coherent perspective that we need to make moral sense of the expanding "library."[29] Kevin Kelly says that cyberspace creates a "new sphere of thinking" that is "relativistic, postmodern and full of uncertainty. . . . Moral certitude becomes more and more difficult to find."[30] The sheer magnitude, the dynamism, and the proprietary nature of our information undermine our ability to assess it—to determine how good or incisive the information really is and even what it means for the quality of our lives and our communities. We might be more informed than previous generations, but we are no wiser or more virtuous. Even our newspapers prove it, with an endless supply of stories of social conflict, domestic violence, and political corruption.

Recognizing our condition as tired Web surfers with little clear direction, someone created a Web page titled "The End." Surfers who landed on this site found the following thoughtful copy:

The End

Congratulations!
You have finished the Internet
(This is the last page)

Thank you for visiting

There are no more links.
(You must now turn off your computer
and go do something productive)[31]

Whoever created this Web page had discovered a bit of low-tech wisdom amidst the ongoing babble of cyberspace. "There's fifty-seven channels and nothin' on," sings Bruce Springsteen.[32]

Overcoming Bandwidth Envy

In 2001, *U.S. News & World Report* featured a cover story on traffic gridlock in American cities. According to the article, since 1982 the amount of time that Americans spend in traffic had increased 236 percent. In large cities, the combined morning-evening rush hour had doubled to almost six hours. If these data are accurate, drivers devote a staggering amount of their discretionary time to traffic jams alone. Analysts say that traffic congestion costs Americans a staggering $78 billion annually in lost time and wasted fuel.[33]

Although some drivers are moving closer to their workplaces to shorten commutes, the overall traffic situation is worsening. A Chicago commuter who discovered every alternative route home jammed one night, finally just rolled up her windows and screamed primordially. It did not make her feel any better, however, and it certainly did not improve her traffic situation. A clinical psychologist who counsels married couples who commute by car from a bedroom community to Silicon Valley says that half of his clients are dealing with commuter-related stress. For those who cannot find local work or move closer to their jobs, he advises rigid scheduling. "If you're going to have to have this kind of life, you have to schedule the sex, you have to schedule the quality time with the kids, exercise, dates between Mom and Dad." Otherwise marriages will "just slip away," he warns. We could try to solve such social problems technologically by building more roads. But most people say they would prefer instead either improved mass transit or less-auto-dependent communities.[34] They imagine *social* as well as *individual* solutions, and *cultural* as well as *technological* possibilities.

The problem of auto gridlock reflects a recurring dilemma: how to identify and accept human limitations. Unbridled technological change disrupts our ways of life, resulting in cultural chaos and accompanying moral confusion. Even the construction of highways disrupts the neighborhoods and carves up the social landscape into new units based on class, race, and income. Moderation, one of the oldest virtues, is crucial yet rare in high-tech endeavors. Rather than assuming that the answer to any moral quandary is more technology, we need a virtuous sense of technological moderation that balances unbridled change with cultural continuity. Moderation admits that both excessive and insufficient messaging lack virtue. Setting reasonable technological limits enables us to dedicate time and energy to noninstrumental pursuits that are crucial for living a good life. Limits also help us to make our informational pursuits themselves more healthy and worthwhile. If we direct too much of our energy to managing messaging, we become amoral information junkies. Saturated with information, our hearts grow cold to the greater good. Moderation, on the other hand, enables us to balance the moral and the technological so that we can live with greater moral integrity.

One of the moral dangers today is mastering informational techniques while losing our grip on responsible living. We can easily slip into the habit of doing some things primarily because they are technologically feasible, not because they are intrinsically right to do. Our minds imitate databases, processing greater amounts of information, when they should be making more responsible judgments. Stephen L. Talbott warns that the database is a metaphor for the "scattered mind—the mind that feverishly gathers trinkets here and there, convinced that, somehow, a big enough pile of such notions will magically coalesce into one of those new paradigms said to be taking shape all around us."[35] Information gridlock induces moral paralysis.

Our overreliance on informational ways of knowing deflates the meaning of intrinsically moral language. For instance, informational phrases such as "distance education" and "database research" lack the moral contexts of earlier practices; words such as "teaching," "learning," and "lessons" carry a moral weight that evaporates in discussions about informational education. We find ourselves talking about the entire educational enterprise apart from our responsibility to become better persons, caring neighbors, and wiser citizens. New educational technologies certainly can deliver information, but can they also cultivate careful discernment and good judgment? Lacking any sense of technological moderation, we accept a morally vacuous concept like "unlimited bandwidth" as representing a worthy telos.

In the information age, technological language takes on a moral weight that it hardly deserves. We equate informational abundance with goodness and progress, as if all information and all uses of information technologies are worthwhile. We find it difficult to limit voluntarily our use of informational language and technological metaphors; the cybernetic language of technique invades all areas of life, from religion to sexuality. The very concepts of "doing right" and "being good" give way to notions of "doing much" and "being effective." Under the spell of amoral techno-speak, we cast the kind of convoluted language that Samuel Beckett in *Waiting for Godot* calls "quaqua"—meaningless, self-referential chatter that fails to orient us to truth and wisdom.[36] T. S. Eliot laments, "Where is the wisdom we have lost in knowledge? Where is the knowledge we have lost in information?"[37] Says Madeleine L'Engle, we all depend "too much on knowledge, and not enough on wisdom."[38]

The evaporation of moral meaning from our informational language is evident in the way techno-gurus espouse "unlimited bandwidth" as a solution to a myriad of social problems. With little or no regard for the virtue of moderation, technophiles practically venerate *digital bandwidth*—the amount of information that can be transmitted within a fixed period. They so envy digital potency that they become indifferent to the ravages of informational excess. To avoid informational deficiency, they forsake any moral vision predicated on virtuous moderation.

First, the unbridled quest for greater messaging speed discards venerable moral practices that require patience and perseverance. Ironically, bandwidth envy essentially diminishes the value of time as an aspect of what it means to be a virtuous human being. Knowing—being intimate—inherently requires *duration*. We can come to know something or someone only by investing time in the practices of knowing. The so-called conquering of time with instantaneous messaging invariably retards our capacity to know anything of great importance. Increased bandwidth favors the knowing of truncated events and disconnected messages. As we commit more and more time to impersonal, unreflective, rapid-fire messaging, we have less and less time left to commune intimately with neighbor, God, and creation. Instead of limiting high-tech bandwidth to protect the kinds of virtuous relationships and practices that take time to cultivate, we dedicate more and more of our limited time to instrumental pursuits and amoral activities. We become machine-like creatures, uploading and downloading messages, organizing them into folders, burning them into new storage media, and printing them off to our heart's content. While greater bandwidth promises to save us download time, it invariably leads to new informational endeavors that consume more of our "free" time for intrinsically moral practices.

Second, we bring to added bandwidth additional information of dubious merit, including mediocre, extraneous, half-baked, and even disingenuous messages. In an article entitled "The Search for Intelligent Life on the Internet," Amy Harmon says, "At a moment when the world's need for information has never been greater, the Internet's role as the ultimate source of unmediated news has been matched only by its notorious ability to breed rumors, conspiracy theories and urban legends."[39] Greater bandwidth is like a gift certificate; we feel we must buy something, regardless of whether we truly need it. We have time left on our monthly cell phone contract, so we start calling distant acquaintances, even though we have nothing to say and no real desire to listen to them. On the Internet, greater bandwidth inclines people to massage their egos by publicizing their own two cents worth on message boards and email lists. Computer-mediated communication "so lowers the threshold for voicing opinions," writes Robert D. Putnam, "that, like talk radio, it may lead not to deliberation, but to din."[40] People find themselves collecting links for Web sites, compiling tired jokes, visiting trivia sites, tracking stock prices by the minute even if they trade by the month, searching for Hollywood news, and conducting other wasteful excursions. After the terrorist attacks on the World Trade Center and the Pentagon in 2001, the Web and email were ablaze with rumors. The events elicited torrents of unsubstantiated reports, including a message that the French astrologer Nostradamus had predicted the tragedies. Pollster George Gallup Jr. explained, "As the saying goes, the problem isn't Americans don't believe in anything. It's that they believe in everything."[41]

Scarcity, not abundance, usually denotes value and leads us to be more thoughtful about our use of resources. If we have to invest our limited time and energy into an activity, we are more likely to be committed to it. "This is the grave threat of the technical," writes theologian James M. Houston, "that it appears to make available readily, easily, universally and even instantly what was once scarce and valued. Commitment then ceases to be an exercise of the soul."[42] Online publishing proves this point. The number of trivial, inane, and self-inflated Web sites is astounding.

Third, increased bandwidth devalues human communication because of the ease of making and distributing digital copies of information. Walter Benjamin suggests that the ability to mechanically reproduce cultural artifacts tends to render the originals less meaningful—less like special icons and more like everyday artifacts.[43] Cyberspace devalues digitally reproducible messages even more. According to what I call the *Law of Digital Markets,* the free, instantaneous copying of messages transforms human communication into a more abstract, market-driven phenomenon with no intrinsically moral purpose or value. Wide-open informational markets produce a kind of digital trash analogous to the waste produced by fast-food restaurants. Our Web surfing, for example, creates a perfect copy of every site that we visit, but we eventually dump most of this information when our computer cache discards old files. We grab the information we need to fulfill our short-term instrumental need and then deposit the rest of it into the digital trash.

Whereas moral discourse requires contemplative consideration—time to consider what is worth remembering and repeating—digital copying is largely a matter of instantaneous impulse. The concept of unlimited bandwidth appeals to our desire for greater individual indulgence, and market availability and personal desire become the ipso facto guides to informational action. Perhaps the greatest example of this phenomenon is the explosion in online pornography. Porn merchants pioneered e-commerce technologies, including shopping-cart ordering and online credit card payment. They also devised ways of transmitting large-image files through narrow bandwidths and were early adopters of streaming video.[44] Copying pornography has never been easier. Individuals can quickly and anonymously act on their sexual impulses with immediately discardable images. The Law of Digital Markets suggests that digital copying fosters such selfishly instrumental uses of information.

As expanding digital bandwidth facilitates copyability, it leads to moral decay, unless we expend time and effort cultivating habits of the heart. Whereas digital messages can easily be reproduced, moral culture has to be nurtured painstakingly from generation to generation, one word or gesture at a time. We cannot cut and paste moral wisdom and virtuous character from one person or culture to another. In fact, we constantly have to renew nontechnological customs such as family meals and hospitality that preserve virtue through time. Generally speaking, these kinds of time-intensive habits give our lives moral significance, whereas frenetic informational copying renders our lives more meaningless. Like a gluttonous eater, the ravenous consumer of bandwidth can lose any sense of the goodness of moderation.

Fourth, increased bandwidth further fragments society by expanding specialized messaging at the expense of shared culture. What I call *Balkan's Law*—the Balkanization of cyberspace—holds that "like interests" coalesce online—whether political, professional, consumerist, religious, or sexual.[45] Greater bandwidth does not bring all people together as much as it fosters the growth of tribal interests, from professional groups to political movements. As we see already with digital television and the Web, increased messaging space produces special-interest content that gobbles up much of the added bandwidth. Moreover, market specialization and audience segmentation give digital empires opportunities to divide and conquer both public interests and traditional social institutions. In a digital environment, even individual family members can avoid each other by surrounding themselves with their own favorite music, television programs, and Internet chat channels. Each citizen can collate political information purely in tune with his or her assumptions. In a high-bandwidth universe, we can more easily align ourselves with special penchants and preoccupations that are disconnected from a shared public life and from cultural traditions.[46]

We can begin to see the value of bandwidth moderation by contrasting Gilder's gluttonous vision of unlimited messaging with the monastic reading of books. In the Rule of St. Benedict, for instance, monastic reading *(lectio divina)* was meaningfully slow. Each monk received one book to read annually, rereading it meditatively throughout the year. St. Anselm's "Meditation on Human Redemption" (1090) describes such reading: "Taste the goodness of your redeemer . . . chew the honeycomb of his words, suck their flavor which is sweeter than honey, swallow their wholesome sweetness; chew by thinking, suck by understanding, swallow by loving and rejoicing."[47] Reading was not valued for speed or instant copyability but for its intrinsic, time-honoring meaning. To read was to become intimate with the God-breathed wisdom in a text.

The pace of wide-open bandwidth works against such moral intimacy, diverting our attention from one missive to another. As suggested in chapter 1, our relationships with texts become promiscuous, with no fidelity to overarching truth or wisdom. Rather than reading any particular text carefully, we skim through information, bouncing from one Web site, email message, or satellite channel to the next one. Reading increasingly becomes the fragmentary consumption of scattered information from the flotsam and jetsam of distant databases. Today, online information is the database junk that we scan the quickest, with little moral consideration. We do not need to limit our reading to one book per year to regain some of the spirit of St. Anselm's meditation on redemption, but we do have to be far less promiscuous and far more moderate in our reading habits.

Consider also the example of Václav Havel's philosophical and political treatise, *Letters to Olga*. Unjustly sentenced in 1979 to four years in a maximum-security Czech prison for opposing the communist regime, the playwright saw his personal "bandwidth" to the outside world reduced to a trickle—four handwritten pages that he could send only to his wife each week, with no guarantee that the prison censors would permit delivery. These letters became his only regular and direct means of communion with the outside world, as well as his sole opportunity for creative literary expression. Prison authorities imposed restrictions on what he could address in the letters, forbidding him to write about prison conditions. In spite of these limitations, writing the letters became his passion behind bars. It gave meaning to his life in prison, helping him endure the emotional and intellectual burdens of confinement, as well as providing a morally reflective practice. "The letters," recalls Havel, "gave me a chance to develop a new way of looking at myself and examining my attitudes to the fundamental things in life. . . . In time I learned how to think ahead and arrange my thoughts in thematic cycles, and to weave the motifs in and out of them and thus—to build, over time, my own little structure, putting it together something like my plays."[48]

As the monks savored reading one book a year, Havel came to cherish his letter writing partly because of its limited bandwidth. The "cost" of every letter—the sheer moral weight of each of his words when he could share so few of them each week—forced Havel to judge carefully what was truly worthy of reflection and expression. Writing out of his commitment to democracy and inspired by his growing recognition of the mystery of being and the value of human life, Havel composed through these letters a significant work of political philosophy.[49] He invested personal time, intellectual creativity, and moral passion in a selfless project that nobly serves the traditions of democratic theory and practice.

If we responsibly moderate our informational desires, new technologies can afford us a greater degree of peace and harmony in everyday life. Using email, for instance, offers the possibility of avoiding some intrusive telephone calls and organizing our correspondence around a ritual of focused writing and reading. But do we have the patience and self-discipline both to restrict the extent of our emailing and to prevent it from chopping up our everyday lives into attention-diverting bits and pieces? Limiting our bandwidth can foster deeper relationships and moral coherence. Today, we are still apt to cherish the personal letters we received from our grandparents. But will our grandchildren care to keep and reread any of our email?

Realizing Our Broken Messaging

During the mid-1990s, the *New Yorker* published a cartoon that depicted a dog sitting in front of a computer screen, chatting with another canine located somewhere in cyberspace. "On the Internet, no one knows you're a dog," remarks one hound to the other.[50] The absurdity of the cartoon reflects the habits of online messengers who conduct pseudo-intimate chats with unknown others. Anyone can pretend to be anyone else online, without the normal etiquettes of mutuality and trust. The everyday customs of social propriety do not fully apply in cyberspace. Online, every one of us supposedly has the power to be both anyone we want to be and no one at all. In fact, being no one and everyone are two sides of the same dilemma in cyberspace. If we take on too many aliases, we may lose our real selves. We might as well be dogs.

Human communication depends not just on power and technique but also on shared understandings. In the age of cyberspace, we mistakenly equate transmission with communication. We celebrate the invention of messaging technologies such as the Web without considering whether they will actually improve our capacity for understanding each other. Being intimate with information—with someone's *message*—is not the same as being intimate with the *messenger*. Cyberspace focuses our attention too much on the power of communicators to transmit and receive messages and too little on our responsibility to strive for shared understanding.[51] This creates a particularly odd state of affairs online, in which nearly everyone is expressing opinions but few people are comprehending them. Greater messaging capacity seems to exacerbate this situation.

Today's expanding information infrastructures generally do not foster shared knowing as much as selfish *messaging:* transmitting and receiving information via digital systems without giving much consideration to the messages. These systems generally facilitate quick and efficient messaging, not shared understanding, extensive conversation, or even real communication. Digital messaging environments promote the ease of transmission and rarely facilitate careful communication. As a result, our own online missives increasingly take on the character of commercial mass media—short messages designed to gain attention rather than to engage in real dialogue. Shared knowing requires patience, sincerity, and dialogue, whereas cyberspace emphasizes speed, facade, and transmission. Like the advertising business in general, cyber-communication is premised on quick message delivery and immediate message impact rather than on gradual discourse toward shared understanding. Cyberspace further blurs the distinction between information and propaganda. A *Business Week* reporter says that online the "Great Wall between content and commerce is beginning to erode."[52] Wolff says in *Burn Rate* that online the "ordinary conventions of context—that is produced by a third party whom we cannot vouch for—the reliability of provenance, the one generally consistent point of pride in a media world, were being sacked. The inherent problem of the Internet, that it lacked clear authorship and responsibility, was being compounded instead of solved."[53]

Similar to mass media, most cyber-messaging aims more for instrumental impact than for mutual understanding. Digital media are now part of an "enormous communications industry" that is "stamping out words like buttons."[54] But expanding our capacity to manufacture and distribute messages does not necessarily inspire us to better communication. On the contrary, industrial-grade messaging depersonalizes human interaction. It rarely improves our capacity to empathize with each other or helps us to love one another as distinctive persons. The power to send the same message simultaneously to dozens of friends or millions of potential customers is not a communicative ability as much as a messaging ability. Improved messaging techniques create an illusion of greater communication; an email inbox stuffed with messages, for example, gives us the false impression that we are relationally rich persons or even that we know a lot about what is happening in the world. "Let's see if someone loves me," say college students as they check for incoming email messages. The possibility for more intimate email discourse, for instance, is real, but our hectic lives and unmoderated uses of the technology work against intimacy.

Of course, we could try to nurture practices that facilitate communication rather than messaging. We could limit the number of people with whom we exchange email messages, thereby providing more time and attention for reading, contemplating, and composing messages—as most people still do with handwritten letters. We could also distinguish between email missives that should rightly be only instrumental—such as setting up an appointment time or requesting particular information from someone—and the more personal and relational messages that should be considered in the same vein as handwritten correspondence. But as we adopt the digital systems, we normally adopt *digital practices* as well. The greater the bandwidth, the more difficult it is to avoid transforming nearly all of our emailing into rapid-fire messaging.

Perhaps most important of all, high-bandwidth cyber-messaging depends on low-tech relationships in and through which people form shared meanings of particular words, phrases, ideas, sentiments, and the like. We tend to band together in "speech communities" with a common culture and conversational practices. Religious groups, for example, do this at the theological level so believers can converse meaningfully about God, evil, and salvation. These communities of common discourse are also communities of interpretation that maintain the collective memory of a people, including its common understanding of the contexts for communication—such as worship and prayer in religious communities. To be a good messenger, then, is partly to participate in the ongoing memory of the community—its natural history, preoccupations, and distinct identity. We learn, maintain, and alter the meaning of "good" communication by participating in such communities. This occurs even nationally, for instance, as Americans cultivate a common language for discourse about democracy, justice, civil law, and so on. Communities of interpretation do not have to agree on everything in life, but they do have to share enough culture that they can use a common corpus of words and meanings to engage in shared activities, including the pursuit of virtuous character.

Cyber-messaging tends instead to fragment messages by stripping them of shared meaning. Janet H. Murray celebrates the "procedural authority" of online messaging; she believes that the lack of fixed online "authorship" and the relatively collaborative nature of messaging (everyone can alter and retransmit messages) create a fairly open and democratic medium for storytelling.[55] Richard Lanham similarly praises digital information for being "dynamic rather than static, bi-stable rather than mono-stable, open-ended rather than self-contained."[56] But such symbolic ambiguity can also undermine the shared meanings that we need to live in communion with others. With the new technologies we do gain additional liberty to interpret messages in our own personal fashion, but we can simultaneously lose the shared culture that stabilizes life, confers accepted interpretations, and engenders mutual responsibility. As Manuel Castells suggests, our cultural expressions become "abstracted from history and geography" as they are increasingly mediated by electronic communication.[57] The overall thrust of online messaging is a kind of open-ended temporariness of brief encounters. Cyberspace thereby adopts the character of American life in general, with floating workers and mobile people who often are unable to make any long-term commitments to their communities.[58]

Cyberculture implicitly defines messaging as *individual* interpretation rather than *shared* interpretation. Through a kind of solipsism, cyberculture equates reality with individuals' own notions or interpretations of it. The cyber-ideal is every person being free to express his or her own idiosyncratic observations, like one mongrel in a pack of barking dogs. This is why subscribers to email lists (sometimes called "listservs") rarely strive for consensus or even value the common good. Instead, email lists are often forums for libertine self-expression and dissension—extensions of ego over community. C. A. Bowers argues that technological approaches to human knowing assume that "ideas and values are individually centered." In other words, we presuppose in high-tech culture that the individual should be "the ultimate arbitrator of what knowledge and values will have authority."[59] Of course, this is not entirely bad, since it has the potential to gather into discourse the more marginal viewpoints held by fewer numbers of persons. Nevertheless, cyberculture puts so much faith in self-interpreting information that there is less room left for shared knowing and common pursuits.

Given its emphasis on individual interpretation as well as its bias toward instrumental messaging, cyberculture weakens the relationships among messages, communicators, and communities of interpretation. Information takes on short-term significance apart from community life. For example, people use email to circulate stories, chain letters, data, and jokes with no original attribution and no expectation of subsequent dialogue about the original messages. Also, individuals publish their own home pages filled with egocentric information, from favorite foods to recommended Web links, but usually devoid of the broader social context for their lives, such as their neighborhoods, their voluntary associations, or their philosophies of life. Most personal home pages even presuppose that people do not have philosophies of life, only individual likes, dislikes, and related opinions. In cyberspace, individuals can visit one another's Web sites with no real communion between the two persons. To visit a Web site is little more than registering a "hit" by clicking the mouse on a hyperlink. Usually there is no discourse, only messaging. What does it mean to message for one's own pleasure, without any obligations to others or even any desire to work toward shared understanding?

In cyberspace, we approach communication superficially, like surfers skimming through Web pages. One of the most influential Web-design gurus, Jakob Nielsen, claims that only 16 percent of Internet users actually read Web pages word-by-word. He concludes that Web writers should compose about half as many words for the Web as they would for the printed page.[60] Internet researchers similarly discovered that Web surfers are too impatient to read much; surfers are "basically scanning. There's very little actual comprehension going on."[61] Such brevity may be a virtue if the purpose of communication is purely instrumental, such as conveying information about stock market conditions, baseball scores, and weather forecasts. But what if our purpose is noninstrumental and intrinsically moral—such as becoming genuinely intimate with a person or community, conversing about life, sharing in the fellowship of kindred spirits, mentoring colleagues, and nurturing children? Cyberspace is then at best an ancillary messaging medium rather than a prime location for cultivating shared knowing and moral wisdom. The real value of online communication, then, is largely instrumental—such as getting information, sending a message, setting up appointments, and making contact.

In one sense, context-free, informational messaging is personally liberating. We can each enjoy more information and a wider variety of online relationships without ever having to face the burdensome tasks of reconstructing contexts, deriving shared meaning, or even making moral decisions. Unencumbered by social conventions, we can interpret messages according to our own fancies. According to this perspective, we should not feel burdened by the desire to know *with* others, since we can never know them for certain. Who is to say that one person's *cant* should never be another person's *credo?* After all, we might assume, the truth of one era becomes superstition in a later one. By regulating the freedom to message, we run the risk of missing new discoveries, novel perspectives, and creative innovations. From this frame of reference, cyberspace seems like a route to a more free and open society unburdened by moralistic contexts, tarnished memories, and unfulfillable obligations.

In another sense, however, cyber-messaging leads us to meaninglessness. It tends to discount shared understanding, dismiss traditions, obviate moral obligations, and usher in personal instrumentalism as the

de facto "ethic" for all messaging. If more and more of our time is dedicated to exchanging voluminous amounts of information with impersonal
databases, we will be less likely to commune responsibly with people in
our own domiciles and neighborhoods. According to one major media
industry forecast, consumer spending per person on the Internet grew
faster than any other medium in 1999, and by 2004, consumers will average 228 hours annually in their use of the Internet.[62] Meanwhile, escalating messaging speeds and shifting message contexts create more guesswork, rumors, and questionable suppositions about what people mean. In
spite of our information abundance, we will make even more hasty, mis-
leading, and unfairly critical judgments about individuals and cultures.
This kind of messaging might not bring us into shared understanding as
much as it will stir up impatience, jealousy, and greed. Of course, there
are fine exceptions, such as private email lists through which colleagues,
friends, and family members carry on civil and even relatively intimate discourse. In general, however, unless we leaven cyber-messaging with shared
moral practices and commitments to dialogue, we will increasingly find
ourselves efficiently recycling largely meaningless messages.

Conclusion

In the film *Where the Heart Is,* the "welcome woman," Sister Hubbard, meets the young, pregnant Novalee, who was abandoned at a Wal-
Mart by her boyfriend. The Pentecostal Hubbard aims to give Novalee
some advice. "You read the Bible?" asks Hubbard. "Not as much as I
should," replies Novalee. "Good," says Hubbard with conviction. "Folks
read too much of it, they just get confused. That's why I like to hand out
just one chapter at a time. That way folks can deal with their confusion
as it comes."[63] We all need time to deal with our confusion in a message-
saturated world.

Faster messaging cannot automatically foster the most moral and
intimate human practices. Along with greater messaging power,
increased bandwidth tempts us to squander our time and talents selfishly with little moral reflection and deliberation. Unless we counterbalance our cyber-practices with habits of the heart, we are far more
likely over time to fall selfishly into cultural chaos and moral confusion.
Envying digital bandwidth is simply not a virtue, only evidence of an
insatiable desire for more information.

The quest for more bandwidth can be a manifestation of the insatia-
bility of human desire. Bandwidth envy can become a "pleonexic"
desire—an insatiable drive for more and more of something to the point
at which the desire is no longer good. Cyberculture wrongly embraces

this disordered desire as if it were intrinsically good and right. St. Augustine believed that we should direct such deep ardor only toward the Creator, because compulsive and insatiable human desires otherwise lead to idolatry.[64] The monks overcame such idolatry both by limiting their spoken and written bandwidth and by morally contextualizing their reading as part of the human search for God's goodness. Havel's letters similarly transcended pleonexic idolatry by affirming the intrinsic value of human life and the overarching need for human responsibility. Mired in pleonexic intemperance, we tend to desire greater information without considering the virtue between excess and deficiency.

Unlimited bandwidth, as a goal in and of itself, merely favors informational quantity over virtue. Pursuing bandwidth without a moral vision leads to digital styles of life directed intrinsically toward "having" rather than "being." To borrow a phrase from Pope John Paul II, we seek more messaging power "not in order to be more but in order to be able to spend life in enjoyment as an end in itself."[65] In the era of domestic landline modems and corporate local area networks, we see the ravages of intemperate uses of excess bandwidth: email overload that swamps workers; growing conflicts among people who stereotype each other based on their digital messaging; seemingly endless numbers of Web sites that offer no ideas or expressions worthy of public interest; frustration over the difficulty of locating dependable information online; and millions of hyperlinks that do not work and informational pages that are out of date. These kinds of problems reflect the chaos of a high-bandwidth system in which people have neither the time nor the inclination to be responsible stewards of their own communication.

While we struggle with digital avarice, however, much of the world lacks even some of the basic technologies that we take for granted. Only about 8 percent of the world's population has access to the Internet.[66] Many nations cannot afford the necessary infrastructures. Sixty percent of the earth's inhabitants have never even made a telephone call, and half of the population lives where there are no nearby phone lines.[67] Even the technology-rich United States has an "info-gap" between those who have access to digital technologies and those who do not. We grow indifferent to such disparities because of the digital nooses around our own necks that tug us toward pleonexia.

Unbridled bandwidth easily becomes an entropic diversion, following us everywhere via cell phones, personal digital assistants, pagers, and laptop computers. If we increase our bandwidth intemperately, without also renewing our responsibility, we run the risk of eclipsing the potential value of cyber-innovation to society. We will soon "have nothing to say to each other, or really no time to say it," writes Paul Virilio, "and above all, we shall no longer know how to go about listening to or saying something."[68] The content or meaning of our messages is already becoming less important to us than the speed of delivery. Instead of gaining wisdom, we may find ourselves digitally shackled to trivial, harmful, and manipulative messaging systems. We gain more messaging options but not necessarily better communication. Indeed, we might find that informational abundance further confuses us about the nature and purpose of living. In the digital future, our communities will reflect even more the confusion of Babel.

Of course, we can still enjoy the power that messaging technologies seem to give us. But using power wisely is a great and difficult task. As Clifford Stoll suggests, the equating of raw information with power is a corruption of Francis Bacon's famous dictum that knowledge is power. Most likely Bacon was referring to Proverbs 24:5: "A wise man has great power, and a man of knowledge increases strength."[69] Power is meant to be moderated by wisdom, especially moral wisdom. Whatever level of bandwidth we achieve with groundbreaking innovations, its human value is always limited by our own "moral bandwidth" as fallible persons.[70]

Rather than rediscovering the moral nature of our being, we trap ourselves in forms of cybernetic messaging that demand more and more of our time and attention. Unless we learn informational moderation, our lives will consist of spending longer periods with larger databases, wider networks, and speedier messaging. Cyberculture offers us no means to rise above the entropic noise, no dwelling place to catch our breath, gather our wits, discern our course, and become more intrinsically moral people.

One of the great American myths is the inherent benefit of unfettered movement and constant change. As Henry Adams wrote in his autobiography, speaking of himself, "What he valued most was Motion, and what attracted his mind was change."[71] To some extent, constant motion is a particularly American sickness now spread like a virus through cyberculture. If we are not able to slow down enough to rediscover moral wisdom, our high-tech endeavors will create ever more diversionary noise, resulting in thinner lives. "Remote from the natural world and wired into a workplace that never shuts down," writes Dorothy C. Bass, "we are in danger of slipping into an existence that is always winter and never Christmas."[72] We do not need unlimited bandwidth as much as we need refreshment through time-consuming disciplines such as contemplation and conversation. We need to learn how to moderate the transient traffic of bits and bytes so that we are able to listen to the nontechnological voices of virtue.

chapter three

Seeking Wisdom
in Tradition

■ The high-bandwidth world of informationism is not ultimately satisfying. As a result, today we see all kinds of countercultural movements that question the value of frenzied cyber-messaging. Among the more prominent alternatives is the "simplicity movement" that arose during the 1990s, particularly among overworked managers and technicians in urban areas. This movement calls people out of the information glut and into a more serene world of inner peace and personal joy. Using common-sense ideas, it contrasts the undisciplined life of the infoholic with self-disciplines such as working less, simplifying lifestyles, saying no to others' requests for our time, eliminating unnecessary personal possessions, and focusing on what "really matters."[1] "Maintaining a complicated life," says simplicity advocate Elaine St. James, "is a great way to avoid changing it."[2] The quest for a simpler life often reveals how informational busyness prohibits us from attending to the meaning of our lives.

Simplifying our lifestyles is a good step away from the hectic world of informationism, but it will not necessarily enable us to practice the habits of the heart. Although a simpler lifestyle gives us an opportunity to reflect on the essence of life, it might not be any more coherent than informationism. Bucolic attempts to de-technologize our lives can easily slip into radical individualism and focus us even more determinedly on the present, with little respect for the wisdom of the past. Slowing down our rate of retrieving and disseminating information is a necessary but insufficient step in our journey toward reclaiming the habits of the heart. In the United States, we are especially apt to try

69

something new without considering alternative ways of life in the past. John F. Kasson writes that a "striking number of people still place their hopes almost totally in technological innovations to rescue us from the problems that beset us." Instead of seeking such "idealized retreats," he says, "we need to recover a meaningful sense of historical connections in order to allow ourselves to live more fully and creatively in the present and to provide the basis for a sense of connection with posterity."[3]

This chapter first argues that instead of grabbing greater bandwidth or scrounging after more information, we need to locate a few "first things" that we can count on to begin making our way wisely through the information society. One way of discovering these initial beliefs is through considering the root beliefs of a religious tradition. The Hebrew and Christian traditions maintain an overarching *metanarrative*, a sacred story of a people's historical relationship with the Creator and with other faithful souls. Participating in such a tradition enables us to join the discourse about the metanarrative—what the tradition says is important about life and how we can find meaning, coherence, and wisdom in the midst of information overload. The traditions of *revealed religion*, in which God has revealed truth to humankind, direct us in how to rebind broken relationships among people, God, and the creation. In the Hebrew tradition, faithful people seek *shalom*—right relations of peace and justice. Religious tradition helps us to rebind our lives by commending to us senses of *proportion* and *judgment*. We cannot discover such virtue in raw information, only in time-honored moral practices that flow from people's faithful commitments.

The second section suggests that a crucial moral practice in religion is *listening*. Quickly sending and receiving short digital missives will never direct us to shalom. Many people have reached a point technologically where most of their communicating is only unreflective and trivial messaging. In the information age, we might be losing our capacity to listen and thus to become intimate with the moral wisdom embodied in religious practices. It may never even occur to us that listening can be a virtuous practice of willful obedience to truth. To listen is to give attention to the "other"—even to the divine other.[4] From the perspective of cyberculture, listening is inefficient, old-fashioned, and impotent. Yet listening, like nonviolent social protest that seems to lack any action, can morally revitalize us, build community, and promote social justice as well as personal responsibility. Listening provides the symbolic space for human beings to reconsider who they really are, whom they should trust, and how they should then act. Listening to a religious tradition, in particular, is a spiritual excursion out of the noise of cyberculture and into conversations about the eternal habits of the heart. The faithful listener hears two major messages that point to virtuous living: *gratitude* and *responsibility*. Living gratefully and responsibly binds us to the journey toward becoming virtuous people.

The third section suggests that we are all responsible not just for seeking virtue but also for passing it along to each generation. Every generation is protean and must discover virtue all over again from earlier ones. Virtuous people are *traditores*—"handers over" of the narratives and related moral wisdom within a religious tradition.[5] These traditions can foster a *shared memory, caring practices,* and *mutual accountability*.

Reaching from Chaos to Tradition

No matter how much technology and education we acquire, we are apt sometimes to wonder if there is more to life than information and technique. In *Sweet Thursday*, John Steinbeck describes the second thoughts of Doc, who lives in Monterey, California, and is collecting and selling specimens that he gathers from the area tide pools. Doc contemplatively realizes that the end of his life "is now not so terribly far away. . . . 'Have I worked enough? Have I eaten enough? Have I loved enough?' All of these, of course, are the foundation of man's greatest curse, and perhaps his greatest glory. 'What has my life meant so far, and what can it mean in the time left to me?'" Finally, Doc wonders, "And now we're coming to the wicked, poisoned dart: 'What have I contributed to the Great Ledger? What am I worth?'"[6] These kinds of cosmic questions should haunt residents of the information society—if they take the time to listen to the meaning of their own lives.

Information technologies extend the scope of human messaging, but they do not alter our essential dependence as human beings on language, story, and image to understand who we are and what our purpose is on earth. All human cultures rely on nonscientific forms of knowing to interpret the meaning of life. The problem of "processing" life's information—if we should even call it that—is inherent in the ways that we as humans interpret the world around us. We ask questions about life because our existing understanding is not adequate. We seek to know more intimately who we are and how we should live.

Moral wisdom depends especially on our nontechnological ability to use language well to interpret the meaning and purpose of life. If we desire to know the cosmic picture of life, not just the minutiae of each day, we are bound to consult sages more than databases, to engage in dialogue rather than send messages, and to consider long-standing metanarratives rather than faddish theories. We can make coherent sense of information about life only if we first articulate an overarching notion of where we came from, where we are headed, and where we should direct our energies. Then we will be able to direct ourselves to what is right in the cosmic order of life, not just what is most immediately effective and efficient for today.

Concerns about our value as responsible persons, about the ends to which we should live, and about the type of contributions we might make to our world are deeply religious and necessarily moral. One engineer in Silicon Valley says, "Things are always becoming obsolete. I've put in so much, but the products are gone. I have a sense of futility."[7] Even such mundane or seemingly secular concerns about work can point us to the need for a spiritual reality. What is the real value of work—besides a paycheck? Is there some type of eternal purpose to technological endeavors? Raising such questions can drive us to seek meaning, virtue, and intimacy rather than settling for information, technique, and superficiality. The search for the meaning and purpose of life eventually will lead us out of informationism and into religious tradition.

I use the word "religion" to refer not just to particular religious institutions but more broadly to the ultimate meaning and purpose of existence, along with accompanying practices or customs. The root word *religio* means "to rebind."[8] To act religiously in the world is to rebind the broken cosmos. Religion addresses the most fundamental issues faced by all people in all times—issues of brokenness, healing, and ultimately reconciliation. The purpose of religion is to reveal to people how they can be reconciled to each other, to themselves, to the physical world, and to God. As indicated earlier, in the Hebrew tradition, the great writers of faith referred to this rebinding as shalom.[9] Living in shalom is living a good and right life in tune with the moral wisdom gained through revealed truth.

Ultimately, we should hold all our high-tech endeavors to this test: Do they foster the joy and harmony of shalom, or do they sustain alienation, conflict, unhappiness, and injustice? Seeking shalom helps us to see our informational pursuits as part of a responsible *vocation*, not merely as instrumental tasks or selfish leisure pursuits.[10] Living a religious life means being committed to the rebinding of both private self and public life, to humbly serving one's neighbor rather than merely to exploiting markets, building new organizations, or discovering technological innovations. As Wendell Berry suggests in the title of one of his books, the religious life answers a crucially important question: *What Are People For?*[11] We have to answer that question before we can ask wisely what information technologies are for. Technology is made for human beings; human beings are not made for technology. Religious traditions remind us to keep first things first.

The information society desperately needs such rebinding. The realm of bits and bytes cannot live up to the Pollyannaish predictions of high-tech gurus. For all of their benefits, information technologies can introduce even greater chaos into our lives. We tend to see in such cyber-technologies the enticing potential for us to extend our egos more quickly across space. We also imagine opportunities to exploit markets and make our work more efficient. The sad truth is that we are not interested so much in rebinding brokenness in life as we are in enjoying greater power and control. In short, we are apt to employ new information technologies without considering how they might help or hinder the cause of shalom. Unsolicited prayer requests arriving via email from unknown persons are a strange combination of religious zeal and digital messaging. How are we to assess the validity of such requests? Should we spend precious prayer time on long lists of potentially dubious concerns of which we have no personal knowledge? If we are not careful, our uses of information technology can transform distinctly religious practices into instrumental habits devoid of heartfelt knowing.

Information technology can be cold, impersonal, and frightening. Some of our films and literature imagine an Orwellian future of faceless authoritarian governments that control people with efficient technologies. In the film *2001: A Space Odyssey*, the spaceship computer HAL tries to take over the mission, relegating human beings to the role of technology's slaves. *The Matrix* similarly portrays a technologically dystopian future in which the entire human race is manipulated through technologies that directly program their brains with misinformation about reality. Apocalyptic predictions about technology usually are over-dramatic, but they nonetheless reflect an uneasiness about our growing dependence on information technology. Even our daily struggles to master relatively simple information technologies cause frustration, anger, and despair. We now expect that computers will crash, networks will crawl, and software glitches will destroy our work. We fear both being left behind in the technological advance and being led into a dystopian future.

These kinds of fears are healthy when they remind us of the greater responsibility we have to rebind the cosmos in shalom. Critical discernment can set us apart from the torrents of information and give us a chance to discern reality. Rather than allowing ourselves to be too close to cyberculture, we can distance ourselves from its secular-rational tendencies. In James W. Carey's words, backing away gives us room to "deconstruct the satanic and angelic images that have surrounded, justified, and denigrated the media of communications."[12] But backing away is insufficient. We also need a true vantage point from which to assess our high-tech brokenness. We must be intimate with something or someone real to gain a frame of reference that transcends cyber-culture and overcomes morally vacuous informationism.

One vantage point is the long-standing wisdom within religious traditions. Such traditional wisdom is not always dependable, because human institutions are themselves broken. For centuries, for instance, the Christian church wrongly assumed that the earth was the center of the universe.[13] History documents Christian violence against other believers, supremely evident in the merciless Crusades. Nevertheless, much tradition has withstood the test of time and proven itself far more reliable than faddish theories and ideologies. Rebinding the information society begins when we use the rational power of our minds, guided by the moral wisdom maintained in religious traditions, to show how the prevailing high-tech myths deconstruct themselves. We then discover that the popular mythology about cyberspace is itself a quasi-religious worldview predicated on secular-rational logic and devoid of any truly moral vision of the good life. Religion can help us gain the moral bandwidth and spiritual discernment we need to critique and then renew our informational endeavors.

In contrast with cyber-messaging, religious traditions maintain both messages and contexts within particular practices passed along from generation to generation. They communicate visually and aurally through communal rituals. When Christians celebrate Holy Communion, for example, they recall Christ's words from the Last Supper, watch believers sharing the sacrament together, and taste the elements of the meal. A believer enters into the context as well as the message of the faith; the faith-directing context, the faith-defining message, and the faith-declaring community are united. There are no "virtual" sacraments that merely approximate or emulate real ones; they then cease to be sacraments. Religious traditions sustain particular forms of human experience by maintaining a moral context for the meaning of life—a way of passing along faith and virtue from generation to generation. They co-opt time and space for the purpose of maintaining cultural continuity. This is why religious traditions could never exist purely in cyberspace, where novelty and de-contextualization uproot culture.[14] Traditional practices are still the greatest contexts for binding human communication to moral wisdom.

Religious traditions are the primary carriers of the noninstrumental wisdom we need to counterbalance the secular-rational logic of informationism. Jaroslav Pelikan defines a "tradition" as the "living faith of the dead," and contrasts it with mere "traditionalism"—the "dead faith of the living."[15] David Gross says that a tradition is a "set of observances, a collection of doctrines or teachings, a particular type of behavior, a way of thinking about the world or oneself, a way of regarding others or interpreting reality."[16] I define a religious tradition as a *transcendentally framed and morally directed way of life that faithfully aims to rebind the broken cosmos from generation to generation.*

An authentic religious tradition is not outdated rules, meaningless habits, or petty moralisms. It is the accumulated wisdom and the resulting disciplines, customs, and beliefs that a people carries from person to person through generational time—all of it nurtured as a living dialogue that includes the remembered "voices" of the past. This is why G. K. Chesterton calls tradition a "democracy of the dead" that "refuses to submit to that arrogant oligarchy who merely happen to be walking around."[17] Religious traditions maintain sacraments that help carry the faith by coding it in physical practices. Although such traditions are not completely static, they do seek to preserve what is good and right in human culture. Traditions are carriers of wisdom, of the means and ends of what is true, right, and lasting. Opening our ears and eyes, minds and hearts to tradition can help us to live responsibly, to put our lives in proper order—first things first. If Hans-Georg Gadamer is correct, we can participate in a tradition today by making its historic text and context our own.[18]

The "record" of a tradition, as codified in sacred texts and related writings and practices, identifies where we are to start our search for cosmic rebinding. Whereas information technologies tend to replace wisdom with newer information, religious traditions maintain past revelations that have proven themselves in rebinding the cosmos. Gadamer recognizes that a tradition's metanarrative and past conversations about the metanarrative can be set in documents for later generations to discover anew. He argues that this documenting of the religious past enables us to participate afresh in traditions partly by listening to and dialoguing with the voices of the past ages.[19] Seen in this light, following a religious tradition is not habitually returning to a dead culture but instead a way of remembering proven wisdom in ever-changing cultural contexts. Even the most seemingly routinized religious practices, such as clanging bells that call area believers to prayer at sunrise each day, can remind believers to be faithful practitioners. Because tradition always assumes how the most important "things" are supposed to be in the world, it guides us in morally binding the entire creation, including ourselves, to the telos of shalom. Gross suggests that a tradition must "carry a certain amount of spiritual or moral prestige."[20] Traditional practices—the *doings* of religion—are pathways for sustaining moral wisdom from generation to generation.

The current expressions of a religious tradition, however, are never the last words. A tradition must be flexible enough to seize unpredictable challenges, to address unexpected cultural opportunities, and to overcome its own mistakes. A tradition's memories and records keep it true to core wisdom, but they also document how faithful people have expressed such wisdom in an ever-changing world. Cyberculture is so dynamic that it lacks respect for core wisdom and makes change itself into a symbol for progress. This is why religious tradition is so crucially important in the entropic information age.

Informationism is too morally shallow to direct us as to how we should think about and use cyber-technology. Cyberculture calls merely for more "intellectual capital," "knowledge workers," or broadband communication systems. Such sanguine efforts are little more than attempts to mitigate financial risk and maximize human control over creation. But is risk our root problem? What about arrogance? Irresponsibility? Selfishness? We tend not to ask these root questions because we accept informational versions of social progress—as if technique were religious dogma. To borrow the language of Dietrich Bonhoeffer, informationism now carries the Western world's "cult of reason," "deification of nature," and "faith in progress."[21] In spite of their own weaknesses, some religious traditions have proven themselves over millennia to be sources of deep, lasting, moral wisdom. Tradition can embody what Theodore Roszak calls the "master ideas," the "great moral, religious, and metaphysical teachings which are the foundations of culture."[22] Religious traditions morally leaven the secular-rational techniques of informationism. By becoming more intimate with traditions, we can overcome some of the moral myopia of informationism.

Religious traditions, then, are direction-setting "maps of reality" that generations of wisdom-seeking communities of faith have already charted. They are not finely detailed or perfectly completed maps as much as they are roughly drawn illustrations that tradition-keepers must continually refine and clarify. They provide a hermeneutical language of spiritual and moral insight for our journey through life. The word "hermeneutic" comes from the name of the Greek god Hermes, patron of reading and messenger between the gods and living people.[23] As the myth goes, Hermes was the god of meaning who resisted attempts to limit human understanding to secular interpretations. Religious traditions carry hermeneutical practices and beliefs that enable us to interpret the moral dimensions of contemporary culture. When we follow the metanarrative of a tradition, we relocate ourselves within a moral paradigm that acknowledges a living reality beyond the bounds of informationism. In the Hebrew and Christian traditions, in which God reveals truth to humankind, participating in tradition becomes a means for discovering the wisdom that God has already shared with a broken cosmos.

Tradition provides us with the "oughts" that cyberspace excludes as irrelevant. We desperately need such perspective because, as Martin H.

Krieger suggests, technology is not just a means of innovation but also a "mode of violation." Technological innovation, he says, always "breaks down the conventional and traditional modes of life."[24] It rearranges taboos and establishes new social practices and cultural conventions that often dilute and dissolve older ones. Unless we seek and maintain moral wisdom, our informational efforts can easily violate virtue. Wisdom is one of the four cardinal virtues in classical thought, along with justice, moderation, and courage.[25] Wisdom helps us locate virtue, which in turn supports good customs such as neighborliness, friendship, and hospitality. Moral customs thereby help to lock virtue into culture and dampen the more cold-hearted practices of technique. Blaise Pascal writes that custom is "the source of our strongest and most believed proofs" and has the power to "bend the machine."[26]

The customs inspired by religious traditions can maintain the habits of the heart that foster democracy and protect freedom. This is why many of the most significant social advances in history—from the Civil Rights movement in the United States to the overthrow of apartheid in South Africa—emerged from the efforts of people who followed distinctly religious traditions.[27] As Alexis de Tocqueville explains in *Democracy in America*, Americans' habits of the heart spring from their voluntary commitments to religious traditions, not merely from their participation in civil affairs.[28] Civil society itself depends on underlying communities of moral discourse that nurture moral wisdom, practice moral habits, and sustain virtuous character through time. Religious customs can anchor our habits to moral practices rather than to high-tech mythology.[29] Our religious associations thereby pass along the intimate moral resources we need to cultivate the habits of the heart in an information society.

Hearing the Voices of Religious Wisdom

Julia Barnett Rice campaigned in early twentieth-century America for silent zones on city streets. After Rice got a federal law passed to regulate tugboat horns, she persuaded Mark Twain to lead a silence campaign among schoolchildren who pledged to refrain from making loud and distracting noises near hospitals. Then she convinced New York City council members to put up signs announcing "Quiet Zones" adjacent to hospitals and schools. Soon other cities joined the Quiet Zone movement. Establishing these zones was not only a reaction against noise but also an action in favor of practices such as healing and learning. The advocates of Quiet Zones recognized that stillness and harmony are important aspects of good living.[30] They implicitly believed that quietude facilitates shalom.

Grasping a religious tradition does not begin with clever techniques and crafty plans. It begins rather inauspiciously with listening. If we start with proclamation without first listening, we contribute to the noisy quaqua; the Internet is already populated with opinionated rantings from messengers who do not listen seriously to anyone except perhaps themselves. On the Internet, Robert D. Putnam observes, "Millions more of us can express our views with the click of a mouse, but is anyone listening?"[31] Nor can we start with informational technique instead of listening. Information technology per se rarely leads one to living expressions of wisdom, only to information *about* religion and religious institutions. We carry religious traditions within ongoing, nontechnological customs such as prayer, worship, and contemplation. Only when we intimately encounter believers and God through such customary practices do we begin to hear the heart of a tradition. This is why the prophetic ministry of the Old Testament contrasts the silence of God with the trivial racket of human beings.[32] It is also why the medieval Christian church emphasized contemplation as a route to a living faith and to a deeper fellowship with God. Of all human activities, however, listening is one of the most difficult to grasp because we cannot see anyone doing it. Listening happens in the mind and in the heart—*within* our being. Religious customs can provide the means of hearing with our hearts as well as our minds.

The more racket we create, the harder it is to hear ourselves, others, and God. "Lately I have had too many visits and there has been too much talking," the Trappist monk Thomas Merton wrote self-critically in his journal in 1964.[33] Nowadays, we might say, "Too many emails and too little reflection" or "Too much messaging and too little meaning." The rule in one monastery was not "Do not speak" but rather "Do not speak unless you can improve on the silence."[34] In the information age, we can use the noise of messaging to avoid intimacy with God, just as we use the daily diversions of videos and recorded music to circumvent troubled interpersonal relationships. Throughout the centuries, humans tried to transform religious traditions into "noisy" activities, virtually guaranteeing that they would not hear God because of the resulting racket. Today, for instance, much "church work" makes congregants so busy that they have scant time and little capacity for listening. Cyberculture wrongly assumes that good can occur only when there is a lot happening, especially newsworthy events and technological energy. "The feeling that 'if nothing is happening, nothing is happening' is the prejudice of a superficial, dependent and hollow spirit," writes Václav Havel, "one that has succumbed to the age and can prove its own excellence only by the quantity of pseudo-events it is constantly organizing, like a bee, to that end."[35] Informational motion today is anathema to spiritual intimacy and therefore to moral wisdom.

Religious traditions record in their customs how a people listened to the Almighty and to each other, and then how they responded by seeking to live obediently. The lexical roots for the word "listen" *(akouo* and *hupakouo)* derive from the word for "obedience."[36] When we listen to others, we give them an opportunity to define our reality by revealing things to us; we use the remarkable gift of empathy to put ourselves under their counsel, into their words and gestures. In this way, we get to know another person, including God. Loving God and other people depends on getting to know them intimately by listening to them "with the ear of the heart."[37] As the work of an obedient will, heartfelt listening is fundamentally a moral act that can foster intimacy and bind people together under the authority of God.[38]

This emphasis on listening likely seems ludicrous to minds brimming with informationism. In the information age, we incorrectly assume that we must first transmit in order to become wise persons. We see ourselves as the makers rather than the discoverers of wisdom. We forget that God might have already spoken wisdom and consequently that we will have to listen if we intend to glean it. Nor are we likely today to consider that the religious customs embedded within living traditions are carriers of God's wisdom. Yet even the Bible "speaks" in and through the practices of the community of faith, from listening to the singing of psalms to hearing the preaching of the gospel. Nicholas Wolterstorff calls this the "divine discourse" through which God speaks to and through his people from generation to generation.[39] Only by listening can we search outside ourselves, beyond the techno-clutter, for the ultimate meaning and moral purpose of life. Listening enables us to transcend the limits of the "secular mind" and to cultivate a "sacred mind" humbled by gratitude and anxiously aspiring to know the Almighty and live obediently.[40] Traditions provide the times, places, and practices that give us access to the dialogue that others have had and are still having with God and each other. In the Christian tradition, for example, reciting the Lord's Prayer and celebrating the Lord's Supper bring believers into fellowship with God and neighbor.

What do we hear when we listen to these revelations embedded in the customs of a tradition? We hear something like this: "I created you personally as part of an especially talented species that can celebrate life thankfully and care for this world and your neighbor responsibly." We repeatedly find these two essential messages in the Hebrew and Christian traditions: *gratitude* and *responsibility*. Of course, there are also many nuances to the discourse within particular traditions. But tradition-specific discourse flows largely from gratitude, which is ultimately thankfulness for the creation, and from responsibility, which is primarily service to others. All of us who listen to these two messages are planting our self-identities and intimacies in the wisdom of revealed truth rather than in humanly generated noise. Such roots grant us a sense of responsibility for things greater than our own survival and higher than our own self-interest. Aleksandr I. Solzhenitsyn says that freedom was given to us "conditionally," on the assumption of our "constant religious responsibility."[41] Listening to the wisdom within a tradition can lead us to adopt responsible habits of the heart shaped by gratitude to God and care for neighbor.

Moreover, these two crucial religious motifs, as part of the rebinding of both the exterior world and our inner lives, direct us to the integrity we need in the midst of the cultural chaos of the digital age. As divine "givens," gratitude and responsibility transcend informationism by reordering our views even of informational reality. They are every human being's calling. God calls us to gratitude and responsibility; we listen and then respond by living virtuously. As Walker Percy puts it, religious faith springs from a "metascientific, metacultural reality, an order of being apart from the scientific and cultural symbols with which it is grasped and expressed."[42] In other words, a faithful listener no longer hears information and technique as ends in themselves. Instead, he or she recognizes that all technological endeavors should derive their purpose from the greater mission of thankful responsibility. Without such a moral purpose, cyber-technology becomes a self-defeating endeavor, like that of Sisyphus, who pushes the rock up the mountain again and again. If we depend only on our own techniques, with no external resources, no lasting binding, only one innovation after another, each technique solves some problems but also creates longer-term ones. Undertaken within the truths of revealed religion, however, short-term informational endeavors can become expressions of gratitude and modes of life-giving service that bring some shalom into the world.

Revealed religion tells us that we have inherited the world and everything in it. We did not create the world or even ourselves; all of it, including life, is a gift. We are obligated to accept this inheritance thankfully and to exercise our wills responsibly over the range of our particular part of God's world. We are to be stewards instead of exploiters, listening caregivers rather than noisy messengers, and suffering servants rather than indifferent technicians. Although informationism attempts to situate us in the world as control freaks and efficiency experts, we accept instead the greater calling to moral responsibility. We refuse to venerate information technology per se because we admit that greater knowledge without deeper wisdom is at best a mixed blessing. Our impressive messaging could potentially cut us off from tradition and unravel the tapestries of gratitude and responsibility that bind us to God, neighbor, self, and creation. Revealed religion reminds us to listen and thereby to be thankful caretakers rather than ungrateful domineers. Listening with others in the quiet zones of a tradition gives us a chance to hear, remember, and believe the divine discourse that can direct us to the habits of the heart.

Passing Along Virtue

In her book *Who Are We*, Jean Bethke Elshtain suggests that as "prideful late-twentieth century creatures" we "no longer think of ourselves as *belonging* to anyone or anything. We do not belong—we own; we possess." Those of us in the developed West possess an astonishing array of communication tools, from pencils to laptop computers. Nevertheless, our triumphs frequently ring hollow in hindsight. When we begin to listen to one another, surely we hear this hollowness. "We are," Elshtain adds, "creatures who have forgotten what it means to be faithful to something other than ourselves."[43] As we listen to other faithful people and to the divine Other, we can begin replenishing the moral practices of a tradition. Among these practices are *remembering our stories, caring for one another,* and *holding each other mutually accountable.*

As human beings, we naturally remember through the stories of our own lives and through those of our communities. Typically, our communal narratives recall what the members believe to be good and worthwhile ends. The unity of the moral life, writes Alasdair MacIntyre, is the "unity of a narrative quest." Within this quest we seek to gain more knowledge of "the good" and to bring our individual lives and our communities back to the grace of such goodness. Virtues can "sustain us in the relevant kind of quest for the good, by enabling us to overcome the harms, dangers, temptations and distractions which we encounter, and which will furnish us with increasing self-knowledge and increasing knowledge of the good." Narratives open up traditions of moral wisdom for our understanding, appreciation, and recollection. Religions of "the book"—such as Christian and Jewish faiths—are expressed communally through the memories of a shared metanarrative.[44]

One thing we learn from religious traditions is the importance of habits of remembering. Community narratives are partly a means of recalling the virtuous deeds of past generations and thereby being inspired by them again and again. Of course, such recollecting can be corrupted by nostalgic yearnings, by intentional alterations of history, and simply by faulty memories. Nevertheless, we live within a virtuous community partly by re-remembering the events and meanings of shared narratives from age to age. Theodore Roszak says that memory is "the register of experience where the flux of daily life is shaped into the signposts and standards of conduct."[45]

Information without memory fogs our moral vision. Cornel West says that "we live in a society that suffers from historical amnesia, and we find it very difficult to preserve the memory of those who have resisted and struggled over time for the ideals of freedom and democracy and equality."[46] Many young people today are disconnected from the past, even from the histories of their own families. Their lives are like video games that change regularly with each new program cartridge. When we forget the past, we also lose our footing into the future. We no longer know who we are or where we should be headed.

By contrast, remembering religious metanarratives and their corresponding, time-honored understandings can preserve wisdom. When we go astray, they help us recall the route back to community and to moral wisdom. Gross suggests that remembering enables us to connect with the things that matter most in life.[47] Remembering is one way of keeping what is good, of staying intimate with the right meaning and purpose of life. Memory was even one of the canons of ancient rhetoric. Medieval Christians believed memory was as vital for human beings as their intellect and emotion.[48] "Memory is necessary for all the operations of Reason," wrote Pascal.[49] Whereas informationism emphasizes the transitory and temporal aspects of our existence, metanarrative-anchored traditions highlight the more eternal and cohesive concerns of human beings.[50]

Since each generation must grasp wisdom anew, cultural memory is the glue that holds past, present, and future together at any point in time. All human endeavors have histories that can illuminate both particular cultures and the human condition. The history of cyberspace, for instance, emerges from the stories of pre-Net messaging, from the invention of the telegraph in the mid-nineteenth century to the rise of radio, television, and satellite communication during the twentieth century.[51] Popular technological histories often naively start afresh with each new technology, as if no one learned anything of value from earlier experiences. Are the greed and arrogance of so many Internet companies today really that different from earlier corporate exploits such as those of the robber barons? Do not the varieties of folly emerging in cyberspace—such as pornography and get-rich-quick schemes—merely reflect the types of problems that plagued social deployments of earlier media? A lack of memory makes it more difficult to make sense of the present.

Traditions of revealed religion also emphasize the importance of caring for others. Caring is seeking the best for others by skillfully and empathetically attending to their needs. One of the most virtuous ways for us to live with gratitude and responsibility is to care. Caring for others leads us from individualism into community, where we affirm the intrinsic value of others and where everyone potentially becomes our neighbor. How can we care for people in cyberspace and for a high-tech society overall? How can we become caretakers of these new technologies and caregivers to technicians and information managers?

Caring orients us to real needs and to actual people rather than merely to abstract analyses and expert opinions. In this sense, caring—not technique—is the intrinsic "skill" of responsible serving. Listening to others' stories of life can nurture caring among specific people in actual time and real space. The Internet, on the other hand, easily depersonalizes the very relationships that are meant to be the sine qua non of caring. It makes our listening less inviting and engaging. We can use technologies caringly, but they themselves are unable to care. Only people can care. In a high-tech age, professionalism and expertise join with technology to sabotage care by depersonalizing our storytelling and weakening our capacity for listening.

The Christian faith has long taught the crucial significance of caring. Peterson says that either Christians care or "they don't stay in business very long, or they don't stay credible very long."[52] The term *cura animarum* ("the cure of souls") appears repeatedly in the Christian tradition. The word *cura* combines two words—"cure" and "care." "Cure" is skillfully nurturing someone to health by applying the right knowledge and technique. "Care" is being a compassionate companion to the needy person. The idea of *cura* combines these two in one; the caregiver is tuned to a person's heart as well as to the body, to communion as well as to skill.

Today, we probably know more about caring "than any other generation that has ever lived on the face of the earth," writes Peterson, but people still complain about how they have been mistreated. People say they have been "abused, exploited, organized, bullied, condescended to, ripped off." Throughout history, curing without caring has been an enormous problem for societies. "For thousands of years now," admits Peterson, "bitter stories have been told of the rapacity of priests, physicians, nurses, and counselors, as they move smilingly through our communities in their sheep's clothing."[53] Reintegrating cure and care is crucially important in an information society, since the techniques of curing tend to advance faster than our capacity for caring. In the Christian tradition, acts of caring repeatedly renewed movements and institutions—including the church—that had become cold, calculating, and self-serving. The story of Christianity is meant to be the good news of a caring God who calls disciples to care for the creation and one another.

Each one of us is born into a time and place that presents us with opportunities to care responsibly. We do not have to wait to gain technical expertise or to earn the social advantages of rank, position, or title. Such instrumental thinking ignores the existing range of our effective will. Although today we technocratically perceive ourselves as instruments for control, we are also vessels for caring. We are persons of our times, ushered by the mysteries of providence into particular opportunities to care for others. History is not a cybernetic system moving toward entropy. Neither are our personal lives. We cannot fully control time and place, although we can—and should—seize the opportunities that come before us to act responsibly by caring. Often we do not have much choice about our life's circumstances, but we always inherit opportunities to care because of the brokenness all around us. If we hear via a mass-distributed email about a childhood friend's illness, we could care enough to send a card and note of encouragement or even call the past friend to retell a few stories of grace from years ago. We can care by teaching others strategies for coping with information overload and helping them learn how to use cyberspace wisely. Our own lives should be stories of caring.

Whereas the secular-rational worldview tries to remove suffering from our minds, the responsible caregiver tunes into the world's suffering. No matter how much information we collect and how speedily we distribute it, people will continue to suffer. Alleviating suffering requires that we care enough to sacrifice. "For a people trained in a culture of getting things done (pragmatism) and taking care of ourselves (individualism)," writes Peterson, "the life of sacrifice doesn't seem at all obvious; neither does it seem attractive."[54] If we can hide suffering, we assume, we can avoid sacrifice. So we place suffering people in institutions where the experts can care for them and where *we* do not have to hear stories about *their* suffering. Or we leave the television set or radio blaring as the priest administers last rites to a loved one; the noise gives us a connection to this world and enables us to avoid the thoughts of our own eventual death. Most North Americans today never see anyone die in person—even their loved ones. We watch television, read novels, surf the Web, and go to movies partly to get our minds off our and others' troubles. None of these potentially mind-numbing actions is intrinsically wrong, but today we almost automatically use them to tune out much of the real pain of the world—even the suffering in our families and neighborhoods. We are understandably uncertain about when, where, and why we should invite others' suffering into our lives. But as Václav Havel learned under communist oppression, "the only genuine values are those for which one is capable, if necessary, of sacrificing something."[55] When we hide human suffering behind the noise of messaging, we remove opportunities for sacrificial caring.

Those of a religious faith admit the existence of pain in a broken world and then locate specific brokenness by listening to others' confusion and cries. If we engage in trivial messaging all day long, we can temporarily push the broken world out of our minds and away from our hearts. Over time we can become indifferent to the stories of our neighbors, family members, coworkers, and fellow citizens. Caring is nearly the opposite of such messaging; it listens for the groans of a suffering people. The prophet Isaiah spoke of a "suffering servant" who would one day save the world, not by conquering it with technique but by suffering for it. In the Christian tradition, that servant is Jesus Christ, who suffered on the cross for the sins of humankind. The suffering servant, a perfect caregiver, is our model for responsibly caring for others. Søren Kierkegaard writes, "'Authority' does not mean to be a king, but by a firm and conscious resolution to be willing to sacrifice everything, one's very life, for a cause. . . . This infinite recklessness is authority."[56] We do not suffer with others because we like suffering; we suffer because being responsible people leads us into others' burdens and requires us to endure as well as celebrate life with them.

We also care partly by creating the kinds of technologies that truly serve individuals and society rather than developing technologies merely to advance our personal interests or to bolster our egos. Caring engineers design information technology that is easy to use and requires minimal technical background. Often the free-speech, protect-your-rights rhetoric about the Internet demonstrates a lack of care for people who might have to suffer at the hands of rampant libertinism. Protecting children from online invasions of their privacy and from the ravages of pornography are means of caring. So is pointing out the limits of such technologies and cautioning people about being overly optimistic about technical solutions to fundamentally moral problems. Equipping students and elders with the skills and understanding necessary to find the right online content and to evaluate its sources are also ways of caring. Helping people who spend too much time in cyberspace to rediscover the joy of proximate community is a crucially important means of caring for the quality of their lives. Religious traditions provide practices that help us assess whether the contemporary stories of our own technological lives are in tune with caring. Rather than merely being efficient messengers, we can strive to be stewards of such practices as friendship, neighborliness, and hospitality.

The institutional character of caring is more difficult to discern even though it is crucially important in a postindustrial society.[57] Lewis Mumford distinguishes between "authoritarian" and "democratic" technologies. The more authoritarian technologies are extremely powerful, centralized, and capital-intensive. As enormous, inflexible systems, they are generally insensitive to moral customs. Nuclear power generators and television networks, for instance, depend on elaborate technical systems and bureaucratic administrations. Democratic technologies, on the other hand, are more decentralized and reconfigurable so that different groups can more easily master them and freely refashion them for their own local and idiosyncratic needs. Democratic technologies engender participation and reformation, enabling communities to cultivate techniques that are in tune with their own ways of life.[58] Windmill-driven generators and portable video cameras are relatively democratic compared with nuclear power stations and television networks. Ivan Illich calls democratic technologies "tools for conviviality."[59]

Democratic technologies are presumably more conducive to caring for others. In one sense, the Internet is democratic because it is relatively easy for any literate person to use, because its messaging is distributive (person-to-person) as well as hierarchal, and because the costs of digital messaging are relatively low compared with those involved in operating a printing press or a broadcast station. But institutional realities are always more complex and ambiguous than purely technological realities. For instance, not everyone in society has a computer or easy access to the Internet. Also, few Internet users can write their own software; most of us depend on programs created by engineers in large corporations. Frequently, programs cannot do what we need them to do, in the ways we need things accomplished. In addition, concentrations of capital can direct how people use information technologies. According to one study, over half the time that Americans spend on the Web is spent on only four Web sites.[60] Most of all, cyber-technologies are not always compatible with noninstrumental, local, and dialogic cultures. Instead, they best serve the instrumental needs of marketers and bureaucracies.

Bonnie A. Nardi and Vicki L. O'Day call for "information ecologies" anchored in local communities. They cite schools that established their own guidelines for responsible use of online media.[61] Certainly such decentralized uses of cyber-technologies represent steps toward making them more convivial. But the notion of responsible "use" still identifies people largely as consumers of messages rather than caring, responsible participants in dialogue. Instead of seeking an "information ecology," we should foster "ecologies of shared wisdom" or "ecologies of mutual caring" that embrace shalom. When we focus on information rather than on virtue, we are less likely to create communities where people care for one another.

Seeking justice is one of the most potent forms of caring. Social institutions and technologies that are themselves unjust or that promote discriminatory practices are stumbling blocks to caring. Martin Luther King Jr. wrote in *Letter from a Birmingham Jail* that negative peace is merely the "absence of tension," whereas positive peace is the "presence of justice."[62] Information technologies come and go, but rarely do we assess them as agents of justice or injustice. Instead, we reduce justice to a matter of overcoming the "digital divide" between those who have access to technology and those who do not. We uncaringly equate individual consumerism with social justice. Shalom is hardly equivalent to universal Internet access or a computer in every classroom; such weak notions of justice could merely lead us to enslave every individual to the same technological system. If elementary-age students are not learning to read adequately, for example, computers or Internet access are hardly the best solutions for improving their education. A caring institution seeks a goodness beyond what is required for organizational self-preservation or simply for parity with other institutions. Moral wisdom reminds us that virtuous action is performing *above* normal principles and *beyond* ordinary laws. It captures a "rightness" that is good for actual people in a real place and time, not solely for everyone in the abstract. Communities of revealed religion, for instance, remember stories of justice so that people can recall what justice is and know how to be just.

If personal caring is being a *mensch*—a responsible person of honorable intentions and deep regard for others—then institutional caring is not just being an organization of individual mensches but also a mensch-like community. Both individual and institutional mensches offer us their lives as parables of virtue. Books about Internet companies are loaded with success stories about technological innovations and skyrocketing company stock prices but nearly devoid of tales about mensches. What does this say about the moral character of cyberculture? Why do we talk about Internet geeks, hackers, and spammers but never about Internet mensches or saints? It is even difficult to imagine how a Net saint would live, what he or she would do that is fundamentally self-sacrificial and God-honoring. We have little notion of goodness and rightness within the social use of information technologies. If we desire to use information technology for the purpose of caring, we need a compelling concept of the cyber-commonweal, sustained by stories about virtuous people who use the technology wisely.

Maybe one saintly role model on the Web is Kathleen Wilson, whose own suffering became a context for serving others. She remembers, as a five-year-old bouncing on her grandmother's bed, wondering what special mission God had planned for her. Years later she seemed to have achieved something of a heavenly life, working as a photographer in

Athens, Greece. But soon she noticed numbness and then a tingling sensation in her right leg. Within a month, she was confined to a wheelchair. She returned to her parents' home in the United States and was soon diagnosed with multiple sclerosis (MS). "The first three months were especially difficult," recalls Wilson, "At 3 A.M. you think, 'What am I going to do with my life? I don't even have a life.' So I started surfing the Internet." At that time, there was little information about MS online. Wilson accepted that discovery as the beginning of her life's calling, namely, to create a Web site, MSWorld, where people with MS could exchange information about the disease and communicate with others who had it. "We're all about enhancing the lives of people with MS," she says. "We're into maximizing the joy out of every day." Among her projects is awarding Life Enhancement Grants to enable people with MS to buy means of transportation. "We want to ask people, 'What would you like to do?' Have lunch with your friends every Friday?"[63] Wilson listened to the call to care and responded obediently, regardless of her own suffering.

Finally, listening to a religious tradition can remind us that caring communities nurture people who hold each other accountable. A community's historical narratives carry moral standards that serve as yardsticks for the moral health of people and institutions. Such stories should remind us that we are responsible not just for our own thoughts and actions but also for those of our neighbors. MacIntyre says that we can ask each other for an accounting. We are, after all, part of each others' stories.[64] I am my neighbor's keeper, and he or she is my keeper as well. As our lives intersect, our stories influence each other. We should care about what we all do with cyber-technologies, particularly within the domains of our own communities at work, home, school, and neighborhood. It is not just leaders, government officials, techno-gurus, managers, and experts who are accountable for technological endeavors— although they certainly are. If we take no interest in how our schools or governments are funding and employing Internet technologies, for instance, we probably do not care enough to be accountable with others for our own communities. If, on the other hand, our religious metanarratives reveal our accountability for the world, we are much more likely to become people whom our communities can count on to listen and then to care.

Amidst all the hubbub about cyber-progress, we should remember that virtuous communities are made up of people who listen and who embrace stories that inspire virtue. Throughout history the most virtue-forming stories have come from religious traditions, not from self-help manuals, flow charts, mission statements, or organizational operating principles. In fact, we could ask along with MacIntyre whether it is even possible to cultivate the habits of the heart without narrative-based traditions of virtue. In religious communities, metanarratives inform our personal stories, helping members to remember, to care, and to be accountable. Stewardship requires us to develop technologies that are in tune with our particular narrative traditions, related memories, modes of caring, and forms of accountability. Our tendency toward "one-size-fits-all" products, "out-of-the-box" solutions, and "turnkey" technologies—where only technique defines use—is an unhealthy penchant if we seek to nurture virtue.

Conclusion

Lewis Mumford reminds us that the New World afforded immigrants a land of abundance. "The first promise of the New World," he writes, "was that of renewing the vision of effortless plenty that Old World man had wistfully relegated to the long-past golden age." For a time the "settlement of the New World lifted the fear of poverty, death, overcrowding. . . . Here nature's bounty for once temporarily exceeded the human demand."[65] Manuel Castells argues that we have moved beyond this "Modern Age," in which people believed that reason would enable them to use culture to dominate nature. We are now entering an era in which "Culture refers to Culture, having superseded Nature to the point that Nature is artificially revived ('preserved') as a cultural form."[66] If Castells is right, we are all becoming "environmentalists" in the sense of creating our own artificial environments without appeals to tradition or ears for listening to voices of virtue. Cyberspace seems to offer us paths to such sweet abundance, without the need for moral wisdom. In this mythical perspective, the Internet is the new land of the free, the lush garden of endless delight. It will irrigate our dry hearts and fulfill our fondest dreams—all without recourse to old-fashioned ways of life.

On the contrary, the wisdom of the past is not merely a bias or a prejudice but a necessary source of moral direction. Without historical memory, there can be no wisdom. Deleting all earlier habits of the heart, all wisdom and related customs, all divine discourse in favor of pure information, is not progressive thought as much as scatterbrained illogic. "The present age is demented," declares Walker Percy. "It is possessed by a sense of dislocation, a loss of personal identity, an alternating sentimentality and rage which, in an individual patient, could be characterized as dementia."[67] Even our vast bibliographic projects, such as research libraries and powerhouse databases, need human wisdom if they are to help us find out who we are, where we are located, and where we ought to be headed within the larger cosmic order. "In general," writes Mumford, "New World man wasted the treasures he opened up and he trampled out the very life he had originally quickened to. . . . Had New World man shown more understanding of the whole range of primitive gifts, too often despised and cast aside, he would have left mankind as a whole both wiser and richer."[68] Gratefully accepting God's gifts and then responding responsibly are ways of being wiser.

We have to be particular kinds of people if we intend to act responsibly as caretakers of creation. Responsible stewardship is our *relationship to* creation as well as our effort *exerted on* creation. Just by being good people, we leaven the world around us. In the study of ethics, scholars refer to such good people as those of virtuous character. Plato used the Greek word *dikaiosune*, translated "justice," to capture this sense of virtue.[69] St. Paul used the same word when he addressed the Greek philosophers on Mars Hill about the existence of their "unknown God" (Acts 17:23). But the concept of virtue means much more than legal rightness; it includes all the "ways of being" that identify someone as a person of genuinely good character. Such a lofty notion of virtue challenges the instrumentalism of technique, which wrongly assumes that efficiency and control are inherently good. If virtue guides our high-tech endeavors, we are far more likely to gain real and worthy benefits from information technologies. If not, we will continue to replace the wisdom with secular-rational ways of knowing that are themselves insufficient for rebinding the world. As Elshtain suggests, in spite of all our marvelous communication technologies, we are "not using the ethics that we have, especially we communities of belief that embody a tradition the culture long ago abandoned."[70] Balancing the practical gains from technique with the virtuous gains of moral wisdom is the best synergy that we could hope for in a high-tech world.

Religious people and communities, as they embrace virtue, can become signposts to the hope that this broken world can be rebound— and that it *is* being rebound. The virtue within a tradition ultimately points us upward to a more enduring and right state of affairs. It also inspires us to embrace neighborly responsibility as part of our own identity. As the next chapter posits, such virtue gives us a sense of proportion as humble caretakers in a world filled with technological folly— even our own. This is why we need to assess not just our technological progress but also our moral being. In Solzhenitsyn's language, we should live toward "the fulfillment of a permanent, earnest duty so that [our] life journey may become above all an experience of moral growth: to leave life a better human being than one started it."[71]

chapter four

Laughing Ourselves
to Humility

In 2001, the United States Federal Bureau of Investigation (FBI) caught one of its own agents, Robert Hanssen, selling secrets to the Russians. News reports indicated that the veteran employee had been spying for the Russians for at least fifteen years without drawing agency suspicions. Some reporters speculated that the FBI might never have caught Hanssen without the assistance of friendly Russian agents. But the most stunning aspect of the case, from a technological perspective, was Hanssen's use of FBI computer networks and databases to confirm that the agency was not investigating him. The FBI's own high-tech systems helped Hanssen to conduct counterespionage by verifying that the agency had not detected his activities.[1]

When the case became public, the FBI touted its ability to catch Hanssen "red-handed."[2] Skeptical reporters wondered, however, if the agency really deserved such accolades. They wanted to know why the FBI had failed to conduct regular lie detector tests of Hanssen. Also, they were perplexed by the fact that Hanssen had been permitted access to the FBI's computer files that would have stored internal investigative information about him. Hanssen had even left copies of letters he had written to his Russian contacts on the hard drive of his home computer. He had encrypted the letters, but surely he knew of the FBI's ability to crack such codes. Although the FBI pitched Hanssen's arrest to news media as an agency victory, public information about the case suggested instead that the agency was enormously lax in its procedures for detecting moles. Eventually, FBI Director Louis Freeh admitted that "at the end of the day, all of our systems probably need to be looked at and probably improved."[3] His humility was a refreshing change from the FBI's earlier spin on the fiasco.

The Hanssen episode is a parable about human use of information technology. It reminds us that information technology does not merely give us more managerial control over our own organizations; it also creates opportunities for *mis*-control and *mis*-management. Seemingly "good" technologies often end up in the hands of evil-intentioned people who do foolish and sometimes even horrible things with them. The terrorists who commandeered four jet aircraft in 2001, crashing two of them into the World Trade Center and one into the Pentagon, used Internet terminals at public libraries to organize and coordinate their diabolical missions.[4] Cyber-innovation also creates unintended consequences that are bound to happen. High-tech "revolutions" are two-edged swords that solve some human problems but invariably create new ones, including moral dilemmas.

No matter how bright our technological future may appear, human history tells the real story: Technological quirks can become bugs, bugs can turn into significant problems, and ongoing problems can eventually escalate into disasters. Similarly, human weaknesses become bad habits, bad habits engender character flaws, and the problems of character fall into personal and collective manifestations of evil. Our cyber-endeavors are never free of either technical imperfections or human nature.

The first section of this chapter examines our high-tech projects as forms of human *folly*. We hold to the kind of technological hope that E. I. Smith, captain of the *Titanic*, expressed in 1912: "I cannot imagine any condition which could cause this ship to flounder. I cannot conceive of any vital disaster happening to the vessel. Modern shipbuilding has gone beyond that."[5] We all assume that cyber-innovation is good and unstoppable. But information technology is not always so wonderful, benign, or manageable. Even when we claim greater efficiency and control, we sometimes end up spending more time and energy dealing with technological setbacks, cost overruns, message overloads, and evil uses of supposedly good technologies.

The second section examines the ways that information technologies often create new moral dilemmas, even when they are solving instrumental problems. High-tech gains invariably elicit unexpected moral setbacks. Often we futilely try to solve our moral crises with greater technological innovation, thereby expanding the scope as well as the depth of cyber-related problems. What I call *Fool's Law* postulates that new information technologies never live up to the hype that surrounds their invention; many of the effects of new information technologies are beyond human prediction and control; information technology partly subverts the mission of organizations that adopt it; and striving for technological innovation without fostering the habits of the heart is a recipe for moral chaos.

The third section suggests that we should fear our own technological exploits. We are not merely inept. We are also mixed-up and, at times, strikingly depraved. Failing to care for the creation, we make life unpleasant and sometimes miserable for others. The technologies that make messaging faster can also render life more confusing, stressful, and unsatisfying. Recognizing the potential for moral as well as technical disaster, we need to accept the *humility* that comes with responsibility. Humility is a crucial virtue in the age of cyberspace. It reminds us to accept our technological limits and then to live thankfully within them. Humility leads to a healthy skepticism and even a *reticence:* a willingness, when appropriate, to say no to some technologies or to particular uses of them, while remaining grateful for those that help us to live more fully as virtuous stewards of our time and talents.

The fourth section considers how humor can foster technological humility. The information society elicits comedic commentaries on the plight of people struggling through cyber-mazes. Humor can help us not to take ourselves too seriously. It can also express both subtle and profound insights into the moral aspects of our technological endeavors. Humor especially *fosters a proper sense of proportion, reveals our tomfoolery,* and *cultivates greater patience.* In all three ways, humor regrounds us in reality by reminding us of the gap between our high-tech pronouncements and our actual accomplishments in a broken cosmos. When we laugh together at our high-tech folly, we recognize our common predicament. Then we can give thanks that we, too, have survived the absurdities of the information age while trying to be responsible stewards.

Acting like Cyber-Fools

When the Love Bug computer virus flashed through the Internet in 2000, it destroyed millions of files on personal and corporate machines.[6] News media estimated that it caused over $10 billion in damages to computers from the Pentagon to the British Parliament. Experts quickly determined that the virus originated in the Philippines. Within several days, authorities in Manila concluded that twenty-four-year-old Onel de Guzman, a computer science student, was the likely perpetrator. Not only had he created similar viruses, but he also initially even admitted that he "might" have released the Love Bug. In addition, Guzman had proposed for his college thesis a similar technology designed to gain free access to the Internet by stealing passwords from users. But Guzman could not be prosecuted, because Philippine law had no regulations against such misuses of computers. In fact, he became a national hero and received many job offers from high-tech firms.[7]

This story raises many troubling questions. How could the software of a billion-dollar company—Microsoft—become susceptible to a simple virus program that probably hundreds of thousands of moderately savvy programmers could have written?[8] Why did so many people who received the virus-laden email message open up a file attachment named "I Love You" supposedly received from business associates? Why did Guzman become something of a national hero after perpetrating such an expensive and menacing crime? Unfortunately, the Love Bug virus is not an isolated case of technological folly. A study in 2001 discovered that one out of five company computers is infected by at least one virus.[9]

No matter how diligently we try to domesticate cyberspace, we will discover that parts of it are out of control. Although the technology that undergirds the information society is the product of much rational thought and remarkable technical achievement, its social nature and moral impact largely elude us. Information technologies are already well integrated into many societies, but we can barely discern what they actually have contributed to or detracted from life. But one thing is certain: For all their benefits, cyber-technologies also provide new ways for us to act foolishly. They do not fundamentally improve human nature. Instead, they give people new means of being who they already are—confused creatures with mixed motives and a severely limited capacity to predict the future.

Because of the dominant triumphalistic rhetoric of the high-tech revolution, we lose track of what it means to be a foolish user of information technology. A fool can be well-informed, even quite knowledgeable. His or her problem is not merely technical or informational but rather a lack of wisdom. In short, a fool is clueless about what is truly important in life, the bigger picture of human existence. Whereas the wise person grasps the natural rhythms of life and the essential truths of the human condition, the fool lacks intimacy with the fabric of moral living—love, faithfulness, generosity, and the like.[10] Fools major in the minors. A cyber-fool, for instance, could be highly skilled at managing a digital network but might never consider how to do so responsibly on behalf of a community. Wise people are in touch with moral reality, whereas fools are enamored with relatively trivial and technical matters—like an attorney who masters legal procedures but is clueless about justice.

In cyberculture, computer experts are sometimes foolish wizards. Writers portray some hardworking young technicians as lacking common sense and daily skills, such as eating healthy meals, demonstrating proper hygiene, working reasonable hours, and seeking to do what is obviously right rather than what is expedient. This type of cyber-fool is not primarily a bohemian who discerningly rejects mainstream lifestyles in favor of a more upright way of life but rather a nerd who forsakes healthy living for short-term satisfactions. He or she might think grandiosely, reading the popular philosophy of the wired generation. And usually a cyber-fool celebrates the triumphs of instrumental success—as Guzman apparently did in Manila (according to some accounts, he probably unleashed the virus as a means of proving to his instructors that his thesis proposal had technical merit).[11] In a broader perspective, the techno-fool is only one example of a classic genre of humanity, not an idiosyncratic product of cyberculture. Such fools lack what Václav Havel calls a "metaphysical anchor," a "humble respect for the whole of creation, and consciousness of our obligation to it."[12] In the biblical traditions, the fool is a cosmic dolt who is unaware of his or her deflating foolishness. A fool's technical ability might be impressive, but it is hardly wisdom. The fool's false pride assumes that he or she is the center of the universe and the source of truth, just as kings' jesters had license to do nearly anything to make a point.

Our high-tech endeavors are riddled with foolishness masquerading as progress. Pollyannaish tales of cyber-gurus, technology columnists, and Internet book authors proclaim that we are conquering space, liberating people from the shackles of hard work, and freeing society from the limitations of yesterday's ways of life. But reality reflects a mixed story of winners and losers, irresolvable paradoxes, and inflated promises that are rarely fulfilled. Foolishness never disappears; we merely transfer it to new technologies in later eras. Today, we lie and gossip online as well as in person or in letters. We become technically proficient at meaningless tasks. In a host of ways, we still employ technique when we need virtue and proffer empty rhetoric when our situation demands wise substance. All the while, we cover up our foolishness with endless rhapsodies about our cyber-accomplishments.

In the field of computer security, for instance, most organizations simply fail to take the known precautions. Richard Power, author of *Tangled Web*, spent six years writing about computer and network security. His research included interviews with members of the Computer Security Institute. "The lesson to be learned," he concludes, "is that very few lessons are ever learned." Power says that companies think of computer security merely as a technology issue. "They all want the 'killer ap' for security," he complains. They refuse to accept the fact that security is "not a technology problem. It's a human problem. It's about using common sense."[13]

As we develop new information technologies, our foolishness creates additional moral problems. For instance, many organizations now must hire experts to address security and privacy dilemmas resulting from technological innovation. Some consulting companies even specialize in "computer forensics"—the business of reclaiming from hard drives erased data, such as deleted email messages and word-processing documents.[14] These digital detectives are fueling a "litigation machine" made up of lawsuits based on digital evidence. In the era of purely paper information, such evidence might never have survived the garbage dump.[15] Cyber-technologies create digital "footprints" of erased data that lead computer-forensic experts to formerly undiscoverable "smoking guns." "There are a lot of trial firms," says a privacy consultant, "that see the next LearJet coming from privacy class action."[16]

Consider as well the moral issues involved in employee-employer relations among information workers. Silicon Valley is not just the center of the high-tech industry in the United States but also the nexus for job-hopping by fleet-footed workers who are chasing after the best short-term boost to their bank accounts. During the height of the high-tech boom in 1997, approximately one out of every four employees in the area's high-tech firms changed jobs annually—a rate almost twice as high as the national average and up 60 percent from 1989.[17] Of course, sometimes job changes are genuine opportunities for better work and perhaps even a brighter future. But job-hopping also reflects the foolish idea that short-term self-interest leads to long-term happiness. "There's a price for all the freedom," writes Quentin Hardy. The price includes eighty-hour workweeks, "stratospheric housing costs and a grinding sameness in both the populace and the ugly strip-mall landscape. No wonder that escapism and rootlessness are rife."[18]

Massive layoffs in 2000 and 2001 eventually showed how technology companies had disregarded the welfare of their workers. Many high-tech managers and executives irresponsibly perceived work as a fast-paced game of musical chairs that would result in employees without jobs. J. K. Larsen notes that the most obvious character of Silicon Valley is "incessant change. . . . Employers are only temporary." He suggests that in such a situation one finds "the obsolescence of employees" as well as the "impermanence of personal relationships. . . . Many people find their personal lives fail to find a dependable base."[19] Not surprisingly, current and former employees of transient, ill-fated cyber-companies often angrily denounce the foolishness. One enormously popular Web site became a place for out-of-sorts technology workers to post rumors about impending layoffs and vituperatively criticize executives' actions.[20] Although journalists rhapsodize about the "great" new technologies, they rarely address the resulting social upheavals, especially among workers. As a nation, we naively assume that robust technological expansion will not put the social order at risk.

Faddish technological endeavors nearly always interfere with genuine progress. When we define progress in purely technological terms, we compel ourselves to use the latest technology even when it might not be wise or appropriate. For instance, many college teachers feel compelled to use online student discussion software, to transform their teaching notes into classroom presentations in darkened classrooms, to require students to visit a class Web site every day, or even to encourage students to take lecture and discussion notes on computers rather than in paper notebooks. Similarly, churches install video projectors in order to get the "full benefit" of computer-presentation technology, sometimes resulting in entertainment-style worship services laced with slick slide shows, video clips, multimedia bulletin announcements, and dynamic sermon outlines. These kinds of technological practices often distract a congregation from the spoken message, fragment the liturgical flow, and destroy the solemnity of worship—all in the name of progress. Our knowledge of the existence of technology, coupled with our desire to be progressive and effective, compels us to use it. When the promises of technique seduce us, however, responsibility usually eludes us.

Much of our high-tech folly results from unplanned opportunities to use digital technology selfishly. When colleges and universities jumped on the Internet bandwagon, for instance, they imagined the Web and email primarily as educational technologies for research and collaboration—just as corporations perceived them as potential business technologies. But soon students and employees were using the Internet for personal communication. Email was a great way of exchanging notes with friends and family members. In addition, some students downloaded term papers from the Web—cyber-plagiarism. A few faculty members responded by writing software programs that could sometimes identify plagiarized works.[21] Students and faculty also began exchanging via the Web digital files of recorded, copyrighted music, thereby defrauding the music industry. At one company, 80 percent of the bandwidth was being chewed up by employees downloading pirated songs for free.[22] Accessing pornographic materials online exploded on college campuses and in corporate offices, leading some companies to buy software that would supposedly block employee access to inappropriate materials. As much as 70 percent of the traffic on pornographic Web sites occurs during work hours, presumably via corporate and educational computer systems.[23] Without knowing in advance what would happen, schools and businesses constructed high-speed networks that made it easy for users to participate in all kinds of illegal, unethical, and purely personal activities—all of them funded by employers and schools. Information technologies invariably expand opportunities for foolishness beyond the initial rationales for implementing the technologies.

No matter how hard we try to be wise stewards of cyberspace, we sometimes still find ourselves acting like fools. Some of us find solace in the fact that others demonstrate worse high-tech high jinks. We might personally never create an email virus or intentionally violate the privacy of a colleague's hard drive. Nevertheless, in our own ways, often with remarkable creativity, we, too, act foolishly. We fail to back up our digital files, perhaps putting years of work in jeopardy. We give a friend our computer or network password. We sneak a few peeks at sexually explicit Web sites, pass along email rumors, and lambaste online the dot-com that laid us off, even though our motive for seeking the job was short-term and selfish. Many of these kinds of foolishness would not seem so bad if they were merely isolated events with no grave consequences for others. But they reflect a basic human tendency that plagues our cyber-endeavors, namely, a lack of humility. Like the Love Bug author, we foolishly fail to subject our informational actions to real moral scrutiny.

Pinpointing Our Moral Dilemmas

In 1998, many Japanese patrons began complaining about ringing cell-phones and beeping pagers at public events. Auditorium managers finally gave up asking patrons to turn off the gadgets and pleaded with technologists to solve the problem. The nation eventually announced a government panel that would establish technological guidelines for jamming devices designed to block incoming messages at public places.[24] Although the problem was moral—a failure to be courteous citizens—the solution would be technological. That solution, however, would create other moral dilemmas. What if a doctor attending an event in a jammed concert hall did not receive an emergency page? What if the jamming technologies also affected other electronic devices, such as pacemakers? Why should the concert halls be responsible for the actions of patrons? In the industrialized world, people often naively assume that technological "progress" will eventually solve the problem of human irresponsibility.

High-tech innovations instead tend to compound the moral complexity of our lives, making it more difficult to know how to act responsibly. Information technologies can even spread the impact of our foolishness more quickly through high-speed networks. In a sense, cyberspace widens the range and furthers the means we have to act foolishly. Pinpointing our moral dilemmas becomes increasingly difficult but ever more important.

Email, perhaps the most popular form of personal communication to emerge in the digital age, is a telling example. Today, employees and employers struggle over email usage policies. Most employees use company email for personal purposes, in spite of company regulations that sometimes either limit or forbid employees' personal use of the technology during work hours.[25] The popularity of email at work has even led to a growing software industry that serves employers who wish to monitor their employees' email communication.[26] Nearly three-quarters of the larger American companies record and review employees' email and Web usage.[27] Information technology departments thereby become anti-information departments; their goal is not just to help employees send and receive information but also to prevent them from exchanging particular types of messages. In some cases, digital surveillance of employees extends beyond simply preventing personal email messaging to monitoring all company email for evidence of unethical or fraudulent messages, such as those containing elements of harassment or discrimination, pornographic images, and proprietary company information. Chevron and Microsoft each settled email-related sexual-harassment lawsuits for $2.2 million.[28] The stakes are enormous.[29] The complex ethical issues involved in this kind of techno-snooping cannot be solved technologically. In fact, as we create one counter-technology after another, we hide the moral issues of responsibility under a patina of instrumental nonsolutions.

Often the people who identify high-tech moral issues are not in-house managers or technicians but rather extra-organizational "hackers." The media portray hackers as evil technological zealots, when in fact they are frequently creative and hardworking people who strongly desire to advance information technology for the good of society. Hackers are different from "crackers," who crack into computer systems often with self-serving and even malevolent intentions.[30] The term "hacker" originated as a description of writers of software who "hack" together the code that makes programs work. But the idea of hacking has come to mean in some technology circles a kind of good-intentioned surveillance of cyberspace with an eye toward helping the common users avoid being exploited—a cyber-version of Robin Hood. The "open source" movement, which supports making nonproprietary software code available to all interested parties, is one example of this altruistic intent; long before this movement, however, hackers shared code with each other. To a typical hacker, poorly written code is a testament to foolishness. Moreover, unstable or insecure code is morally wrong. Most hackers exploit network and server weaknesses in order to document how vulnerable such systems really are, not to steal information or destroy an organization's technology.

The truth is that hackers are sometimes the only people willing to point out the moral foolishness behind cyber-hype. In the current era of widespread cyber-foolishness, hackers are whistleblowers who alert the wider world to the folly of corporations and governments that operate vulnerable technological empires. If hackers can break into a federal agency's computer, for instance, so can other governments or terrorists. Hackers embarrass us all by demonstrating that our information systems are overly touted. They often reveal the imprudence within mainstream technology endeavors, becoming the de facto consciences among technologists. Whereas businesses and governments tend to ignore the larger moral issues, except as they affect the bottom line, hackers are often the only people who will admit publicly that the techno-emperor is naked. Some hacker groups even hold to a "hacker ethic," whereas most corporations and nonprofit organizations never establish significant ethical standards for their own information technology departments.[31]

Wasted time, money, and natural resources are other moral dimensions of information technology. Poor stewardship plagues high-tech endeavors partly because management and accountants overrely on the advice of their own technologists or on consultants selected by the technologists. A survey of companies in 1996 by the Standish Group revealed that American companies spend over $250 billion dollars annually on computer technologies alone. Yet the waste is staggering. The same survey discovered that 42 percent of corporate information technology projects were abandoned before completion.[32] Organizations purchase hardware and software that are never used or are employed at a level far below capacity. Entire networks and software systems are scrapped in favor of new ones that never work as well as the older ones. Upgrades, replacements, and maintenance of information technology can easily cost more than the original systems. After two jets slammed into the World Trade Center in 2001, experts estimated that securities firms alone would have to spend between $3.2 and $7 billion to replace their computer systems.[33] It is difficult to imagine the scope of that kind of technological investment, let alone the costs of maintenance and normal replacement on three-year cycles. Our informational progress actually piles waste upon waste, culminating in landfills brimming with paper printouts and discarded computer equipment that is better than that available to most people around the globe. "Despite the industry's antiseptic image" writes a journalist, "making computers is like making sausage, only more toxic and less sustainable."[34]

Most telling of all, no one really knows how to determine total information technology costs, because installing computers and digital networks creates additional, nonmeasurable costs. Business and consulting groups proclaim savings from increased productivity, but such studies usually ignore the resulting unproductivity.[35] Time is lost to personal use of email and the Web, to network breakdowns, to learning new hardware and software, to unnecessary email memos about technology as well as to necessary ones about technology policies and procedures, to finding digital documents, to moving old documents and program settings to new machines, to repairing hardware and software, and on and on. Today, our information technologies are so integrated with organizational culture that they affect everything from meeting times (when the right technology or room is available) to company gossip and organizational morale (at many organizations, employees exchange email messages complaining about organizational officials and policies).

We have reached a point at which relatively inexpensive technological "improvements" can generate enormous nontechnology costs. When regulators changed Texas Instruments' area code in Dallas, the resulting technology costs included roughly $100,000 for operator retraining, directories, cellular number changes, and internal phone system upgrades. But the *paper* costs for new stationery, business cards, and various business forms totaled a staggering $1,200,000.[36] Ten years ago, people proclaimed the coming of the "paperless office." Now engineers and marketers are announcing new technologies that will "give people everywhere the freedom to access and print their e-mail messages, Internet content and other documents at any time, anywhere, from any mobile device, to any printer."[37] We had better order more reams of paper! "Upgrading" to information technologies frequently affects other organizational practices.

Technological progress can cost far more than anyone is able to predict, since every institutional setting is somewhat idiosyncratic and never fully testable. We think of information technology as uniform and evenly dispersed across organizational culture, when in fact its use is highly dynamic and never fully controllable. Technology creates far greater organizational unpredictability—and thus wider variations in cost—than cultural habits that are anchored over time in particular oral and print practices. Who knows when a virus attack will destroy PCs or when a hot news items will lure employees to the Web and away from their work?[38] When employee-to-employee email will lead to office dalliances? When subpoenaed email files will result in a class action lawsuit against a company? The rhetoric about the declining costs and greater efficiencies of information systems usually fails to account for the human dimensions of such systems. One economist says, "When you look at the layoffs, the downsizing, the plant closings, the heightened sense of worker insecurity, the elimination of millions of mid-management positions in the early 1990s, it smacks more of unprecedented cost cutting than increased productivity."[39] Someone has to pay the piper for technological changes.

Fortunately, most of our high-tech tomfoolery so far has not cost human life.[40] The habits of our hearts still retard evil, although periodically history reveals how terribly coldhearted we are capable of becoming. The evil uses of guns, gas ovens, and airplanes periodically remind us how immoral human beings sometimes are. Perhaps most difficult to accept is the fact that even our good intentions can create horribly tragic outcomes. Cyberspace expands the likelihood of major high-tech accidents because the systems are so complex, because the systems are increasingly global, and because the systems' escalating speeds give people less time to think before acting.

Technology represents significant moral costs because our technological endeavors tend to take on a life of their own, apart from our understanding of them and our efforts to control them. Once a human "project acquires a certain size and becomes vested with human dreams of 'progress' or of 'liberation,'" writes Vinoth Ramachandra, "it attains a life of its own, dragging human beings and societies in its wake." As a result, he adds, no one bears responsibility when things "go wrong."[41] The only thing that we can then do to justify the "wrong" is to speak of "accidents" that are presumably outside of human control.

Paul Virilio calls accidents the "intellectual scapegoat of the technological."[42] In his view, high-tech innovation invariably creates accidents, just as inventing the railroad led to train wrecks. The extent to which we cannot fully control our technologies is the seedbed for accidents. Today, he says, cyber-technologies are creating conditions for global rather than purely local accidents.[43] A Wall Street crash resulting from programmed trading could create worldwide financial repercussions quite literally overnight—repercussions even for those people who own no stocks and are not online. Virilio suggests that we do not yet understand what types of massive, global accidents will be possible in a high-tech world; we need new metaphors beyond a "market crash" to describe them adequately.[44] Even if we can describe them, however, we will not be fully able to prevent them because they come with the digital territory. Information accidents will happen. International computer networks will up the moral ante.

We are increasingly captive to the moral dilemmas of Fool's Law, particularly our misguided trust in our ability to control the information technologies that we create. Informationism creates the illusion that we control technology and that we can progress technologically if we are totally self-reliant and fully self-involved. We believe in the powers of new cyber-technologies because we want to have all the technological benefits without any of the subsequent moral confusion and cultural dislocation. The truth is that even the most seductive information technologies lack any intrinsic power to ennoble us. Fool's Law is a lesson never learned. We want to admire the great work of people who engineered and produced jet-propulsion technology, for instance, but we had better remind ourselves as well that even a few evil persons can use it for ill.[45] Perhaps the moral implication of our cybernetic self-delusion is too distressing for us to admit. We lack the necessary humility.

Information technology cannot transcend the gap between expansive human hopes, on the one hand, and the moral limits of actual human knowing, on the other. Moral reality never lives up to our technological rhetoric. Kenneth Burke imagines a short play, "Prologue in Heaven," in which "The Lord" and Satan dialogue about the human condition.[46] An Impresario begins the event with a few observations about human beings who "invent" motives. Seduced by money—the language of the "universal wishing well"—people create *linguistic empires* that rationalize their beliefs.[47] In other words, we concoct self-interested myths that portray the world to our liking. We label technological innovation "progress" and convince each other that high-tech developments portend moral achievements as well. Our cyber-related language is so inflated by allusions to power and progress that we believe our own rhetorical quaqua.

Invariably, such self-ingratiating systems of cyber-expectation collapse. Poor stewardship, unfulfilled promises, negative effects, and accidents sometimes rise above our sanguine rhetoric. Suddenly, we have to account for foolishness, explain the mixed motives, and interpret the gap between what people profess about information technology's benefits and the actual results of cyber-innovation. Often these short-lived revelations about the disparity between rhetoric and reality emanate from religious traditions, in which people still converse seriously about the sources of evil and the ultimate purposes of cultural activity. The heart of this moral dilemma is our trust in the power of information technology to make us better people. Once we recognize this quasi-religious hope in our cyber-endeavors, we face a metaphysical dilemma: Either we accept informational mythology as a viable religion, or we critique it from the vantage point of a nontechnological tradition.

Our high-tech folly, then, stems from a fundamental human defect: our tendency to underestimate the limits of our knowing and overestimate our ability to engineer progress. Our rhetoric *about* technology never equips us with a comprehensive understanding *of* our actual condition. Cyber-endeavors invariably breed larger and more complex technologies than we can fully comprehend, while our language of progress hides our moral impoverishment. Much of our techno-talk about conquering time and space is wishful thinking—as if we can magically call into existence a desired high-tech future. Our cultural language about technology becomes a popular religion with its own sacred words and morally weighted phrases that people uncritically accept as truth. Such "digibabble"—to use Tom Wolfe's term—becomes a quasi-religious language about growing convergence, increased personal freedom, and renewed community.[48] But such inflated idioms never fully correlate with moral reality.

The quasi-religious rhetoric of cyberculture enraptures us with promises of renewed lives, stronger families, more humane work, and supercharged economies. It claims to offer us what every great religion provides, namely, a means out of our predicaments, an ordered cosmos instead of our chaos, and the peace of shalom rather than more conflict and injustice. Havel rightly suggests that we are "looking for new scientific recipes, new ideologies, control systems, new institutions, new instruments to eliminate the dreadful consequences of our previous ideologies, control systems, institutions and instruments."[49]

Fool's Law reveals the moral hollowness of such cyber-hope. The mythos of the digital sublime promises to save us time, make us smarter, and empower us.[50] Meanwhile, our friends get hooked on cyber-pornography. Our children's grades decline in spite of the school district's massive investment in information technology. Where is the moral center of the Internet? Only in our dreams. Where are the medium's boundless power and eternal goodness? Only in our imaginations. Should we laugh or cry? With grace, we start to recognize the foolish rhetoric that we once took for wisdom. The cyber-emperor is nearly naked. We can see ourselves, too, for the cyber-fools we really are. We remember the sent emails we would like to retrieve, the hours we squandered surfing the Web, the rumors we passed along online as fact, the software we bought and rarely used. The resulting frustration and fear should open our hearts to the need for humility.

Falling Fearfully into Humility

When Václav Havel visited the United States in 1990, he delivered an insightful speech about his own fears for the future of humankind. He pictured the world as a growing collection of competing interests—personal, state, national, group, corporate, and the like—with few people and nations concerned about shared interests. "We are still under the sway of the destructive and thoroughly vain belief that man is the pinnacle of creation, and not just a part of it, and that therefore everything is permitted to him," Havel cautioned. Even people who say they are committed to a broader cause, he said, act demonstrably in their own interests. "We are still destroying the planet that was entrusted to us all. We still close our eyes to the growing social, ethnic, and cultural conflicts in the world. From time to time we say that the anonymous megamachinery we have created for ourselves no longer serves us but, instead enslaves us, yet we fail to do anything about it. In other words," Havel concluded, "we still don't know how to put morality ahead of politics, science, and economics. We are still incapable of understanding that the only genuine core of all actions—if they are to be moral—is responsibility."[51]

Gripped by his personal weaknesses in the face of such global problems, Havel spoke several months later in Jerusalem, a hotbed of political discord and a zone of important religious history. Everything worthwhile that he ever accomplished, said Havel, was "done to conceal my almost metaphysical feeling of guilt. The real reason I am always creating something, organizing something, it would seem, is to defend my permanently questionable right to exist." To him, his position as president of a country was a "paradox." How could someone who thinks of himself as powerless be an effective president of an organization, let alone a nation? "The lower I am," admitted Havel, "the more proper my place seems; and the higher I am, the stronger my suspicion is that there has been some mistake."[52]

One of the great problems within cyberculture is the constant motion that keeps us from fearfully contemplating our actual situation. Havel had the strange benefit of years in prison to consider his plight. If we take the time to reflect on our situation, we might conclude that no amount of information technology is going to repair the destruction in our own lives, let alone save the planet. We depend too much on technique to save us from a fall into fear. Only when we give up on our technological faith and accept the resulting fear can we truly act responsibly. When he arrived at the presidential palace after his election, Havel felt profoundly subdued and strangely paralyzed. "I seemed to have suddenly lost all my ideas and goals, my skills, hope and resolve. . . . I suddenly had no idea what I was supposed to be doing." The story of the rise of democracy out of the ashes of communism was already unfolding, but tremendous work lay ahead for Havel and the Czech people. "Somewhere in the depth of this feeling lay fear: fear that we had taken on too much, fear that we wouldn't be up to the job, fear of our own inadequacy—in short, fear of our very selves."[53]

Venerating technique makes life deceptively easy. Rather than seeking virtue, we can wait expectantly for the next round of promises about life-giving technologies. When we fear, however, we begin falling into humility. Rather than marching proudly ahead with our minds in celestial dreams, we fall back to earth, to the dirty but life-giving soil, to *humus*.[54] We should fear the informationism of our age because it lacks humility; it puts us in the business of authoring paeans to efficiency and control rather than first admitting our foolishness. Short-term technological setbacks, from power surges to hard drive crashes, should remind us that we are not fully in control. Perhaps we never were. Fear sets in: What in the world are we to do if we cannot save ourselves? Humility admits our vapid faith in the digital future and questions our capacity to create any kind of technological heaven on earth.

Fear humbles us and can even inspire us to correct our ways. Fear of the divine, fear of letting down our neighbor, fear of being exposed for our poor-quality work, fear of even letting ourselves down, fear of the evil that lurks in our own Faustian hearts—all of these fears and many more can embrace humility while also giving us a clearer view of our obligations as responsible caretakers of cyber-technologies. C. S. Lewis observed that the "genius" in the fall of Faustus was the devil's offer to extend Faustus's power "to the performance of all things possible."[55] Fear that we are like the self-delusional Faustus is a worthy motivation for humble responsibility.

The Danish philosopher Søren Kierkegaard illuminated the relationships among humility, technology, and power already in the nineteenth century. People who seek to be humble must "stand still" before a mirror, he wrote.[56] In other words, we must first honestly examine ourselves to see who we really are—not who we think we are or who others might charitably tell us we are. We must also avoid "busyness, keeping up with others, hustling hither and yon," because such a life "makes it almost impossible for an individual to form a heart, to become a responsible, alive self. Every life that is preoccupied with being like others is a wasted life, a lost life."[57] Instead, we should strive for a life that looks seriously "inward," to everything that is "deeper." We will then recognize that real authority is not power per se but rather a willingness "to sacrifice everything, one's very life," for the cause of truth. Today, the concerns of information technology can distract us even from the responsibilities of neighborly love. Digital messaging offers us a tremendously seductive diversion that seems to meet our every desire. "Preserve me, Lord," prayed Kierkegaard, "from the deceit of thinking that by being prudent and looking after my own interests I am necessarily using my talents aright."[58]

If we lack humility, our technological activities will express merely our own selfish contempt for the world. Wendell Berry recalls inspecting an Amish farm for evidence of soil erosion. Unable to find any, he speculated that agriculture must have been "formed upon the understanding that it is sinful for people to misuse or destroy what they did not make. The Creation is a unique, irreplaceable gift, therefore to be used with humility, respect, and skill."[59] The Amish understand, according to Berry, that agricultural technology must be operated within self-imposed limits; technological gluttony is bound to destroy the earth. In their own tradition, the Amish humbly recognize that technology can violate traditional culture and weaken or even destroy good social customs. They accept reticence in their technological exploits, admitting that humans cannot possibly see all the repercussions of their technological actions. Without such humility, we will never know when to say no to technological innovation and expansion. Moreover, when we say only yes, we lack any kind of moral vision. Most people who seek to use information technology humbly will probably not be as restrictive as the Amish. But if we lack *any* technological reticence, we also lack responsibility.

The virtue of humility directs us away from selfish cyber-desires and toward the needs of our neighbors. Even in a high-tech society, being humble means taking on the burdens of the broken creation rather than merely satisfying one's personal desires. We should question our own journeys into cyberspace, fearing that we may not be properly tending to the creation. In this humble view, technology is no longer an idol, an end in itself apart from the needs of the world. Some of the most radical decisions we make as humble caretakers of the world are those that involve what *not* to do with technology, because in the surrounding culture of gluttony, *non-technique* is rarely considered a worthy option. We need to realize that mindlessly adopting the latest consumer technologies might put us in debt, not just to the bank but even more deeply to arrogance. Humility asks us to justify our technological decisions not on the basis of what they do for our egos but on the basis of caring for others as responsible stewards of the gift of creation. Being humble, then, does not mean that we must reject technology. Instead, it focuses us on serving others in the most selfless and least bellicose way possible. As David Lyon puts it, "Our ancient wisdom tells us to *ask radical questions*, but to *act in the real world*."[60]

Humility is so countercultural today that embracing it will threaten many of the powers of the information age. Humble people are often the truth tellers in a technological community. They do not repeat utopian digibabble or meaningless quaqua. Instead, they recognize human limitations in simple and straightforward language. The real technological prophets are not the savvy prognosticators but rather the concerned naysayers who worry more about the spread of heartless technique than about protecting their own self-interest. He or she is a sharp contrast to the bellowing futurist who disingenuously declares revolution, or the moronic manager who pretends that everything is just fine as long as the bottom line is "good." As a habit of the heart, humility reminds us to fear our own foolishness. Humble naysayers hold themselves and others accountable for digital exploits and informational arrogance. Especially in the secular-rational empire of informationism, the dust of ego and the darkness of self-interest cloud our moral vision. Humility prepares us to be spokespersons for the needs of a broken creation rather than mere champions for the seductive powers of the times.

After recognizing that we are fools, we sometimes gain enough humility to see a bit more soberly the ups and downs of the information age. The road to such cyber-revelation, however, can be a frightening journey: "Abandon All Hope, Ye Who Enter Here," reads the sign over the entryway to hell in Dante's *Inferno*. Perhaps we should hang such a sign over the doorways of every information technology department to remind us of the evils of misapplied technique. Cyberspace today seems to be miles away from such abject evil, but in fact the age of cyber-terrorism might soon be upon us.[61] Although high-tech terrorism will not likely cause the level of destruction of a world war, computer networks are becoming staging grounds for new methods of digital aggression. Cyberspace is not simply a frontier of progress held back by fixable technological snafus but rather the latest extension of human arrogance into new empires. "We must live with the possibility that decisions made in good faith will turn out to be disasters," writes Robert McAfee Brown.[62] Like the satire in Stanley Kubrick's wacky film, *Dr. Strangelove, or How I Learned to Stop Worrying and Love the Bomb,* humor can help us to see the unvirtuous character of some of our technological pursuits.

Humorously Exposing Our Folly

Twenty-something Mike Daisey grew weary of eighty-hour workweeks at the online retailer Amazon.com. Once a true believer in the dot-com lifestyle and an avid fan of Amazon's CEO, Daisey increasingly doubted the company's cult-like mantra that "sending people books was really going to change the world."[63] He also wondered about the ethics of rising through the ranks in the company's customer-service division by reducing the time he spent with each telephone caller—sometimes by simply hanging up on them. For a while, calculating the value of his stock options kept Daisey excited about his job, even with its grueling schedule. But then Amazon's market capitalization plunged, and lay-offs ensued. To make matters worse, Daisey discovered a list of the stock options for people in his department; the rankings put him near the bottom of the list in spite of how deeply he had given his heart to the firm.

Dismayed but not fully defeated, Daisey left his corporate cubicle for the stage. He launched his own one-man, stand-up show that parodied the dot-com world. Titled "21 Dog Years," his loosely scripted, stream-of-consciousness performances recounted his crazy years with Amazon and satirically reflected on the dot-com dream that promised to produce millionaires but often lacked basic business sense. By mid-1998, he told his audiences, everyone who believed in common sense in the Internet industry "had been shot." Believing that his show serves "a better purpose than endless pink-slip parties," Daisey humorously illuminates the folly of the times, including his own naiveté. Daisey's comedy reminds audiences that no one is above techno-folly. One venture capitalist who saw Daisey's performance remarked about early dot-com boom years, "We all want to act like we were above it all, but we weren't."[64]

Freed partly from the suffocating tyranny of technological pride and admitting humbly our need for help in charting our technological futures, we can pursue the habits of the heart that will shape our technological landscapes for the good. Even though this is a serious pursuit, it is also a humorous journey with all kinds of fits and starts. Humor helps us not to take ourselves too seriously or to take our responsibilities too cavalierly. It can reveal truth, embrace gratitude, and identify responsibility in a broken world.

Certainly, not all humor uses laughter morally. Unethical forms of humor contemptuously denigrate individuals and institutions; they rely on derision, malice, and vindictiveness rather than humble satire.[65] Someone who hates, says Havel, does not really smile as much as smirk. Such a person is "incapable of making a joke, only of bitter ridicule; he can't be genuinely ironic because he can't be ironic about himself."[66] Prideful joking, through put-downs and deprecating gossip, is a means of feigning superiority over others. The Internet swirls with folklore and urban legends about those stupid "others" who do not know the difference between a computer mouse and a television remote control, who think that the CD-shelf in a computer is a coffee cup holder. Worse yet, thousands of personal Web sites are small public squares for shouting derisively at particular races, cultures, and lifestyles. Parts of the Web teem with hatred designed to belittle and bemoan.

Good forms of humor, both more civil and more self-critical, illuminate our folly. They aim not to hurt people or destroy relationships but to illuminate and eventually to help heal broken people and organizations. Walker Percy suggests that good satire "is not primarily destructive. It attacks one thing in order to affirm another. It assaults the fake and phony in the name of the truth . . . to affirm the human."[67] Illuminating our folly helps us get our bearings regarding the ridiculous things that we do in the name of cyber-power and cyber-progress. As Brown suggests, humor involves "a willingness to be cut down to size and emerge liberated rather than devastated by the experience."[68] Such humble laughter admits everyone's culpability in human folly. We then laugh not to divide humanity as much as to recognize that we are all members of the same species of techno-fools.

The more complacent we get about high-tech life, the more we need this comedic perspective to keep us honestly humble and sane. "We think we have life all doped out, that we understand how things fit together, that we know our strengths and weaknesses," continues Brown, "and then an unexpected incongruity presents itself, in a joke or an experience or an aside, and we realize that we are not so much in control of things as we thought we were."[69] After surfing the Web, humorist Dave Barry concluded that cyberspace is "proof that civilization is doomed." He discovered online not only pathetic, hostile, and deluded material but also the "tasteless and the borderline insane"—from Web sites devoted to the toilets of Melbourne to those about human testicle consumption, body piercing, and even cussing in Swedish. His book, *Dave Barry in Cyberspace*, is a wonderful romp through cyber-foolishness that simultaneously pokes fun and critically assesses the subject.[70] As we read such a book, we can laugh together, knowing our shared predicament and collectively seeking improvements. Cornel West calls for "subversive joy," the "ability to transform tears into laughter, a laughter that allows one to acknowledge just how difficult the journey is, but also acknowledge one's own sense of humanity and folly and humor in the midst of this very serious struggle."[71] The best humor serves us in at least three ways: (1) giving us a better sense of proportion, (2) revealing tomfoolery in different guises, and (3) helping us to be more patient.

First, humor can help us gain a more accurate sense of proportion. Whether we get terribly excited or deeply discouraged by new information technologies, we tend to give them a more privileged place in our imaginations than they should rightly earn. The hype and spin of high-tech futurists, like the doomsday scenarios of anti-technologists, lack any reasonable sense of proportion. "They say the cars of the future will be equipped with dashboard computers complete with maps and a global positioning device," says comedian Dennis Miller. "Hey, listen, I'm going to the store for milk, I'm not . . . Magellan tracking around the Cape of Good Hope, all right? Tell me, O global positioning device, where can Ponce De Dennis locate the 7-Eleven in my neighborhood?"[72] In

2001, researchers proudly proclaimed that voice-recognition technology had been added to palmtop computers. Demonstrating this "remarkable" technology, a "speech engineer" at IBM asked his palmtop, "How do you feel?" The computer responded, "My battery power is at 83 percent."[73] What a friendly, reassuring answer! As Havel suggests from his experience with European politics, sometimes the most earnest efforts of people "have a way of blending uneasily with what is most comic. It seems that it is precisely the dimension of distance, of rising above oneself and making light of oneself, which lends to our concerns and actions precisely the right amount of shattering seriousness."[74]

Perhaps the greatest sense of proportion that we can gain through humor is realizing the absurdity of using technology to play God. Virilio suggests that the human effort to develop cyberspace is a "quest for God. To be God."[75] All the salvific mythology surrounding our cyber-exploits is truly laughable. Will we really conquer space and time? "Without software," says Barry, "a computer is just a lump of plastic; whereas *with* software, it's a lump of plastic that can permanently destroy critical data."[76] We need verbal and visual reminders of our technological pretensions—just as cathedral roofs sported gargoyles to humble the holy worshipers. Humor can deliver us back to the reality of our limited virtue and remind us that we are hardly God.

Second, humble humor can reveal tomfoolery in all its guises. "No matter what computer you buy, no matter how much you spend," warns Miller, "by the time you get it to your car, it's an eight-track tape player."[77] Only humble persons are likely to admit that they, too, have been sold a high-tech bill of goods. Waste, distractions, interruptions, and breakdowns are all part of our high-tech endeavors.

In 2001, the Bush administration apparently decided that the Internet was not secure enough for governmental communication, so it proposed a new, separate network. As one government official put it, "We need to bifurcate cyberspace: we need to have a secure zone in cyberspace and then we can leave the rest of it as it is today."[78] Translation: "We, the government, might have created this monster, but we cannot control it any longer. It's time to bow out and leave the mess to the market. It's been nice knowing you online."

Barry says he once accidentally posted a private message online, where thousands if not millions of people read it. Later the intended recipient of the message, a British author, posted a message saying that he had heard there was a message going around with his name on it, but he had not seen it. Barry concluded that he had managed to "send this hideously embarrassing message to *everybody in the world except the person who was supposed to read it.*"[79] Having made an "intergalactic fool" of himself, Barry later recounted the fiasco in his book, thereby helping all of us see not only his mistake but also how a revolutionary communication technology can foul up our communication.

Third, humor can engender patience. Without patience, we cannot take the time to be responsible. In a high-tech world, however, more and more people expect immediate service and overnight results. The faster their messaging, the less willing they are to be patient. For example, U.S. citizens are becoming increasingly irate with members of Congress whose staffs simply cannot respond to all incoming email. A study by the Congress Online Project found, "Rather than enhancing democracy . . . email has heightened tensions and public disgruntlement with Congress."[80] In 2001, however, when governmental offices were threatened by the spread of the anthrax virus through the postal system, Congress encouraged citizens to use email to communicate with their representatives.[81] High-tech messaging leads us to adopt machine-like habits with no slowdowns that will undermine efficiency and control. Humility instead leads us to empathize with others by laughing *with* them, not *at* them. If we try to live only by the rhythms of the high-tech clock, we will lack compassion.[82] The patient person lives not in digital time but in humane time. Patience is a means of giving time to others rather than merely claiming it for ourselves or dedicating it to instrumental pursuits.

One popular information-age humorist is Scott Adams, creator of the *Dilbert* cartoons. When Adams started drawing the cartoons, he imagined the corporate creature Dilbert as simply an engineer who had all kinds of things happen to him outside as well as inside the office. When Adams added his email address to the script in 1993, however, he started receiving a tremendous amount of mail from readers who said they most liked the cartoons that depicted Dilbert in his office cubicle, battling the foolishness of corporate life. Adams then redirected the stories of Dilbert, creating a running commentary on the lunacy of corporate life, including technologies such as computers and the Internet.[83] Adams suggested, for instance, that "computer users will become the new sex symbols, because they're the ones with the power."[84] Adams believes that the business cubicle and the corporate need for empowered employees are irreconcilable. "I think that nobody's brain can reconcile these two things. So if you're a creature that belongs in a box, you can't also be a creature that makes important and powerful decisions for the good of mankind."[85] Adams sees his task as not just cartooning but also a means of morally informing us of high-tech idiocy in corporate life.[86]

The profoundly comedic aspects of human life, writes James M. Houston, are "holy humor" that should lead us to take ourselves less seriously and take the divine much more seriously. Such comedy deflates human pretensions and reveals the false idols of our world. Humor, Houston claims, is "both an attribute of our humanity and the rhetoric of God's grace."[87] In other words, the moral fabric of the world gives us a context for true and good comedy. Humor works in two ways, revealing the gap between human pretensions and God's expectations, and comforting us with the fact that there is nevertheless grace in the gap. This is why Kierkegaard wrote that the "more thoroughly and substantially a human being exists, the more he will discover the comical. . . . But the resolution of the religious individual is the highest of all resolves, infinitely higher than all plans to transform the world and to create systems and works of art." Therefore, he adds, the religious person, more than a nonreligious person, "discovers the comical."[88] A world with information technology but without laughter would be a grim, spiritually impoverished place to inhabit.

If there were no moral order, there would be no humor, only chaos. "Only if we are secure in our beliefs can we see the comical side of the universe," writes Flannery O'Connor.[89] Our cyber-endeavors invite humorists to offer wisdom about our wayward innovations and regular foul-ups. The laughter of pretense and incongruity finds prodigious material in the antics of computer and Internet users. Consequently, we should expect great innovations in comedy as well as cyber-technology. "The Software of the Future will . . . be extremely sophisticated," predicts Barry. It will have "so many features, graphics, animated cartoon characters, video clips, etc., that a single program will fill up all the space on your hard drive before you're halfway through installing it. You'll need to purchase several additional computers just to get the program operating to the point where it will tell you the phone number for Technical Support."[90] Of course, the phone line will have been disconnected because the software company will have shifted all customer support to the more efficient Web. If we cannot laugh about the information society, we are taking ourselves far too seriously and finding too little grace in our situation. Everywhere he looks, Miller finds "such a dependence on synthetic forms of communication. Whatever happened to good old-fashioned face-to-face insincerity?"[91]

Conclusion

Carey says that technology "plays the role of the trickster in American culture, at each turn of the historical cycle it appears center stage, in a different guise promising something totally new."[92] The "audience usually identifies with the trickster and thus symbolically asserts itself over the forces of the world." The trickster clouds our ability to see technology soberly. Under his spell, we naively call information technology a mere tool, pretending to ourselves that it is fully at our disposal and can be totally dedicated to our service.[93] We shuffle along, following the idols of efficiency and control toward an increasingly muddled telos. We are so intimately enchanted with this trickster that we cannot see him for what he is, namely, an extension of our own arrogant desires to manipulate and control the world for self-serving ends.

Living in a culture that venerates technique and upholds informationism, the humble person looks like a fool. Even a reasonable reticence about information technology meets with raised eyebrows and incredulous guffaws. To question aspects of cyber-progress is to come across as a self-righteous idiot if not an ignorant Luddite. We have reached a point at which admitting techno-foolishness is itself perceived as foolishness. The person of humble hope and sane convictions has little place in cyber-heaven. Heaven help us, for we are indeed fools. "For every computer error," says writer Joel Makower, "there are at least two human errors, one of which is blaming it on the computer."[94]

In the age of high-speed micro-processors, blazing databases, and seamless networks, human foolishness finds new venues. We become high-tech fools bent on exploiting the apparent power of technique to fashion a better world. Meanwhile, humorists remind us that information technology is not fully under our own control, no matter how many terabytes of file space, megabytes of bandwidth, and megahertz of processing power we have at our earthly disposal. Presumably, the FBI learned this humble lesson in the case of the agent who used the Bureau's own computers to help the Russians.

While we will never overcome all foolishness, we can certainly learn a few lessons, apply them to our lives, and share them with other humble fools. Foremost among these lessons is the fact that we are not God, and hence, we will never be able to control fully our own cyber-endeavors. In addition, we should not look to cyber-technology as a means of salvation. "We certainly want salvation," says Archbishop Charles J. Chaput, "and we acknowledge that salvation is of the Lord—but for many of us tools function as a pretty good insurance policy, just in case. . . . We've learned to trust our own ingenuity because it works. Unfortunately, the construction crew at Babel felt the same."[95] Finally, we ought always to remember that a fool is still a fool—even if the fool knows how to use the latest gadgets.[96]

chapter five

Being Authentic
in Webs of Spin

■ Marcus Arnold joined millions of other Internet users on a Web site called AskMe.com, which helped laypersons gain knowledge by reading experts' answers to posted questions. Marcus seemed to have a natural aptitude for legal matters, so he vigorously posted his own "expert" answers to people's legal queries. In fact, he spent more time on the Internet answering questions than he spent studying at school. He was only fifteen years old. As a self-appointed legal advisor on AskMe.com, he identified himself initially as "Law Guy 1975 aka Billy Sheridan." People rated his answers among the most helpful expert opinions posted on the site, making him one of the top ten legal advisors. He correspondingly upgraded his online name to the more professional sounding "Justin Anthony Wyrich Jr." Soon he was answering as many as 110 questions per day. Marcus could not figure out why grown-ups sought his amateur legal advice, but he was on a roll. Cobbling together the legal tidbits he recalled from watching *Court TV* and surfing the Web, Marcus became the third highest rated legal authority on AskMe.com.[1]

As Web users began asking Marcus for his phone number and fee structure, however, the fifteen-year-old started feeling pangs of guilt. After all, he was not an adult, much less a bona fide legal expert or licensed attorney. So Marcus remorsefully posted a confession on AskMe.com, admitting his age and lack of legal training. Some of the real lawyers on AskMe.com then took Marcus to task, allegedly conspiring to sink his user ratings on the site. A few furious attorneys even sent him email lashings for masquerading as a lawyer. While the legal professionals humiliated Marcus, the non-attorneys came to his defense.

115

They posted new legal questions for Marcus and rated his responses highly. Two weeks after disclosing his real identity, and in spite of all the criticism from lawyers, Marcus became the top-ranked legal advisor on the Web site. The pseudo-lawyer had won the confidence of his pseudo-clients.[2] Or had he?

This chapter first contends that people are using online resources and relationships partly to fabricate human identities, including how people perceive themselves—their self-identities. These cyber-facades can alter how people perceive themselves both online and in the real world. Frequently, searches for self-identities involve searches for intimacy as well. Cyberspace is a growing arena for people and organizations to define personal and shared reality—as Marcus and his "clients" discovered.

Next, it argues that cyberspace actually grants greater power to professional communicators who benefit from economies of scale and publicity. In fact, Marcus's rise to online notoriety illustrates at the personal level the potential for professional image-making in cyberspace. With a clever publicist, Marcus could have gained media exposure and perhaps become an Internet folk hero. A new generation of online *symbol brokers*—such as journalists, advertising practitioners, and public relations professionals—are learning cyber-techniques for influencing audiences' perceptions of reality. Professional symbol brokers now use cyberspace to shape people's self-identities. These brokers help the information industry to establish an identity for cyber-technologies. According to this identity—which I call the *mythos of the digital sublime*—cyber-technologies promote individualism, empowerment, community, progress, and abundance. This prevailing mythos, or mythological story, serves the needs of high-tech organizations by legitimating the entire high-tech project. Moreover, the mythos simultaneously confirms citizens' own technological optimism that information technologies will make people happier and wiser.

The third section of this chapter stresses the importance of regaining *authenticity* in an information society. One of the most significant moral dilemmas in cyberspace is how to say what we mean and mean what we say. Rapid-fire digital messaging turns gossip, rumor, and half-truths into the latest facts. It is increasingly difficult in cyberspace to know who says what, what he or she really means, and whose self-interest is shaping online rhetoric. Pseudo-attorney Marcus charmed many of his online clients, but we cannot be sure that they believed he actually knew the law. Perhaps the people who gave him high ratings were merely trying to make fun of lawyers. Worse yet, the entire fiasco could have been a publicity stunt cooked up by publicists at AskMe.com. If cyberspace is to avoid disingenuous persona-making, it must cultivate authentic communication anchored in shared commitments to *truth-fulness*, *empathy*, and *integrity*.

Identifying Ourselves

In Lisa Rogak's novel *Pretzel Logic,* Emily attempts to do a favor for her lately distant and irritable husband by putting some bills in order. As she sits down at his computer to download the necessary files, she discovers something deeply vexing—a trail of sexually explicit pictures, Web links, and chat-room visits suggesting that her husband had been searching online for gay intimacy. Stunned by her discovery, Emily fearfully confronts her husband. Sure enough, he is gay. In his view, their marriage has been a convenient facade, not a source of true intimacy. Moreover, his new self-identity is incompatible with heterosexual marriage. Before long, they divorce.[3]

Cyberspace is partly a new arena for human beings to access the kinds of resources that enable them to explore new self-identities. As Emily's husband showed, information technology provides a way for individuals to escape their current social relationships and enter into new relationships that redefine who they are. Just as people for hundreds of years have used printed materials to explore novel ideas, to learn about forbidden practices, and to explore exotic subcultures, many people today journey through cyberspace into otherwise hidden ways of life. Cyberspace is another route to *Playboy, National Geographic, Ms.,* and all kinds of lifestyle "destinations." The writings of Sherry Turkle, Richard Holeton, Indra Sinha, Andra Sinha, and others describe how many people use cyberspace to expand the boundaries of the self by taking on different personas and trying out new relationships.[4] In Richard Lanham's phrase, words pixeled upon a personal computer screen shift us from a "closed poetics to an open rhetoric."[5] The Internet becomes a place for anonymous self-discovery. Images, hyperlinks, and descriptive prose are resources for *bricolage:* new identities pieced together from online odds and ends.[6]

In cyberspace's open rhetoric, growing numbers of people imagine self-identity as a fluid product of ongoing self-discovery. Moreover, the anonymity of online communication seemingly makes such self-discovery far less risky and more intimate. "We who populate cyberspace," writes Howard Rheingold, "deliberately experiment with fracturing traditional notions of memory by living multiple personae in different virtual neighborhoods. . . . The way we use these words, in stories (true and false) we tell about ourselves (or about the identities we want people to believe us to be), is what determines our identities in cyberspace."[7]

Cyberspace creates an arena in which some people believe they can act on the wishes of their hearts to become particular kinds of people.

We can see this defining of personal identity in the mind-boggling growth of personal home pages, online journals, and personal Web-cams broadcasting from bedrooms and living rooms. In 2000, there were 5.5 million personal Web-cams in use, and annual Web-cam sales were expected to skyrocket to 38 million by 2003.[8] These types of Web sites are often individuals' searches for an identity amidst the alienating forces of modern industrial life. "I have a hard time confronting people or saying what's on my mind," says one twenty-year-old online journaler. "If something's really bothering me, I'll come home and put it in my journal. Other people will read it and say, 'Don't worry about it. Things will get better.'"[9] He discovers online the kind of social support he finds more difficult to receive from the "offline" world. This pseudo-intimacy with strangers helps him to accept his social awkwardness as a part of his identity. By expressing himself online and corresponding with those who read his expressions, he is able to construct a more satisfying sense of self.

More than any previous technology, cyberspace symbolizes the hope that individuals can redefine their own and others' views of themselves. Erik Davis argues in *Techgnosis* that "information technology transcends its status as a thing, simply because it allows for the incorporeal encoding and transmission of mind and meaning." Every "significant new device of communications," he claims, enables people to "partially reconstruct the self and its world, creating new opportunities (and new traps) for thought, perception, and social experience."[10] Derrick de Kerckhove—dubbed "Canada's media prophet laureate"—even suggests that personal identity will become a major form of social entertainment as people "produce" their own self for others.[11] Kenneth J. Gergen argues that new technologies "saturate" us with opposing options for identity and enable us to maintain a growing number of friendships. But he also suggests that this expanding range of identity choices tends to weaken all identities, making them more dynamic and expendable.[12] If such observers are correct, information technologies give us greater freedom to alter our personal identities, while simultaneously rendering all identities more subjective and disposable. Today, many people's senses of who they are flow at least partly from their participation in cyber-messaging. When American Airlines announced the availability of fast Internet access on its planes, a company spokesperson said, "More people want and need to stay in touch with their lives while they're in the air."[13]

Some people journey into cyberspace, therefore, not just for information but to be acknowledged as living persons and thereby to gain a personal identity. For them, the unacceptable alternative seems to be a kind of spiritual death—a disappearance into the forgotten, where they are cut off from others, unable to be intimate, and lacking a meaningful self-identity. "For everyone is pained," writes Milan Kundera, "by the thought of disappearing, unheard and unseen, into an indifferent universe, and . . . wants . . . to turn himself into a universe of words."[14] The Internet gives millions of people additional means of expressing themselves, relating to others, and forging identities out of seemingly intimate encounters. This might be why, as Kevin Robins and Frank Webster suggest, our current surge of technological utopianism "coincides with a certain strand of postmodern thinking, one that considers identities in terms of choices and options."[15]

This remarkable human capacity to define reality through the use of communication technologies includes how we conceptualize cyberspace. Our Internet-related philosophizing, predicting, and proclaiming define the medium as a route to meaningful self-image. One of the major advocates of this kind of rhetoric was Pierre Teilhard de Chardin, whose work influenced media theorist Marshall McLuhan. As writer Tom Wolfe explains, Chardin predicted early in the twentieth century that God was using technology to unite "'the hitherto scattered' human race into a single 'nervous system for humanity,' a 'living membrane,' a single 'stupendous thinking machine,' a unified consciousness that would cover the earth like 'a thinking skin,' a noösphere."[16] McLuhan later transformed the concept of "noösphere" into his own notion of the emerging "global village," a secular version of the Christian idea of the eventual unity of all believers. McLuhan imagined that the Almighty is present in technology, converting the world to a common faith.[17] According to this kind of rhetoric, Holy Communion and full spiritual intimacy are just around the technological corner, only a few megabytes or nanoseconds away. Much of the popular philosophizing about cyberspace captured this rhetoric of impending intimacy and divine fellowship— as if Web surfers would find online the most satisfying modes of being and the most meaningful collective identity.

In spite of our hope that new technologies will enable us to form better identities, using cyber-technologies is a subjective art that never quite fulfills our desire to know who we are. In fact, the Greek *techne*—the root word for "technology"—is also the root for the word "art."[18] Artisans use "techniques" to create artifacts, just as engineers and programmers use techniques to design and run digital machines. In other words, all of us who use the "tools" of cyberspace actually are creating "artistic" identities, fabricated versions of reality. Instead of precisely exchanging information, we are artfully framing both the internal and the external world. Nearly instant opinion polls on the Web, for instance, supposedly give us a snapshot of public sentiment, when in fact they are little more than pseudo-concrete descriptions of people's reactions to simplistic statements. Informational databases are techniques we use to try to understand the world outside our heads. But the search engine software is nothing more than a system that abstractly determines how relevant particular Web sites are to given search terms.

As an artistic endeavor, information technology is never rhetorically neutral. It always plays creatively with our minds, shifting our perspectives and tilting our perceptions of reality. Communication technologies can even "possess" us in the sense of captivating our imaginations and focusing our attention. The stock market, for example, can take on a kind of mythological reality in people's collective minds, apart from the actual market and its everyday operations. Along with similarly minded people, we might "read into" news reports various economic meanings, such as "impending collapse" or "bull market." As we listen to people in cyberspace and other media, we "talk ourselves" into attitudes about particular equities and general market conditions.[19] Most of what we claim to know about the world, such as the functioning of the economy, we actually acquire only secondhand from media experts, who themselves are "artists" who fashion versions of reality. Cyber-identity is always somewhat illusory.

In the 1990s, for instance, journalists and economic experts together conjured up the idea of a "New Economy." Soon millions of people were using the term to describe a booming stock market fueled by investor euphoria over technology companies that actually offered little promise of profitability. The label was more of a wish than a reflection of economic wisdom. By speaking, reading, and writing the words "New Economy" over and over again, we invoked a new economic identity predicated on the value of growth and innovation rather than profit—after all, most of the new technology companies were losing money even as their market capitalizations skyrocketed. Capital poured into equities markets, and stock values rose precipitously. We told ourselves that capitalism had finally sprung free of industrial business practices. A new, high-tech world was supposedly upon us, one characterized by "friction-less" trade and "high-efficiency" growth—a kind of hyper-capitalism. Never had "more money been made in a shorter period of time," waxed a high-tech CEO. "The convergence of the economy and the stock market and the Internet phenomenon—it's magic."[20] In turn, people's newfound psychological hopes influenced the market itself by accelerating demand for high-tech equities and fueling the flow of capital into technology companies.

By 2000, however, economic reality confounded investors' perceptions of the New Economy. Dot-com revenues looked increasingly anemic. Some technology companies even went bankrupt as capital dried up. The market eventually buckled under the weight of negative economic data and increasingly skittish investors. We might have talked ourselves into an economic slowdown, if not a mild recession, as the gap between investors' previous euphoria and the declining economic conditions grew painfully obvious. Our rhetorical hopes could no longer support the mass-mediated descriptions of reality. We lacked enough lucky charms to forestall a precipitous decline in technology companies' valuations, leading to a widespread economic slowdown. Maybe our rhetoric about the New Economy was feigned intimacy; we thought we knew more about high-tech economies than we really did. In any case, the euphoric identity we had hung on the term "New Economy" was fading. We discovered that our perceptions of reality were dramatically dissonant with the underlying facts. One of the few technology CEOs willing to challenge publicly the New Economy rhetoric throughout the 1990s was Intel's Andy Grove, who called the term "ill-defined and imprecise. I can't be a believer in it unless you define it."[21] Of course, the term's imprecise, mythical meaning is precisely what attracted so many enthusiastic believers.

We typically derive our understandings of the meaning and purpose of information technologies from the mass-mediated stories of innovation. Even the idea that the Internet empowers us comes from the overarching tale of high-tech progress. As we identify with such stories, we take up their technological rhetoric as our own. We buy into these commonplace understandings in an attempt to make sense of complex social and cultural processes that no one fully comprehends. Like Emily in *Pretzel Logic* or technology investors in 2000, however, we sometimes have to face the fact that identities and realities do not always fit well together. We are not always as intimate with reality as we presumed, in spite of the wealth of available information.

Challenging the Symbol Brokers' Myths

In an essay titled "The Soul of the New Economy," Scott Stossel identifies a new professional genre he calls "the Businessman as Revolutionary." Citing the success of the high-tech business periodical *Fast Company*, Stossel argues that New Economy aficionados combine the corporate ethos of *Fortune* with the countercultural bravado of *Rolling Stone*. *Fast Company* recognizes, he claims, that the real potential of the New Economy is more rhetorical than economic. The phrase "New Economy" is a selling tool, an attractive new image of the businessperson as a chic revolutionary rather than as one of the "suits." Many people, writes Stossel, "fancy themselves" as the next dot-com CEO and spend too much time "on airplanes to industrial parks or in cubicles crunching numbers." *Fast Company* "capitalized on the latest fears and dreams of these people: it told them they were cool." The magazine's hip culture gave aspiring revolutionaries the high-tech language that differentiated them from old-style capitalists. The Internet, for instance, signaled "the end of business as usual" and produced "smarter markets." Stossel suggests that business "co-opted counterculture" as New Economy workers learned how to pour the old wine of corporate capitalism into the new wineskins of the information mystique.[22]

One result of this hip capitalism is an emerging generation of "symbol brokers" who speak of faith in professionalism while practicing technique.[23] Symbol brokers are professional communicators who "broker" mass-mediated messages between different audiences. They include journalists such as those at *Fast Company* and in the mainstream media. They also include advertising practitioners and publicists who broker symbols on behalf of clients who seek to influence public opinion or buying patterns. These kinds of professional communicators "mediate" versions of reality by manipulating symbols, from words to images. *Fast Company* brokered a hip new concept of capitalism for information workers who sought satisfying self-identities in tune with the rhetoric of the New Economy.

Professional communicators take on greater power in the cyber-age because culture is less fixed in tradition and consequently more malleable. Richard Lanham suggests that in the information society human attention is in especially short supply, prompting people to "use a variety of rhetoric as the 'economics' of human attention-structures."[24] Through both covert and overt means, professional persuaders have gained new venues for diverting our attention to messages that match their clients' interests. Computers and data networks offer unparalleled potential to segment culture into markets and to pseudo-personalize messages for individuals within larger audiences. Symbol brokers now have greater means of identifying particular audiences with specialized messages.

Symbol brokers take on special significance in the United States, where cultural tradition is less coherent and more fragmented. As James W. Carey suggests, nineteenth-century Americans largely lacked a shared culture and thus had to maintain community life through various forms of public communication, such as discussion, debate, and negotiation. "Social order was neither inherited nor unconsciously achieved," writes Carey, "but actually hammered out as diverse people assembled to create a common culture and to embody that culture in actual social institutions."[25] Looking toward the future rather than glancing back to the past, Americans optimistically created and re-created a common life through one form of communication after another, from town meetings to the press, and eventually through electronic and digital communication. Americans repeatedly envisioned the latest communication technologies as tools for re-creating communities that they assumed could no longer be sustained purely on the basis of historical practices and traditional habits.[26] In other words, Americans' search for identity has been collective and public as well as personal and private.

Building such shared public life is not primarily a technological feat, although it now requires communication technology. Conducting town hall meetings or discussing politics over lunch are still important forms of democratic discourse, but they cannot sustain national life in the information age. Citizens look beyond their local communities to the media for help in locating and sustaining shared identities. More and more of our public communication necessarily occurs "out there," in the media, not in our own intimate realms of neighborhood, meeting hall, or cafe. As a result, we increasingly depend on media professionals to nurture our public discourse, to represent us, to express for us what we supposedly believe, value, and feel. The 1992 Pontifical Council for Social Communications document titled *Aetatis Novae (Dawn of a New Era)* says that "the power of media extends to defining not only what people will think but even what they will think about. Reality, for many, is what the media recognize as real."[27] Instead of participating in public life, for instance, we are apt merely to consume the news reports written by professionals, along with a few letters to the editor or special columns composed by non-journalists. But the media are not neutral conduits for our own ruminations and discussions; they are social institutions managed by professionals whose own interests are also at stake. Even the journalists know that their reporting has to sell newspapers or attract audiences for advertisers.

Cyberspace does not enhance citizens' participation in our common public life nearly as much as we think. Within particular social groups, such as religious denominations and business professions, symbol brokers still use *specialized* media to link elites with their audiences. Some specialized Web sites, for example, report *on* and *for* the computer industry, relying extensively on expert columnists, reporters, and interviewers. *Fast Company* became one of the chief spokes-media for young workers who identified with the rhetoric of the New Economy. It and similar periodicals solidified the social values of information workers who wanted to be part of a new, presumably better way of doing business. Generally speaking, technology-related industries rely on such specialized media to create their own professional ethos as much as to address everyday tasks, issues, and solutions. Edward Yourdon says that within the field of computer programming, for instance, professionals "depend almost entirely on trade journals, vendor literature, and marketing representatives to explain what the major hardware and software companies are doing."[28]

Within the *general* media, such as local newspapers and cable news networks, professional communicators represent social groups to the general public as well as to each other. Professional journalists, for instance, translate the sentiments and practices of the high-tech business community for the general public. During the 1990s, reporters "taught" Americans about the ethos of the New Economy. They popularized terms such as "Information Superhighway" and "cyberspace" as labels for understanding the so-called information revolution. Borrowing the language of cyberspace primarily from experts in industry and academy, journalists helped establish a national consensus about the apparent benefits of information technology, from more efficient manufacturing and distribution of consumer goods to better-informed citizens.[29] Although some journalists questioned the rhetoric of cyberspace, most of them cheerfully reported the views of wide-eyed futurists and sanguine industry spokespersons. By the late 1990s, the new mythos of the digital sublime had become the core of the public imagination about information technology. Americans hailed the coming triumph of information over ignorance, innovation over stagnation, and speed over slowness.

Symbol brokers are not nearly as independent-minded or altruistic as we might assume. These professional communicators do not necessarily believe personally in the messages they publish or broadcast. Although a symbol broker might be interested in persuading audiences to affirm his or her personal beliefs—for example, a newspaper columnist might advocate a political stance—most professional communicators are paid to express the views of clients, not their own views. Advertising and public relations practitioners normally advocate their clients' views. They are what St. Augustine, himself a rhetorician, called *venditor verborum*, or "sellers of words."[30] Meanwhile, journalists depend on the ideas provided by experts and officials who claim special knowledge but also have their own careers to advance. Through a kind of professional consensus, reporters return regularly to the same pool of pundits, such as outspoken industry CEOs, economists, computer scientists, quasi-academic techno-gurus, and especially book authors.

As suggested earlier, symbol brokers in the 1990s used their intellectual talent and communication skills to create an ethos for the information revolution. Because the Internet was for most people a new medium "making itself up" as it went along, it was "particularly susceptible to the art of spin." Michael Wolff recalls what those who worked in the industry in the 1990s believed: "Optimism is our bank account;

fantasy is our product; press releases are our good name."[31] *Fast Company* did its part by helping to fashion a new, evocative image of the information-age worker as a hip revolutionary with New Economy sensibilities and supra-capitalistic instincts. Using case studies of high-tech companies, peppered with psuedo-philosophical essays about new business strategies and theories, *Fast Company*'s symbol brokers—reporters, editors, freelance writers—attracted a readership of info-workers who wanted to believe they were on the cutting edge of revolutions in both information technology and business. The new high-tech ethos served the magazine by attracting readers, served advertisers by delivering the hip audiences to them, served the emerging cyberculture by spreading its tenets, and even advanced a pop spirituality that validated the underlying faith in digital technologies' ability to usher in progress. *Fast Company* told inspiring stories about the information revolution to those involved directly in it as well as to the wider public. The accuracy or validity of its techno-tales was less significant than the overarching ethos—the cyber-identity that readers found so appealing. Taken as a whole, these technological stories served implicitly as a secular metanarrative about social progress.

Thomas S. Valovic describes similarly how *Wired* magazine, the most visible and arguably the most influential of the periodicals for the *digerati* and their followers, "developed hype-generation into an art form with its unique way of casting the starkly technical in quasi-poetic terms." News reporters who covered the Internet "gravitated to *Wired* and to its coterie of writers, editors, and techno-groupies." Fusing technology with popular culture, *Wired* anchored its own commercial success to its ability to express the cyber-myths: "The digital revolution was here to stay, it was unstoppable, and left to its own devices without interference from government it would bring about some sort of new-world order. *Wired* would be the serialized equivalent of Martin Luther's ninety-five theses nailed to the door of All Saint's Church." In reality, *Wired* rarely addressed the tough questions, such as the pitfalls of hyper-technologization, including its impact on the moral fabric of culture. The magazine's views, says Valovic, were predictable and insular, not truly novel and open-minded.[32] *Wired* reinforced the prevailing libertarian notions of information society—all to its own interests and those of its board and consulting *digerati*. Paulina Borsook similarly concludes, "Although *Wired* maintains a posture of celebrating the cacophony and all the lack of prior restraint Net culture has to offer, in fact, it is not open to points of view other than its own, as bounded a set as *The National Review* or *The Advocate*."[33]

To keep us enchanted with new technologies, symbol brokers create what Jacques Ellul calls "explanatory myths."[34] As tellers of the mythos

of the digital sublime, brokers repeatedly parrot the idea that technological innovation is social progress, that the information highway will
educate people more effectively, that the Internet empowers most individuals to become publishers, that cyberspace enhances democratic participation, that digital technologies are making American business far
more competitive—and many more upbeat tenets that most of us want
to believe. Regardless of whether they are true or false, these kinds of
myths affirm our faith in information technology. They also falsely convince us that we understand the role of technology in our lives and its
impact on society. Symbol brokers help spread such myths by expressing them in simple, attractive language that makes sense to audiences.
Advertisements, in turn, rely on the myths to create evocative images
for high-tech brands. Television commercials for cyber-related products and companies tell us about speed, efficiency, and progress—the
alleged benefits of cyberspace. We seek such coherence from everyday
media reports, secondhand news, and personal gossip. Over time we
tend to adopt such myths as our own, becoming personal carriers of
tales told by the media and techno-experts. Steeped in such mythical
commonplaces, we often fail to recognize that even the most appealing
explanatory myths can also be self-serving messages. In effect, these
myths take on a life of their own, driving our collective cyber-endeavors. Once a human project becomes "invested with human dreams of
'progress' or 'liberation,'" writes Vinoth Ramachandra, "it attains a life
of its own, dragging human beings and societies in its wake."[35]

In the process of extolling these explanatory myths, symbol brokers
frequently simplify and sometimes even distort technological reality.[36]
John Perry Barlow, co-founder of the Electronic Freedom Foundation,
suggests that "the media exist to confirm the delusions of the crowd,"
to "reify every hysterical belief that the mob might suddenly espouse."[37]
Although he overstates the case, Barlow rightly recognizes that symbol
brokers either create or shape widely shared public opinions. Our shared
public views on cyberspace, too, reflect often-repeated sayings about
"new technologies" that "conquer space and time," "revolutionize our
lives," "rebuild community," and "save time." Symbol brokers repeatedly reformulate the same types of myths for each new technological
innovation, thereby affirming the apparent veracity of the myths
independent of their application to specific technologies.[38] Some edu-
cators and politicians also use the myths to persuade students and voters, respectively, about the benefits of information technology. These
myths form the core of the high-tech ethos and help to justify our extensive investments as a society in cyber-technologies. But whether they
are true or false, they give us no moral bearings on information tech-

nology. They keep us from asking deeper and more nuanced questions about the goodness and rightness of cyber-developments.

In the age of cyberspace, public relations is a particularly pervasive form of symbol brokering. In *The Internet Bubble,* Anthony B. Perkins and Michael C. Perkins describe how spin artists fueled the prevailing cyber-ethos in the 1990s.[39] High-tech companies formulated compelling tales that attracted venture capitalists and generated client publicity— what they often called "buzz" in the industry.[40] Investment bankers operated "spin desks" that allocated "chunks of hot new stocks to the personal brokerage accounts of corporate executives, venture capitalists," and other friends.[41] They also worked the technology trade shows and pitched story ideas to trade and general-interest media. These symbol brokers even represented the emerging *digerati,* building their notoriety, booking speaking gigs at industry gatherings, helping them secure book contracts, and publicizing the resulting titles. Meanwhile, public relations practitioners assisted politicians, business elites, and technologists who sought to associate publicly their own endeavors with the positive ethos of the information revolution. Publicists disseminated and intensified—if not created—the personas most associated with mythos of the digital sublime.

The story of cyberspace, then, is partly a tale of how symbol brokers spun sublime myths about cyber-companies, personas, and technologies. Internet companies' business plans, advertising campaigns, press releases, and media interviews persuasively advanced a mythology that praised personal empowerment and individual freedom, declared the renewal of community life, and asserted the emergence of a New Economy that would magically render the old one obsolete. In effect, symbol brokers sold a willing public on the optimistic messages that it wanted to hear, thereby also serving the venture capitalists and Wall Street observers. With few exceptions, critics of the new technology gained relatively little publicity.[42] Even intellectuals became "supporters and evangelists of technology," says Paul Virilio.[43] Brokers merged public hope and industry rhetoric, elevating the Web into a medium of mythological stature—all to great media fanfare and Wall Street jubilation. Perhaps no media mythos was ever packaged, distributed, and commercialized more quickly and effectively.

In the process, however, high-tech companies became some of the most disingenuous self-promoters in the history of business. New e-commerce companies spent millions of dollars on brand advertising designed to position them in the capital markets as trendy businesses with New Economy zeitgeists. Perkins and Perkins document how the so-called New Economy was not so much about creating viable technological innovation as it was about creating media hype over the next big company public stock offering.[44] They quote a partner with a Silicon Valley investment company: "We've stopped putting the effort into actually trying to build a company. We've put our effort into building stocks because you can do that pretty quickly."[45] In fact, advertising became one of the largest expenditures for new technology companies trying to create a distinguishable symbolic presence amidst the cacophony of start-ups all trying to gain investors' attention.[46] There has probably never been more money spent on consumer advertising by a new industry in its early years than the expenditures of the dot-com companies between 1997 and 2000.[47] During the 2000 Superbowl television broadcast alone, over ten dot-coms spent an average of over $2 million per thirty-second spot. The company HotJobs.com had already spent $2 million for advertising during the 1999 game, when its total revenues were only $4 million.[48] Investment banks and Wall Street typically invested more energy building the images of new firms than in actual technological innovation. Enamored with the potential of creating organizational personas through mass communication, these high-tech suitors heartily embraced advertising as an instrument of persuasion. In the process, they followed in the commercial footsteps of their low-tech predecessors who had learned the value of advertising and public relations in print and broadcast media.[49]

Symbol brokers collaborated with venture capitalists to convince the public that technology firms were far more solvent and better positioned in the market than they actually were.[50] *PC World* contributing editor Stephen Manes wrote already in 1999 that new companies were often "obsessed with stock price [rather] than product quality." He further observed that technology firms tended to release company financial data that were "often incomplete, inaccurate, or both." Manes concluded that "data quality" had become about as important to the Web industry as "software quality" was to the computer industry.[51] Similarly, Po Bronson in *The Nudist on the Late Shift* portrays Silicon Valley as a world of images, hype, and buzzwords spun by a host of wacky characters who delude themselves as much as they con others.[52] In *Burn Rate*, Web-company CEO Wolff wonders if he might get rich for being a visionary or a charlatan—two closely related self-definitions in the early days of cyberspace.[53] Successful dot-com CEOs had to be more skilled in the techniques of brokering a corporate ethos than they were at building a viable company.

As the Web itself became a commercial medium, advertising and public relations agencies scrambled to become "full-service" organizations attuned to helping clients create cyber-identities. Millions of dollars of advertising revenue flowed to the Web in the form of banner advertising, sponsorships, and affiliation agreements.[54] Even personal home

pages proudly displayed software company logos and trumpeted particular brands of information technology. Hillary Rosen, president of
the Recording Industry Association of America, said that thanks to the
Digital Performance Right In Sound Recordings Act of 1995, the Internet had become one of the greatest promotional tools for the music
industry. "Instead of only selling a full album of packaged goods, artists
and record companies are looking at subscription services, singles and
compilation downloads, artist packages, on-line jukeboxes and so many
more."[55] In spite of the ongoing battles that the entertainment industry
would have with Web sites over the downloading of copyrighted entertainment, cyberspace had become one of the most important promotional media in the industry's history. "'High-tech' is now, in reality,
'high commodity,'" wrote a computer columnist in 1997. "Every technology innovation generates its own commoditization," he added.[56] One
venture capitalist called this brokering "a reality-distortion field."[57]

Today, the Web is not so much a forum for public discourse as it is
one more arena for symbol brokers to legitimate their clients' ethos.
Pam Alexander, a public relations professional who specializes in high-
tech clients, says that her model of persuasion is built on "overcom-
municating." "We bring an intensity and a sense of urgency," she says.
"There are so many opinion leaders in so many different segments. To
do an effective job, you need to be on top of that. With the rise of the
noise level, communications people like us are more active than ever in
setting the agenda. We influence what gets discussed in the industry we
serve."[58] "Hype happens," reports *Computerworld* magazine. "Venture
capitalists want to get their hooks in a hot company first. Reporters want
to get the big story first. Analysts want to make predictions first. And
everyone wants to feel like an insider. Don't you?"[59] Even the MIT Media
Lab deliberately set out to coin a brand name and establish a high pro-
file in the popular media.[60] Symbol brokers help all of these parties build
the mythos of the digital sublime—all the while benefiting from it.

Cyberspace surely gives many individuals new means to communicate privately and publicly, but it also strengthens the role of symbol
brokers as public propagandists. Cyberspace both cultivates and depends
on propagandists who are becoming increasingly skilled at building their
clients' personas. These brokers view cyberspace not as a forum for civil
democratic discourse, authentic communication, or sustained truth
seeking but as an arena in which they can use the power of images and
the spell of stories to fabricate cyber-identities for people, companies,
and technologies. Symbol brokers helped create the mythos of the digital sublime that equated information technology with inevitable social
and technological progress. They told us repeatedly what we wanted to
hear, namely, that cyberspace could do almost anything we wanted it

to do.[61] The Internet became a symbol of technological innovation, economic expansion, community leaven, individual empowerment, educational resources, and democratic liberty. Even though we tend to think
of them as independent communicators, journalists, too, joined the chorus of praise. The rhetorical battles among symbol brokers today concern which organizations and individuals will most persuasively link
their own images to the overarching cyber-mythos, not whether the
mythos captures the real nature and impact of cyberspace. As *Fast Company* discovered, the soul of the New Economy is hip hype.

Looking for Authenticity

In *The Difference between God and Larry Ellison,* Mike Wilson describes
the culture of the Oracle corporation under its legendary CEO. Wilson
suggests that the defining characteristic of Ellison's style of leadership,
and the resulting corporate culture, was the drive to win. Employees
were not encouraged to be ethical as much as they were exhorted to be
successful, to boost the bottom line by practically any means necessary.
According to one former Oracle board member, Ellison failed to establish for the company a "magnetic north," a "common direction." The
CEO never offered a "sense of how things would or would not be done."
Oracle salespeople, for instance, promised to deliver to new clients some
products that were yet to be invented.[62] The motto seemed to be, "Make
the sale first, and worry about creating the products later."[63] If Wilson's
assessment of Oracle is accurate, the corporation's culture lacked moral
fabric; it legitimated the practices of success-driven employees. The
main corporate end, success, justified the instrumental means of doing
business profitably in a high-tech society.

Cyberculture as a whole fosters the kind of logic that helped Oracle
become one of the largest and most successful software companies.
Disingenuous posturing toward the public and clients has become part
of the high-tech story of winning by necessary means. The high-tech
sector is now oriented almost solely toward efficiency and control, with
little concern for a virtue such as authenticity. The resulting communication tends to be hyperbolic and disingenuous. Every organization
claims to have the best product or service, the most visionary business
plan, and the most empowering corporate culture—a logical impossi-
bility. Nor is there any moral accountability. Cyber-technology becomes
one more means of conforming the world to people's selfish desires, not
a way of responsibly building trust and serving one another.

Cybernetic messaging contributes to the unbinding of the world in
many ways, but one of the most significant is how it rejects the virtue

of *authenticity*—saying what we mean and meaning what we say. Authenticity is fundamental to healthy human relationships in every area of life as well as one of the great characteristics of responsible communication. It requires us to know who we are, to present that known self to others, and to avoid persona-building activities. In a similar vein, Wendell Berry suggests that responsible speech requires the speaker to "stand by it, be accountable to it, and be willing to act on it."[64] Cybermessaging, by contrast, often does not meet the standards for such authentic discourse. It suffocates virtue by giving us the unbridled freedom to be all things to all people, to give ourselves over to the highest bidder or to the most persuasive master. In this sense, the information age needs less professional technique and far more authenticity, particularly the *truthfulness, empathy,* and *integrity* on which authenticity depends.

Truthfulness is one of the most important signs of authenticity in human communication. A virtuous person is both a truth seeker and a truth teller. He or she recognizes that the full truth is far more but never less than factuality or correctness; truth is often wonderfully complex and mysteriously elusive. But a truthful person nevertheless desires to be filled with truth and thereby to be a conduit of truth for others. Truth tellers necessarily question the prevailing explanatory myths, recognizing that inauthenticity plagues professional life and infects even high-tech symbol brokering. They bring a spirit of truthfulness into professional and personal relationships, making associations less instrumental and more humane. Truth telling obligates us to far more than simply creating versions of reality that are in tune with our own interests or with those of our employer or client. When we seek the truth, we try to embody truth in our lives, to be carriers of reality rather than fabricators of virtual reality. Truth telling is one means of orienting ourselves to "authentic being" even in the midst of cyberculture.

Historically speaking, religion has encouraged people to seek higher truth, not to be content with what is purely convenient or what is merely in one's own interest. Religious traditions usually aim to rebind people to the truth so that they may become truth tellers. An inherently religious search for truth is not like nitpicky informationism but a quest to know God and neighbor. American political life, for instance, is anchored in the truths revealed in the Declaration of Independence, including the truth that we are endowed by the Creator with certain unalienable rights. All truth telling requires authenticity on the part of all parties making the promises. When we play with the truth for personal gain, we unbind reality and shirk our obligation to be truth tellers. We reject any deeper, moral understanding of truth in favor of a purely instrumental one. Content with being instrumentally successful, we fail to see both the beauty and the honor in being truthful persons.

Lacking any internal commitment to truth seeking, cyberculture encourages us to believe in everything in general. Databases and high-speed networks foster a technical form of relativism that can fashion almost anything into truth. This kind of high-tech openness disperses and dilutes our understanding of reality. Truth becomes little more than the latest findings, most recent data, or most popular interpretation—with no deeper sense of revealed truth. We see ourselves as purely social constructions, as mere reflections of constantly fluid self-identities and inherently disingenuous intimacies. This is partly why symbol broker-ing is so commensurate with the information age. Symbol brokers need not believe in anything except their ability to influence an audience. It is also why Internet messaging, which typically lacks real intimacy, as a medium is particularly conducive to deception. Unethical investors, for instance, use Internet chat areas and bulletin boards to hype com-panies and inflate stock prices before selling their own shares—a prac-tice sometimes called "pumping and dumping."[65] Participants in cyber-sex often lie online about their real identities and then deceive their real-life partners about the online involvements. Cyberspace is filled with practices that distort truth and embrace the efficacy of deception. The medium's practices invite us to "pump and dump" versions of truth as a means of getting whatever we want.

Religious tradition, on the contrary, focuses our vision on reality while stabilizing our identities within communities of truth-seeking discourse. Communities of religious truth seeking can anchor us in mutual com-mitments to honesty that serve partly as the moral foundation for dem-ocratic society. If we do not resist deception in all its forms, we lose much of what it means to be created as human beings with cosmic responsibilities. We become, like our machines, incapable of knowing who we really are and how we should truly live. Truth telling is a moral decision with profound implications for the information age. It orients us away from technique—mere means—and requires us to integrate our means and our ends, our method and our telos. Without the virtue of truth seeking, communication falls into a merely secular pursuit that relies on technique to manipulate. The only way forward is to live the truth. We all should do our best, wrote Alexis de Tocqueville, to "prove that the interest of each is to be honest."[66]

Authenticity also embraces *empathy.* A commitment to truth telling alone can, of course, lead us to become arrogant propagandists for our own understandings of reality. As word-vendors, we forget that no mat-ter how many facts and how much data we have, the full truth is beyond our grasp. To be authentically human is partly to admit our own limited visions of reality. We are human beings, not gods. Often we see truth only vaguely in the shadows of life. The technologist might thrive on the rush that comes from figuring out how to make a cybernetic system work, but even he or she recognizes that the next technological disaster might be around the corner. Our ability to know the world intimately and to control all of its forces will always elude us. Nevertheless, collectively we can know more than we do as individuals. If we listen to each other, embracing the fact that others may know more than we do, we can gain insight and wisdom beyond our own penchants. This kind of empathetic knowledge is far more valuable than our illusionary control of the world. Submitting to a greater truth, discovered outside ourselves, is one of the most authentic human virtues. It is nothing less than a declaration of our dependence on each other and ultimately on the Creator. Being empathetic is one way of living within such a declaration.

Empathy requires us to forego our own rhetorical agendas at times for the sake of considering others' interests rather than our own. The rhetoric of technological progress all too often fails to include the voices of those who will not enjoy progress. "Admittedly," says one West Coast techno-guru, "we shall abandon part of the population to their fate when we enter the cyberage, but *techno is our destiny,* the freedom high-tech machines give us is the freedom to be able to say 'yes' to their potential."[67] Where is the empathy in such rhetoric? "In order to swim you must take off all your clothes," writes Søren Kierkegaard. "In order to aspire to the truth you must undress in a far more inward sense, divest yourself of all your inward clothes, of thoughts, conceptions, selfishness. Only then are you sufficiently naked."[68] "Empathy" derives from the Greek *empatheia,* which literally means "entering into suffering, being 'in passion,' with one another."[69] St. Francis's famous prayer says, "Lord . . . may we seek not so much to be understood as to understand."[70] Empathetic living is bearing the truth of life together, carrying each other's real joys and burdens. Symbol brokers are too inclined to empathize only with their clients or their peers rather than with their broader communities.

Empathy also opens our hearts and minds to our own consciences, because it permits the possibility of discovering that *we,* too, are self-delusional and disingenuous persons. Václav Havel's comments about politicians could help all symbol brokers in the contemporary world: "Rather than merely seeking to satisfy the many special interests and pressures they must accommodate, they should listen more to the voice of their unique, individual conscience."[71] In other words, our own consciences can challenge the explanatory myths that sweep across the information society. Cyber-technologies themselves do not stimulate our consciences, since they keep us so busy messaging. By empathizing with our consciences, we can gain a more moral grasp on reality. In the Christian tradition, contemplation is an important practice for seeking both our conscience and the revealed conscience of God.

Finally, empathy assents to the possibility that we might be able to identify with humanity—with the broader truth of the human condition, not just with our own experience or that of close friends. Even our daily conversations tend to be so instrumental and superficial that they block out the possibility of empathizing with the human condition as well as with particular people or institutions. We get so caught up in the routines of daily life—answering email and ordering fast food—that we lose track of the possibility that ultimate truth and goodness could speak to us even through our common humanity. To put it in spiritual terms, our informational practices and technological ruminations are not sensitive to the inherently sacramental qualities of human existence. In the age of information, we grow morally and spiritually tone deaf. We empathize only to the point of pragmatic need, not to the level of human connection. We empathize via public polls and market surveys, not with the heart. As a result, our moral spirits atrophy. We find it more and more difficult to recognize goodness, truth, or beauty amidst the messaging of every day. This is partly why sentimentality is so common in secular-rational cultures; superficial emotionality substitutes for epiphanic experiences. We enjoy films and television programs, but our own morally thin lives seem unworthy of greater significance. Technique sponsors its own forms of techno-piety devoid of deeper empathy with the human condition.

Perhaps we need to institute heart-wise habits that soften our non-empathetic practices. We can, for instance, sequester email messages that deserve reflection and prayer, putting them in a separate file or on a personal digital assistant that rings several times a day, calling us out of our busyness and into solitude. We can also consume less news, giving us more time to consider the meaning and impact of particular news stories. Amidst all our messaging with friends and colleagues, we will sometimes hear whispers of pain, doubt, and fear. If we can teach ourselves to pick up on this evidence of people's needs, we can then pursue the kind of dialogue in person or on the telephone that enables us to empathize.

In a world of hype and spin, empathy can lead us to authentic testimony. Cyberculture equates self-existence with the power to change the world. "I message, therefore I am" could be one of the credos of the information society. Instead, "As pride presumes, so does humility confess," writes Augustine. "Just as there is presumption in the one who wishes to appear what he is not, so is he a confessor who does not wish that to be seen which he himself is and loves that which He is."[72] Unfortunately, such humble testimony rings hollow in a high-tech world. But if we do not know ourselves, if we are not intimate with others, if we have no sense of the deeply moral character of life, if we cannot even remotely imagine our obligations to the truth, our lives will invariably testify to the hollowness of our being. If all we can hear is empty rhetoric, then all we can say is similarly devoid of moral meaning. If, on the other hand, there is indeed something worth being committed to, if there is real meaning and purpose in life, if there are cosmic responsibilities that inform our moral imaginations, then the testimonies of our lives should be rich and full. Our lives can then be faithful expressions of truth. "Who is the authentic individual?" asks Kierkegaard. "One whose life, in the fruit of long silence, gains character and whose actions acquire the power to excite and arouse."[73] He adds, "It is absolutely unethical when one is so busy communicating that he forgets to be what he teaches."[74] Being authentic persons is one way of testifying to the truth.

When truthfulness and empathy merge in our lives, we can also live with *integrity*. Cyberculture often forgoes integrity in favor of libertine messaging. Where is the unifying center—the integrity—of cyberspace? Perhaps no question is more important for societies that are fabricated increasingly out of technique. Are we as human beings more than the sum of our skills and techniques? Is there not much more to life than creating and consuming information, as well as purchasing and using the equipment that enables us to expend time messaging? Is there a deeply binding purpose to our efforts and even to our very being? If not, perhaps we are nothing more than morally mercurial personas with an inexplicable talent for influencing one another and with an insatiable desire to make the creation fully subservient to our own interests. Where is the integrating principle that illuminates the value of all others? Can we reasonably have faith in any integrating idea, belief, or person?

Secular-rational cyberculture substitutes information for integrity. It conceives of all messages as information—all the images, words, and sounds we can disseminate, along with the feelings and sentiments they elicit. Cyberculture dismisses the search for unifying integrity as purely romantic or nostalgic. While we may "still be vulnerable to talk of inspiration, destiny, or a glorious past," writes Kenneth J. Gergen, "such language is usually limited to contexts of marginal status—ritual ceremonies, fund-raisers, or Sunday morning services—far from the marketplace, halls of government, and other places where the 'important decisions' are made."[75] In short, the very concept of integrity seems old-fashioned and constricting when contrasted with the sea of available information. We are far more apt in a high-bandwidth environment to approach life as a smorgasbord of consumer options rather than as a unifying endeavor. By advocating consumer choice over moral virtue, however, we deny the possibility of living with integrity. Our lives become database productions that deliver whatever information is called for in a given context.

High-tech culture is so acutely instrumental that it can easily blind us to our own inauthenticity. Under its influence, we focus on building an effective persona that will win friends and advance our careers. Cyber-culture even turns us all into symbol brokers, putting our communicative talents up for sale in the marketplace of technique. Many young dot-com workers found themselves falling into this moral trap in 2000. When the high-tech sector plummeted, some of them left the industry to regain their moral bearings, but others so loved working for technology ventures that they accepted any offer in a tight job market—even positions with online pornographers.[76]

Human beings display an extraordinary capacity to compromise the honest search for truth and even to dismiss the quest itself as foolish. Havel says that "with the loss of God, man has lost a kind of absolute and universal system of coordinates, to which he could always relate anything, chiefly himself." As a result, we live "as if we were playing for a number of different teams at once, each with different uniforms, and as though . . . we didn't know which one we ultimately belonged to, which of those teams was really ours."[77] We "merge with the anonymous crowd" and "flow comfortably along with it down the river of pseudo-life. This is more than a simple conflict between two identities," concludes Havel. "It is something far worse: it is a challenge to the very notion of identity itself."[78] Cyberspace is one "place" where people can create so many contradictory self-identities that they no longer have a coherent self and therefore no possibility for authenticity.

Of course, inauthenticity is not a new human problem. Augustine faced it in his day as a teacher of rhetoric. He began to wonder if it was right to offer his rhetorical skills on behalf of any cause. So he retired from his teaching position rather than continue to do what he could no longer authentically support. He refused to be a for-hire symbol broker. "Tongues that appear to be offering helpful advice can actually be hostile opponents and, in offering love, may devour us in the way people consume food," Augustine wrote in *The Confessions*.[79] As he matured in faith, however, Augustine realized that persuasive communication was not itself evil. In fact, the church needed wise and eloquent spokespersons for truth. How could falsehood be challenged except by the speech of those people who are committed to truth? To remain silent could at times be virtuous, but silence could also be irresponsible in situations that call for open, authentic communication. Augustine finally realized that the trouble with so many rhetoricians—symbol brokers of their day—was their willingness to persuade people to believe in anything; these professionals' only obligation was to the power of rhetoric itself, not to a moral vision that would require them to use rhetoric on behalf of truth.[80] The modern symbol brokers who are now taking hold of the Internet need to hear Augustine's call to authenticity. So does Oracle's Ellison and every Web surfer.

Conclusion

Journalist Chip Scanlan wonders if digital technologies are necessarily a blessing for news reporting. "Journalism has come a long way from the days when a reporter needed little more than a pencil, paper and telephone," he observes. Cell phones, laptop computers, and personal digital assistants are common among reporters. Moreover, journalists increasingly depend on the Web and email to collect story information and communicate with sources. But Scanlan also wonders if technologies' power to remove "obstacles of time and distance" creates "an unwelcome buffer between the reporter and the public." Too many stories already are "reported by telephone," he argues. They "lack texture, completeness and accuracy that only person-to-person encounters can bring." Although many young reporters find such personal contacts "awkward and uncomfortable," adds Scanlan, they remain "the lifeblood of good journalism." He concludes that the "most essential tools for a journalist aren't dependent on a computer chip, but a reporter's mind and heart. They are the very human qualities of curiosity, integrity and empathy."[81] Without such habits of mind and heart, journalism itself slips into cold and frenzied messaging that lacks virtue.[82]

High-speed messaging and informational databases do not necessarily improve human communication. Along with such technological achievements we have re-adopted inauthenticity, which acutely undermines relationships and stymies our attempts to be moral persons. Inauthenticity devalues the content of our language, rendering it either purely instrumental or vacuously relative and confusing. We lose the dignity of speech as a means of upholding shared understandings and embracing community. We also replace virtuous living with technological savvy. We find it increasingly difficult to practice what we preach because we are not sure what we believe, let alone what we should present as our beliefs. Only the efficacy of technique seems to be a viable means of upholding our value as persons. Valovic says that "not only are many of the values of digital culture not 'religious' but they might well be described as ethically challenged." He suggests that "the new technocrats" are "interested in nothing less ambitious than reinventing society in their own image. To a large extent, they see certain anchors of traditional culture as standing in the way of their vision of a new society."[83]

In the information age, we still need symbol brokers who are skilled at interpreting human life for different groups. Michael Oreskes rightly points out that the more glutted we are with information, the more vitally we need people who can help us separate the wheat from the chaff.[84] If symbol brokers act responsibly, they can help us recover the authenticity of personhood and the broader integrity of life. We depend on our storytellers, for instance, to grasp the inherent meaning and purpose of our existence. They can reveal our common humanity and our shared brokenness. Journalists, novelists, and playwrights are particularly important. Priests and prophets are no less critical to our social well-being today than they were in religious history. We also need oral storytellers—such as humorists, balladeers, and narrators—who can work within the live moments of our daily routines to resuscitate real meaning in the midst of our instrumental endeavors. Most of all, we need empathetic communicators who are not merely brokers but are themselves deeply committed to the narratives they craft. In other words, we need authentic communicators who personally commune with others through the integrity of their stories.

Such authentic storytellers can challenge us to reconsider the mythos of the digital sublime. With their help, we can question the excessive optimism that pervades public discourse about cyberspace. We can then discover what is truly new and what is merely recycled propaganda. As Harold Adams Innis suggests, it might be that as "modern developments in communication have made for greater realism they have made for greater possibilities for deception."[85] Information technology is not a *deus ex machina* that will improve everything we do, so long as we do not stand in the way of its triumphalistic ride to cyber-glory. Perhaps the greatest folly in such rhetoric is a technological utopianism that paints a glorious cyber-future as inevitable. When journalist Steve Lohr addressed the mythos of the New Economy in 2001, he concluded that the term "was a symbolic shorthand for the power of technology to transform the economy, investment strategy, business thinking, even modern culture." That "theory," he writes, "requires some revision, to put it kindly. Its biggest problem came first—the word new. Almost nothing about the rise of the Internet in the 1990's was really new."[86] Why did it take so long for a few journalists like Lohr to transcend the myth?

The most compelling alternatives to secular-rational authenticity emanate from revealed religion. Whereas New Age religion generally embraces the contemporary fascination with technology and virtual reality, the Hebrew and Christian traditions remind us of our broken pasts and our capacity for self-delusion.[87] We desperately need to hear words of judgment as well as celebration. Authentic discourse rightly challenges the power of secular empires, including informationism. Most of all, the wisdom embedded in religious tradition, when let loose within society, can redirect us toward authenticity. Morality is meaningless if we cannot rebind our language to truth. Without the moral stability of revealed religion, we will continue to be swept up in the winds of inauthentic propaganda and the waves of brokered consumer desires.

chapter six

Striving
for Cosmic Diversity

■ Writer Anthony Walton argues that African-Americans have always suffered as a result of technological innovations. He says, "The history of African-Americans since the discovery of the New World is the story of their encounter with technology, an encounter that has proved perhaps irremediably devastating to their hopes, dreams, and possibilities." From the caravel ships that enabled the Portuguese to "rule the waves from West Africa to India," to Eli Whitney's cotton gin that boosted the American slave economy, and now to the high-tech revolution that largely excludes blacks from meaningful employment while welcoming them as consumers, African-Americans have been exploited rather than empowered by technological innovations. According to Walton, the underlying problem today is that black "folkways"—conscious patterns of thought and belief—"do not encompass physics and calculus." Blacks do not see becoming an engineer or computer scientist as a "way up in the segregated Black community."[1]

Walton's essay reveals not only the dearth of African-American participation in the wealth generated by information technology but also the remarkable lack of noninstrumental diversity in high-tech culture. High-tech endeavors usually require a wide range of technical skills, but they also display a pausity of virtue. As argued in this chapter, the technical vision of those who chart our informational futures is extremely limited and severely unaccommodating to moral cultures. Informationism and its accompanying instrumental practices spare little room for a diversity that includes virtue. As Walton writes, the people who design the machines are "not intent on unleashing chaos; they are usually trying to accomplish a task more quickly, cleanly, or cheaply." Nevertheless, he adds, "As the world gets faster and more information-centered, it also gets meaner: disparities of wealth and power strengthen; opportunities change and often fade away."[2] As we become information rich, we also tend to fall into a moral myopia that excludes noninstrumental values from shaping cyber-endeavors. We lose the broader scope of virtue.

The first section of this chapter examines the influence of high-tech gurus who supposedly know the truth about information technology. Cyberculture now supports its own stable of columnists, reporters, public speakers, and book authors whom people look to for sage advice. The Internet, in particular, provides a new arena for media personalities to hawk their ideas, elevate their social status, and deepen their influence on the broader society. Indeed, the business of creating and marketing cyber-personas is now a major industry. Like New Age prophets, these experts claim to have "Gnostic" truth—secret, quasi-religious revelations about ideas and practices that supposedly will empower individuals and organizations. In the end, however, cyber-personas typically equate intelligence with simplistic slogans that merely repackage the mythos of the digital sublime. Perhaps most telling of all, the notion of diversity held by cyber-personas rarely recognizes the need for moral wisdom in cyber-endeavors.

The second section assesses the role of information workers as the chief architects of the cyber-project. Technicians and managers, in particular, expertly build and employ efficient messaging technologies. Working with a boyish adolescence, they transform their entrepreneurial endeavors into games of technical skill that lack a moral vision. The result is a stultifying *techno-correctness*, a presumed way of thinking predicated on instrumental means, unquestioned ends, and professional interests. In the 1990s, many of these information workers hoped to get rich through company stock options—and some did. They worked grueling schedules that tethered them to increasingly meaningless work routines. Their labor became their lives, collapsing moral vision into short-term camaraderie and superficial playfulness.

The third section calls for *cosmic diversity* as a means of including moral perspectives in the processes of cyber-innovation and informational administration. The information society needs a more diverse notion of "knowledge workers" that includes essayists, poets, playwrights, public intellectuals, clergy, and laypersons—all people who can imagine a society that values not only technique but also joy and good judgment. These kinds of technologically marginalized people ask some of the toughest questions about the nature of cyberspace—questions about peace, justice, and goodness. Most of all, we should admit religiously derived moral wisdom into our collective discussions of the meaning and purpose of information technologies in the contemporary world. Any public discourse about information technology that precludes the habits of the heart will likely fall prey to the prevailing techno-correctness, which limits how we can comprehend both the value and dangers of new media.

This chapter concludes with a brief theological look at the meaning of diversity. Cultural diversity has long retarded evil as well as renewed the creation. Diversity and unity each depend on the existence of the other. When they are in balance, both moral vision and technological innovation thrive. The Christian doctrine of the Trinity—the three in one, unity with diversity—captures the positive role of diversity amidst unity. Whereas unchecked diversity can lead to libertine chaos, and forced uniformity can result in instrumental monopolies of knowledge, cosmic diversity, as derived from God's own diversity, embraces the uniqueness of persons and cultures while simultaneously affirming our common humanity.

Recognizing High-Tech Personality Cults

CEO Jeff Dachis became a celebrity among the new guard of dot-com millionaires. His Boston-based Web consulting and design company, Razorfish, caught the initial waves of growth and capital investment and went public in 1999. Dachis's own stake in the company netted him a paper value of $77 million when the company's quarterly revenues were only $15 million. Nevertheless, Wall Street rallied around Razorfish, partly because Dachis was such a charismatic salesman for the Internet as well as his own company. He claimed to know the secrets of the New Economy. According to Dachis's revelations, companies were either "in" or "out" of the New Economy, and Razorfish was deeply in. He exhorted his employees—called "fish"—to "be the brand!" Staff apparently responded wholeheartedly to Dachis's rhetoric, even to the point of making clients feel stupid if they did not understand Razorfish's tribal language. "There are sheep and there are shepherds, and I fancy myself to be the latter," Dachis told the *New York Times*.[3] He did not need any diversity of thought; he knew truth. One of the cockiest of the new guard of techno-gurus, Dachis tirelessly promoted himself and Razorfish. He symbolized a rising style of high-tech CEOs—part celebrity, part philosopher, and part preacher, with a moralistic air of superiority.

The Internet fosters waves of new celebrities who establish high-tech personality cults through both new and traditional media. Hopeful information workers seek advice from these prestigious experts, who dispense novel ideas and predict success for all followers who obediently adopt their techniques. Like Dachis, these gurus develop their own rhetoric of success anchored in the prevailing public myths about the information revolution.

Personality is one of the major means of transcending informational entropy in the cyber-age. Public personality—*persona*—gives people someone to look up to and to believe in when public information seems confusing and incoherent. Journalist Steven Brill, sporting his own media persona, argues that the "currency we all trade in today is information, and we're bombarded from all sides by Internet sites, web newscasts, 24-hour cable news stations, infomercials, hundreds of magazines, newspapers, trade publications, docu-dramas, newsletters, and 'Who's on your pager?'" According to Brill, although we live in an information society, we still need a "single entity" to tell people "what they can and what they can't rely on." He even predicted that his *Brill's Content* would become the "arbiter of the information age," the "bible" for the "new century,"[4] whereas in a few years it was defunct. Brill's guru-esque rhetoric is both revelatory and self-promotional, claiming the power to transcend the anonymity of many voices with one intimate voice of clarity and conviction.

Given the chaos of the digital media environment, we seek coherent and compelling voices of authority, persons of clarity and vision who can help us overcome our confusion. Consultants, academicians, CEOs, and other experts step into the void, supposedly explaining our plight and offering practical if not sage advice. Two writers in *Forbes ASAP* suggest, "For a technology company to succeed, the CEO needs to be more than just a business tactician; he or she must also be an articulate speaker and advocate, able to hold his or her own among the pundits and authors who populate such gatherings."[5] Building a persona is one of the chief rhetorical strategies in the information age. A persona is a form of branding, a means of distinguishing and drawing attention in the midst of the information glut. It is also a vehicle for enhancing social status through the imaging of professional expertise.

Cyberspace, like Hollywood, uses personas to organize online and offline information. After all, an effective persona can advance the interests of the sponsoring organization. High-tech trade shows, for instance, rely on celebrity speakers to capture potential registrants who seek professional enlightenment. The number of technology speakers grew from roughly two hundred in the 1970s to more than four thousand in 1999.[6] A successful trade show depends "heavily on the keynote speaker or speakers it can advertise—even if only for cameo appearances."[7] The growth of the New Economy was a tremendous boon to the booking agents and publicists who create personas for conventions.

Technology-related book publishing sells inspirational techno-cate-chisms authored by the same cyber-gurus. Book publishers realize that a persona is just as important as substantive ideas in selling supposedly efficacious techniques to the unenlightened business and technology wannabees. As one CEO told his ghostwriter, "I think of you as a plumber. Maybe the world's best plumber nonetheless. And I think of this book thing like a clogged drain. You're hired to make the problem go away. Once you do, I'll take a look." The ghostwriter explains that a "silver-bullet solution" can make an otherwise unknown person into a cottage industry. Today, he claims, guru wannabees view their books as promotional techniques that can generate million-dollar consulting opportunities and four- or five-figure public speaking opportunities.[8]

The techno-gurus use some of the rhetorical strategies of preliterate cultures, such as moralistic categories of good and evil. Seeing the world as made up of black and white forces, they imagine reality in essentially spiritual terms as a struggle between two moral forces. Razorfish's Dachis distinguished between those who are "in" or "out" of the New Economy—as if the stereotypes could match complex reality. After CEO Gil Amelio left Apple Computers in 1997, he even referred to the company as a "religion" and a "cult." The corporation could survive only with "glamorous" leadership, he insisted, because of its cult-like ethos. "It's the cult. There's an enormous amount of positive energy in the company. . . . It's what kept the . . . thing afloat through some of the most incredibly bad business decisions I've ever seen anywhere."[9] Apple sur-vived partly because of the moralistic tribe of Mac users who venerated Apple machines, identified the company with righteousness, and looked at its chief competitor, Microsoft, as an evil empire. Apple even hired Mac "evangelists"—a title originally held by Apple booster Guy Ka-wasaki—to sell software developers on the Mac operating system.[10] When Apple co-founder Steve Jobs returned to the company after Amelio's departure, he was touted as the savior who would faithfully redeem the beleaguered company.[11] Such moralistic categories usually lack dis-cernment, but they are frequently good for business, rallying the tribe around the techno-righteous leader.

The phenomenal growth in the number and popularity of technol-ogy-related experts also reflects followers' thirst for the "secret" knowl-edge that will presumably reveal powerful ideas and practices. Hopeful that the right knowledge and techniques will give them influence among information workers, they look to apparent experts for special insight. Particularly appealing to wannabees are personas who claim to be able to reveal secrets about the deeper meaning and real muscle of cyber-phenomena. Like early church Gnostics, they create their own "cult" of revelatory ideas and practices—supposedly the deeper insights into the mysterious reality of cyber-phenomena. Canadian communication theorist Marshall McLuhan, *Wired* magazine's self-appointed patron saint, dispensed such secret wisdom in the 1960s and 1970s. Today, people still read McLuhan and other gurus—the "fathers" of the "church of informationism"—hoping to gain revelatory insights into cyberspace. Like religious saints, deceased techno-gurus serve as symbolic vessels for people's everyday entry into furtive understanding; such gurus witness to their self-discovered "truth" and inspire others to faithfulness. Popular gurus help to justify, motivate, and charm the legions of information workers.

The rhetorical foundation for most techno-personas is usually one simple but evocative concept: an emotive idea, angle, or metaphor that leaps out at audiences and gives them the impression that they have finally discovered truth. Each guru has his or her own technological rhetoric sprinkled with supposedly profound new truths and riveting stories of success. In fact, anyone can create revelatory terms that sound profound: "backwards networking," "one-to-one empowerment," "leveraged bandwidth," "creative disengagement," "techno-visualization," "cyber-harmony" (I just made these up). Creative literary agents and ghostwriters help wannabees devise the rhetorical messages that will create the next best-selling cyber-pundit.[12]

High-tech gurus use their charismatic power supposedly to unlock the secret doors to efficiency and control. Speeches and books herald the fact that one or another persona knows these truths and will share them with others for the price of admission or the cost of a book or newsletter subscription. George Gilder, one of the most revered techno-gurus, offers cyber-punditry via his writings, speeches, and his own investment newsletter.[13] Secret knowledge cannot be devised, the gurus suggest; it can only be revealed by those who have already been enlightened. Therefore, information workers and managers depend on the gurus for authentic insight—or so they think. The proliferation of published and spoken punditry regarding cyberspace testifies not just to the rhetorical skill of techno-gurus and their symbol brokers but also to the inability of technicians and managers to find their own ways through the mazes of modern technology. For them, diversity of thought sometimes means little more than allegiance to one or another personality cult.

Gilder preaches "telecosm," an emerging world of instantaneous communication and abundant bandwidth. His popularity stems from his remarkable facility for combining spiritual, moralistic, and technological rhetoric in the form of Gnostic insights. His book, *Telecosm*, is one of the most telling expressions of such personas. The former speechwriter claims in the book to be able to reveal for readers the secrets of the emerging "telecosm" that can "banish all the glass and unveil new cathedrals of light and air alone." Thanks to the magic of light-based digital messaging, he says, we are experiencing a "new canonical abundance." All the leaders of the "world economy are changing course to ride the tides of light." The "conceptual foundation of the computer age," continues Gilder, is now "reduced to irrelevance" in the face of a "new sphere of cornucopian radiance." Like a techno-priest, Gilder claims to explain where the new "promethean light comes from (the science story), how it is taking over (the engineering story), who is fighting it, who will ride it to victory, and what it all means."[14] Writer Po Bronson calls Gilder "a new generation of rogue futurist, contentious and dangerous: he's the Tupac Shakur rap master of futurism." But Bronson also recognizes that Gilder has a "missionary's drive" and speaks with "a preacher's fervor."[15]

Gilder's moralistic framework divides the cyber-world into the good people who champion innovation and the bad people who lack faith in the power of information technology to save the world from virtually everything. Gilder calls the debates about cyberspace and the New Economy "a religious war. With any technology that's changing the world as deeply as the Internet, religious wars are inevitable." He predicts that technophiles "are going to win because we have a vision of change and redemption." Gilder even chides his enemies for being "stuck in the zero-sum assumptions of the premillennial era." He calls for "overthrowing the power and principalities of the old order."[16] Like other new-order prelates, Gilder co-opts the language of religious tradition persuasively to gather his flock of faithful believers around the veneration of information technology. He even positions his critics rhetorically as faithless, heretical souls. For true believers such as Gilder, technological salvation is only a few inventions away.

Similarly, Oracle's Larry Ellison rhapsodizes about the power and impact of information technologies. He uses a rhetoric of predestination to describe the impending future of cyber-technologies. "By combining all information—numbers, texts, sounds, and images—in digital form, and making it available everywhere, and by making it infinitely manipulable, the information highway will utterly change our lives," he predicts. In spite of his pseudo-spiritual verbiage, however, Ellison displays no interest in any particular religious tradition. His technological salvation is cross-denominational, trans-religious, supra-spiritual. Ellison even claims that in the emerging future "people will scarcely be able to remember what life was like before."[17] In other words, information technology will render history and tradition gloriously irrelevant. Technique will supercede wisdom. Digital storage will replace human memory. Data will be the only intelligence our species will need. In Ellison's scheme, this future is presumably inevitable—like the preordained conclusion to history foretold in the biblical Revelation of John. The Internet, he proclaims, is "collecting all the knowledge of mankind and making it available in digital fashion—reliably, securely, and economically."[18] Of course, he is the expert who can point the way into this Promised Land. Cyber-gurus like Ellison become our prophetic tour guides to the emerging digital heaven. Rarely do they inform us, however, that the tour is also a public relations event on behalf of a specific company or more broadly for the mythos of the digital sublime. Nor do they admit the moral vacuity of their technological vision.

Today, the fields of business management, entertainment, and information technology all rely on the persona-oriented techniques of Hollywood. Matt Drudge, who gained a substantial online following through his Web-based news reporting, mimics the self-promotional efforts of mainstream news celebrities. He hosts a radio program as well as edits his Web site, *The Drudge Report*. He also cowrote *Drudge Manifesto*, a book typical of the chatty techno-philosophies aimed at mass audiences. Rhapsodizes Drudge, "In the same way Gutenberg's Bible hastened the End of The Church's stranglehold on fifteenth-century Europe, in the same way Thomas Paine rallied troops to fight King George, in the same way Upton Sinclair cleaned up the meatpackers with a single stroke, the Internet is liberating the Great Unwashed." Coauthored with Hollywood's Julia Phillips, Drudge's manifesto craftily combines self-promotion, technological prophecy, and altruistic rhetoric about the rebirth of muckraking in cyberspace. The Internet "supercedes every mode of communication ever invented," claims Drudge. Recalling the night that he scooped mainstream media by publishing online the story about President Bill Clinton's affair with White House intern Monica Lewinsky, Drudge says, "It was the night the gates blew open." News, he claims, "was no longer controlled, and never would be again." Thanks to cyberspace, "Anyone from anywhere can cover anything. And send it out to everyone." Drudge positions himself rhetorically as just a former "nobody" who managed to seize the power of technology on behalf of the people.[19] His persona is both populist and high-tech—a powerful combination that enables him to avoid charges of elitism while claiming the power of the information revolution to build a cottage industry around his persona.

Audiences apparently desire to become quasi-intimate with personality cult leaders who are rhetorically rich but morally impoverished. The fact is that most cyber-celebrities offer us little or no virtue. At best, they promulgate enchanting but simplistic insights into information technologies. At their worst, they self-interestedly frame their rhetoric merely in terms of people's unrealistic hopes and dreams rather than in terms of reasonable truth. They tell us what we *want* to believe, rather than what we *should* believe. Their storytelling weaves "a few ambiguous shreds of evidence into orderly narratives" that reassure us even when they are dead wrong.[20] In the process, cyber-gurus' propaganda serves their own interests far more than it does the common good. As Wendell Berry writes, "There is no group of the extra-intelligent or extra-concerned or extra-virtuous that is exempt."[21] We all contribute to the tomfoolery that masquerades as wisdom and to the creative destruction that we mistakenly believe is progress. Most techno-gurus' packaged slogans promise far more than they could ever deliver. Certainly we should admire great thinkers and persuasive communicators, but not when their messages merely rehash the morally vacuous mythos of the digital sublime. Celebrity and virtue do not mix well. The former appeals to the value of the market, whereas the latter looks to ultimate goodness or rightness. Most of all, the techno-celebrity cults limit the diversity of our moral discourse by focusing our attention on gimmicky solutions, hollow hopes, and moralistic stereotypes.

Checking the Authority of Experts

When Alexis de Tocqueville toured the United States in the 1830s, he marveled at Americans' commitment to both equality and individualism. He concluded that in America all people are rational enough to take care of their own affairs. Observing the nation's rapid industrialization, however, he feared that escalating mass production might create an intellectual gap between those who work in routine production jobs and those who manage industrial organizations. Production-line laborers might never have the opportunities afforded managers to develop a wide range of intellectual abilities. Tocqueville imagined this knowledge gap as the beginning of a possible aristocracy based on intellectual accomplishments. The drive for material well-being in America, he concluded, could lead over time to what we now call *meritocracy:* an intellectual elite that enjoys greater material wealth and elevated social status.[22]

Tocqueville's fears were prescient wisdom. Even in the age of inexpensive computers and extensive online networks, we face remarkable inequalities of knowledge in North America, let alone around the rest of the globe. This knowledge gap is not merely a disparity in people's access to technology; it is a breach between narrowly specialized and instrumental forms of knowing, on the one hand, and more general and moral perspectives, on the other hand.

Tocqueville was correct in that an advanced industrial society elevates expert knowledge over other ways of knowing. The vast majority of jobs within the high-tech sector of the economy are similar to earlier industrial production work. Hardware and software technicians, network administrators, computer programmers, and the like frequently have little opportunity to participate in more intellectual organizational endeavors, such as establishing an organization's mission and purpose and developing a corporate strategy. Lewis Mumford observes that "the very success of mechanization puts the products of high technology under the control of routineers, lovers of compulsion and conformity, whose chief concern is to keep the wheels moving smoothly."[23] The new "knowledge workers" derive their authority from the specialized skills and procedures that enable them to make systems "work." They are not knowledge workers in Tocqueville's broader sense of relying on wisdom or at least deep intellectual understanding. And they certainly are not knowledge workers in the sense of cultivating distinctly moral habits of the heart. In contemporary society, both expert technicians and managers—*information experts*—are voices of technical authority within their own domains. They largely determine the informational systems used by business, education, government, and nonprofit organizations.

Tocqueville did not grasp in his time that so many workers would become specialists with broad authority within their professional domain. The rise of the managerial class during the twentieth century spread technique-based expertise across society. Most important of all was the rise of *managerial* knowledge workers who rely on data-driven decision making rather than intellectual or moral understanding. In other words, many managers are informational technicians who rely on database and communication technologies that are themselves the work of expert technicians. Like technologists, these managers aim for greater production and distribution efficiencies and for more control over markets. In short, information managers "specialize" by relying on detached, quantitative ways of knowing—what was earlier called informationism. In too many instances, their chief responsibility is to be *effective* managers of information, not to be *responsible* stewards of the resources for good purposes. Caught in an informational meritocracy, they elevate technique over moral vision.

This lack of moral vision occurs because knowledge workers affirm monopolies of knowledge that make specialized, informational techniques the predominant ways of knowing. As C. A. Bowers notes, technicians and information managers aggressively "commodify activities, forms of knowledge and social relationships that previously were the basis of reciprocal responsibility and bonding in communities."[24] The cyber-celebrities keep alive our hope in human personality and secret revelation, while the information experts use their expertise to rationalize every area of life. The specialist system leads to a society in which most of us can do only one thing well—work within our own narrowly defined area of professional expertise.[25] "In living in the world by his own will and skill," writes Berry, "the stupidest peasant or tribesman is more competent than the most intelligent worker or technician or intellectual in a society of specialists."[26] As information experts define intelligence for lay persons, there is little room left in society for nontechnical, nonmanagerial, and noninformational ways of knowing. This is why we tend to think of the Internet, for instance, as serving primarily an instrumental rather than a moral purpose. We imagine the Web as a means of collecting and distributing information for the purposes of efficiency and control. We even talk about how we can "manage" our email and Web-derived information. This kind of managerial rhetoric comes closer than any other metaphor to defining the Web.[27]

Professional specialization values the voices of technical expertise in society over practically all others. The resulting "informational diversity" becomes little more than a narrow hodgepodge of competing professional interests and instrumental skills, with little or no moral insight. As Berry puts it, under the "rule of specialization," society becomes more intricate but less structured, more organized but less orderly. Our disintegrating communities lose "the necessary understandings, forms, and enactments of the relations among materials and processes, principles and actions, ideals and realities, past and present, present and future, men and women, body and spirit, city and country, civilization and wilderness, growth and decay, life and death—just as the individual character loses the sense of a responsible involvement in these relations." Human life, Berry concludes, "scatters itself out in a reckless horizontal sprawl, like a disorderly city whose suburbs and pavements destroy the fields."[28] Cyberspace itself manifests that type of disorderly city of chaos.

Cyberculture privileges informational expertise over non-technical ways of knowing. It imposes managerial values on people's use of informational technologies rather than adapting the technologies to people's existing cultures—their organic ways of life. Instead of integrating Internet technologies into existing communities, we reshape our work and play to fit the routines of information technologies. In other words, we learn technology from the experts who develop it and adapt our lives accordingly. If technologists were committed to building community more than to developing technology, for instance, their innovations would likely be much friendlier to nontechnological ways of life. They might create classroom presentational technologies that are both teacher and student friendly. Some digital white boards on wheels, for example, can be written on with colored markers and the resulting notes or illustrations saved to a disk and eventually sent via email to students. Compared with Microsoft PowerPoint, which is clumsier, relies on more regimented "templates" and requires a fair degree of technical sophistication to use, the digital white board maintains more of the personal style and conviviality that surrounds traditional blackboards. Computers and networks would better support noninstrumental practices and noncommercial purposes. Instead, we find ourselves living under the implicit philosophy of techno-correctness, where to be "right" about anything is little more than to be technically sophisticated about it—to be a specialist who knows how to make technology work. By and large, information experts are not paid to be culturally sensitive or morally good, only to be technically successful. Their task is simply to get the desired results, to engineer ways of accomplishing specified goals. This monopoly of informational expertise partly explains why we rarely talk about cyber-technology and virtue in the same conversation.

Moral diversity is much broader than techno-correctness. To the extent that information workers operate only within an instrumental view of life, they are more like technocrats than virtuous people. Moreover, to the degree that they have little or no cognizance of their larger cosmic obligations, they are creating cultural uniformity rather than diversity. Bowers says that scientists and technocrats, in particular, are creating a "world monoculture" that disrespects "culturally diverse traditions of local knowledge."[29] This kind of narrowly instrumental vision shapes the perspective of many information experts. As the experts rely on the expertise of each other and profess autonomy from the rest of society, they elevate themselves above all competing visions of the meaning and purpose of life. Cyberculture subtly introduces us to a new form of Manichean thought, which simplistically divides the world into the information-rich and the information-poor, the techno-savvy and the techno-stupid, the cyber-expert and the layperson. Walker Percy calls this kind of dichotomy a "misapprehension of the scientific method," an "idolatry" that results in both "the radical and paradoxical loss of sovereignty by the layman" and the "radical impoverishment of human relations."[30]

Václav Havel also challenges such techno-correctness. "The mystery of Being and the meaning of life are not 'data,' and people cannot be separated into two groups, those who know the data and those who don't," he writes. "None of us becomes greater than anyone else simply by virtue of having learned something the others have not, or rather by coming into the possession of some fundamental 'truth' that the others, to their misfortune, have not discovered."[31] Instead, Havel suggests, our task, regardless of our professional expertise, is the same: to live with a "faith" that sincerely "believes in life, in the world, in morality, in the meaning of things and in himself." Our "relationship to life" should be informed by "hope, wonder, humility and a spontaneous respect for its mysteries." Moreover, we should not "judge the meaning" of someone's efforts merely by their "manifest successes, but first of all by their 'worth in themselves.'"[32] Havel criticizes technological expertise for its lack of intrinsic moral purpose.

The prevailing techno-correctness overshadows the moral problems. We find ourselves disgusted by what some people—such as online pornographers—are doing with cyber-technology but simultaneously convinced that effective informational techniques are empowering us to achieve social progress. Yet such an unethical endeavor as peddling smut is itself often the product of highly skilled information experts working at the cutting edge of Internet marketing and promotion. In a sense, pornographers are among the champions of the new technologies, savvily building high-tech organizations and garnering customers to make profits.[33] Techno-correctness gives neither them nor us the basis for judging *any* uses of information technologies. It never requires us to ask any moral questions or fulfill any moral obligations. This is partly why information workers generally lack any distinctly moral discernment with respect to cyber-technologies. Moral discernment depends on extra-technological understanding.

In *Post-Capitalist Society*, Peter Drucker suggests that we now face the challenge of integrating the various specialized "knowledges" into a coherent whole.[34] But what kinds of integrative principles will enable us to accomplish this? The specializations themselves lack broad coherence with other specializations. Knowing how to design a computer or organize a database requires no overarching moral facility for wisely integrating technique into community life. We gain the specialized expertise of professional work—of collecting and applying information to technical needs—but we increasingly lose the more general disciplines of moral living, from loving our neighbors to being hospitable. Whereas nontechnical cultures take a holistic view of life, information experts adopt specialists' views predicated on the power of each expertise to usher in progress.

High-tech organizations extend the moral poverty of techno-correctness to all employees by espousing hollow rhetoric about how new technologies supposedly empower all workers. Charles Handy reveals that technological organizations were among the first to replace the word "manager" with seemingly more inclusive terms such as "team leader," "project head," "coordinator," and "executive."[35] These early adopters shifted management from a definition of status or class within an organization to an activity that could be taught, learned, and developed, presumably by anyone.[36] In one sense, this managerial transformation served society by making it possible for a wider range of people to become managers. In another sense, however, the new concept of learnable managerialism created a more limited notion of what it means to be a manager. Managerialism became a particular way of thinking and working, a professional ethos with its own expert knowledge and tribal skills. Today, this kind of managerialism is largely a matter of managing information technologies and the resulting information.

Moreover, the ethos and skills of information management are based on standards of efficiency and control, not on intellectual insight, let alone moral responsibility. Managers of information can become mere technical manipulators within organizational systems. "Manipulation" and "management" both stem from the Latin root *manus* ("hand").[37] Under such managerialism, information workers dispassionately "handle" the information that dictates the destinies of others. "My nightmare scenario," writes Sven Birkerts, "is not one of neotroglodytes grunting and wielding clubs, but of efficient and prosperous information managers living in the shallows of what it means to be human and not knowing the difference."[38] Today, workers at all levels—even entry-level fast-food employees—learn that informational technique is the core value for modern work, professional success, and social progress.[39] But such technical work can easily slip into a demoralizing instrumentalism that lacks a human dimension. One Web worker says, "The sad reality is that for all the well-deserved excitement the web generates, working on the web can be one of the least exciting things in the world, like being a cook at the Normandy invasion."[40] Although many information experts try to transcend such instrumental boredom by finding a higher meaning in their work, usually there are no pecuniary or social status incentives to do so.

Experts who capitulate to techno-correctness can lose some of their capacity for being responsible persons. A modern professional who is merely technically oriented is an example of what the French call a *déformation professionale,* a malady that commonly takes a particular form within a profession.[41] Moral maladies are among the most frequent deformations in high-tech work, since technique itself rarely offers workers an ethical compass. High-tech modes of organization and production establish a secular monopoly over other practices. To become technically sophisticated professionals, workers adopt the prevailing standards of technique—such as writing efficient software code or building e-commerce Web sites that yield higher-than-average sales per visitor. Speed is critical too, since competitors will soon learn the same techniques. But moral cracks appear in such a profession, because building a profession for people to value technique over responsibility is little more than a way of legitimating moral deformation. One study discovered that Internet executives were four times more likely to have "unsavory backgrounds" than executives in other industries.[42] Such findings should cause us to consider what happens morally when techno-correctness suffocates moral responsibility. The pace of growth and the instrumental character of cyber-companies make them increasingly susceptible to moral failure. Perhaps the lack of moral responsibility is the overriding *déformation professionale* among information experts.

The rise of techno-correctness in the age of cyberspace also reverts adults, particularly men, to moral adolescence. The thrill of technological expansion and digital control has led many information experts to approach their labor as a form of boyish play. Managers and technicians who focus almost exclusively on getting results are akin to male adolescents who lose themselves in the enchantment of competitive video games, oblivious to the world around them. These male-dominated professions generally disregard some of the human capacities that women tend to accept much more quickly and naturally: a sense of moderation in conflicts, a desire to empathize with others, a respect for people's intuitions, and a recognition of the sheer joy of relationship apart from any instrumental interests. Software engineer Ellen Ullman calls this instrumental approach to high-tech work the "cult of the boy engineer."[43] The computer society, says David Hillel Gelernter, is not "almost all male" but rather "a little-boy society, part of an ongoing infantilization of the society over the last half century."[44] Gelernter concludes that computer culture is "a spiritually impoverished world."[45] People need to "get over their boyish excitement, stop playing games, and get serious," he warns.[46]

Younger information workers have been particularly willing to adopt this boyish zeal in their work within high-tech companies. David S. Bennahum describes in *Extra Life* how computers thoroughly enchanted him as a child. "Cheap and omnipresent machines, so easy to slip into; they seduced us—me and so many of my friends. We just disappeared one day, stepped into the arcades and vanished, reemerging years later as adults."[47] One wonders how they matured, how they learned about life, and what kinds of social experiences they missed as adolescent videophiles. The possibilities of turning their adolescent dreams into careers led many teenagers and college graduates to technological or managerial professions. Whether an MBA or a software engineer, they could continue "playing" with informational technologies, without great concerns about the moral integrity of their work.[48]

Silicon Valley and other high-tech centers became occupational arcades, inviting talented young people into adolescent time warps that delayed their emotional and moral maturation. A programmer remarks in *Microserfs* that high-tech cultures "purposefully protract out the adolescence of their employees well into their late 20s, if not their earlier

30s. . . . I mean, all those Nerf toys and free beverages! And the way tech firms won't even call work 'the office,' but instead, 'the campus.' It's sick and evil."[49] Paulina Borsook describes in "Cyberselfish" the young technology workers in Silicon Valley who are "violently lacking in compassion." Like "privileged, spoiled teenagers everywhere," she says, "they haven't a clue what their existence would be like without the bounty showered upon them."[50] Work is a form of play with personal rewards but little sense of moral obligation.

The thrill of being part of a new company is a siren call to young people looking for techno-adventure if not early financial rewards. *NetSlaves* describes the situation: "People are nuts, no matter what profession they're in, but people forced to work like dogs with the carrot stick of stock options and 'untold' wealth dangling under their noses are especially nuts."[51] Like adolescents, many information workers feel unencumbered by family, church, and even moral conscience. The pace, dynamics, and bounties of high-tech ventures outstrip any deeper moral sensibilities. In fact, older computer experts and experienced business executives alike sometimes feel like aliens in this strange land of boyish enthusiasm; if they venture into Silicon Valley's arcade-like world, they become immigrants to a youthful culture of puerile technicism.

The instrumental, adolescent culture of information managers and technicians simply has no interest in defining the contours of moral life. No matter how diverse it might appear on the outside, its core is univocally amoral. Silicon Valley opened its doors to information workers from overseas as well as to bright, young technicians and managers from the United States. But such color-coded diversity is the mythical facade, not the internal reality. Cyberculture's own consensus excludes beliefs beyond the bounds of secular-rational thought. Like an immature adolescent, it has all the energy and none of the moral wisdom of adulthood.

High-tech society increasingly depends on expert knowledge and technical skills that are inadequate for achieving moral wisdom. Techno-correctness is too narrow and self-seeking, devoid of the broader perspective that we desperately need to enter the cyber-future responsibly. Cyberculture becomes, in the words of Ruth Conway, "the creation of those who feel themselves young adventurers cut loose from the familiar norms and structures of authority and who are seized by the impulse to try anything at the whim of selfish fancy."[52] Glorifying such technological adventurism, we encourage technicians and managers to run society for us. In the process, we contribute to monopolies of instrumental and expert knowledge rather than to a vocational diversity that includes moral responsibility. Paul Virilio wonders, "Might not the acknowledged disturbance of the maturation process, with its intellectual, sexual, affective and psycho-motor disorders, and the immaturity of individuals who remain arrested in childhood, be the logical outcome and final manifestation of technological defects which have become hereditary?" He adds, "Let us be in no doubt about it, then, technological progress is merely completing the juvenile revolution of the past century. As with Italian mime-artists, transformed into caricatures of children, play is now everywhere."[53]

Especially in high-tech organizations, information experts often lack an intrinsic sense of responsibility for the greater good. They seek and reward only impact, not virtue. Their cybernetic language predisposes moral autonomy. If techno-correctness steers us toward the *is* of informationism, we need to revive the *oughts* of moral responsibility. Tocqueville recognized that meritocracy is indeed a threat to the egalitarian nature of democracy, but he could not have imagined our current scenario: We fail to merit those who cultivate a higher sense of moral wisdom. Masters of technique increasingly rule the information society like lords of cyber-expansion. Moreover, we find it increasingly difficult to tame their technical fanaticism, because we cannot envision a diversity that would truly respect moral wisdom.

Fostering Cosmic Diversity

In the mid-1980s, student Shuichi Inagi installed his first computer in the bedroom of his Tokyo home. Little did he realize that five years later, employed by a Japanese textile business, he would become the company's resident computer expert. Along with his official job in marketing, he taught company superiors how to use computers and the Internet. He even enabled some of his superiors to become more technologically proficient so they could retain their jobs. At the same time, however, he unwittingly contributed to the erosion of Asia's traditional social order. In Confucian societies, older people were long presumed to be more knowledgeable; patriarchs were the founts of wisdom and the possessors of authority. The rapid expansion of computers and digital networks in Asia began shifting informational authority to younger people. The technical skills of youth challenged the traditional wisdom of experience. "Everything is being undercut," says George Yeo, Singapore's minister of information and the arts. "Older hierarchies can no longer be sustained." In his view, even governments cannot delay the computer age; they must either accept the information society or watch it arrive without their consent. Such tradition-shattering technology becomes an "underground railroad for arbitraging inefficiencies."[54] If tradition is inefficient, it can be replaced with information technologies.

While observers of social change are quick to point out the power of cyber-technologies to challenge traditional cultural hierarchies, they rarely suggest any alternative moral vision. As John Seely Brown and Paul Duguid put it, "Information technology has been wonderfully successful in many ways. But those successes have extended its ambition without necessarily broadening its outlook. Information is still the tool for all tasks."[55] Or as Stephen L. Talbott suggests, "Automation tends continually to reduce the higher work to mechanical and computational terms."[56] If such technologies indeed shift authority from particular social groups to other ones—such as from elders to youth, or from community storytellers to data processors—how are we to determine if the resulting changes are good or bad? We should not be content with this longing for greater efficiency and control. Intrinsically worthy purposes—such as freedom, justice, and peace—should inform our judgments about information technology. But how can we identify, in the midst of our technological activities, a kind of self-interest that is truly well understood? Whom must we include in any such discussion?

Tocqueville gives us a clue in *Democracy in America*. Examining the moral fabric of American society, he discovered gender diversity and with it a religiously inspired moral diversity. Whereas men in the 1830s concerned themselves with the more instrumental pursuits such as business and politics, most women domesticated the hearts of family members. He suggests that "it is woman who makes mores." Women, he argues, are particularly important in our attempts to embrace well-understood habits of the heart, because religion "reigns as a sovereign over the soul of woman."[57] In other words, women were more suited than men for carrying on religious activities; consequently, they were also more intimate with the moral sentiments that leavened self-interest throughout society.[58] Regardless of how relevant this gender difference is today, the maintenance of religiously inspired, unselfish social mores is just as important now as it was in the 1830s.

Religion, more than any other social force, connects Americans' practical activities and instrumental interests to their social mores. Religious beliefs and religiously inspired obligations can soften our otherwise purely selfish endeavors. Without a morality grounded in intrinsic responsibilities toward others, we easily focus only on immediate self-interests, on the power of information technology, and on the authority of professionalism. *Cosmic diversity*—a diversity predicated on universal human responsibilities rather than on merely tribal interests and instrumental logic—restrains our parochial rush to techno-correctness and deflates our fanatical informationism. If human diversity does not include cosmic morality, it will consist of little more than the competing special interests of information workers and their gurus.

Cosmic diversity, contrasted with secular-rational diversity, encourages us to include the insights of revealed religion in our discourses about digital technologies. It requires us, as caretakers of creation, to develop a moral language of responsibility that transcends purely personal interests, professional concerns, and technological efficiencies. Such cosmic diversity is not a collection of competing self-interests but an open discourse that welcomes people who are striving for a deeply human and a more fully moral understanding of our technological condition. Cosmic diversity invites nonexperts and even critics of information technology to our discussions about cyberculture. Of course, scientists, technicians, managers, and other experts should participate in our conversations about the information society, but so should people whose knowledge and wisdom come from personal experience, moral reflection, and religious conviction. Cosmic diversity stretches beyond expert training, formal education, professional involvements, and official duties. In an age of experts and specialists whose frames of reference tend to be dictated by professional considerations, cosmic diversity deepens our moral imaginations. It prevents one area of life, namely, the technical and instrumental, from gobbling up the moral and spiritual dimensions of human existence.[59]

Among the most important people to invite to our ongoing conversation about information technology are contrarians who seek to grasp the moral drawbacks wrought by instrumental achievements or professional specialization. As the Archbishop of Denver, Rev. Charles J. Chaput, puts it, the "information highway must not bypass humanity." We need responsible leaders who will "think deeply, not just about where we're going, but why we're going there."[60] Sometimes those who have failed in technological endeavors are particularly savvy critics. Too often we chart with great élan our apparent success stories, while failing to share our technological mistakes. Responsible critics carry on an important tradition of moral reflection about the ultimate value of purely instrumental pursuits and overly technological ways of life. "What means do you use in order to carry out your occupation?" asks Kierkegaard. "Are they as important to you as the end? . . . Eternally speaking, there is only one means and only one end: the means and the end are one and the same. There is only one end: the genuine Good; and only one means: to be willing only to use those means which are genuinely good."[61] We need the Kierkegaards of today at the table with us. Cosmic diversity includes the critics who reach beyond self-interest to a more fully human responsibility anchored in virtue rather than technique. Contrarians such as Albert Borgmann, Talbott, and Virilio represent important voices of reasonable dissent that stretch our understanding of the moral dimensions of the information society.[62]

Cosmic diversity includes the search for wisdom, not only the drive for more informational control. The cosmic mind should ask, "What is the significance of this technology for our lives as human beings and for our responsibility as caretakers of the world?" If the primary impact of information technologies is on how we form identities and intimacies, then we should not reduce our discussions of cyberspace to matters of pecuniary gain or technological innovation. In the words of Archbishop Chaput, information technologies are among "these things that shape the soul."[63] Cosmic diversity broadens and deepens our understanding of the effects of cyber-technologies, enriching our dialogue with a wider range of moral questions about who we are and what we are called to become. Cosmic diversity strives to include wise voices that are not mere personas created by symbol brokers, stylized by professional communicators, and animated by charismatic celebrities.

Cosmic diversity expands our conversation to the margins of high-tech society, where people are less enchanted by techno-correctness, frequently more concerned about moral issues, and willing to challenge techno-correct orthodoxies. The margins, says Berry, close in on orthodoxy and "break down the confidence that supports it, to set up standards clarified by a broadened sense of purpose and necessity, and to demonstrate better possibilities." As Berry points out, the idea of accommodating the margins—what he calls "diversity within unity"—underlies the United States Constitution and Bill of Rights. America was not intended merely to permit or tolerate divergence from popular thought but to use dissent by turning a "curious eye to the margins, eager to see what may have been tried and proven there."[64] In the information age, although tradition is marginalized, it nevertheless survives in the cracks and interstices on the margins of society, where it eludes the "prying eyes of the state, the market, and the media."[65] Viewed as light from the social margins, cosmic diversity illuminates greater moral capacity than is possible in mere professionalism and technicism.

Cosmic diversity shifts our moral confidence from the legions of specialists, experts, professionals, and celebrities to broader, more inclusive human discourse. It goes well beyond concerns about the "digital divide" between people who have access to cyberspace and those who do not. It requires *inclusion in moral discourse*, not merely *access to information*. Striving for cosmic diversity is not a cure-all for working our way out of high-tech dilemmas, let alone for charting a perfect route for the use of information technology in schools, governments, businesses, and voluntary associations. But it is a way of expanding our moral knowing beyond the monopolies of technical expertise and the shibboleths of info-gurus. Today, we too easily seek the advice of experts and the jargon of pundits when we ought just as readily pursue the insights of neighbors, friends, and other nonprofessionals. Often amateurs are the real lovers of a trade or practice, since they are not motivated primarily by professional status. Cosmic diversity challenges the informational status quo by ensuring that the weak and relatively powerless will have a voice in the discourse about our cyber-future. Without such diversity, we will continue to witness what Alfonso Gumucio-Dagron calls "electronic apartheid,"[66] or what Robert S. Fortner calls "excommunication."[67]

Cosmic diversity can help us to see the moral narrowness of techno-correctness. The Hebrew writer of Ecclesiastes tells us that all human effort is vanity—that all our work is futile because ultimately we and our impressive technologies will turn to dust. Are any of our cyber-endeavors truly worthy of surviving our own deaths? Is there anything inherently good and right in our informational models of efficiency and control? Thinking cosmically about information technology is one way of getting moral and even eternal issues on our agendas. Gelernter rightly argues that the computer scientists who design our everyday technologies should study the liberal arts, so that the work of their hearts, minds, and hands might produce artifacts of higher beauty that fill our lives with more joy and delight and that inspire us to reach higher.[68] When Shuichi Inagi began teaching his superiors how to use computers, he probably had no idea that he was part of a technological movement that would erode some of the honor traditionally granted to Japanese elders. Once he recognized what was transpiring, however, he needed to consider the value of traditional wisdom as an alternative to technical knowledge. Otherwise he would become just one more expert in a rising tide of specialists who had no ear for the noninstrumental margins, no true sense of the moral capacity within cosmic diversity.

Conclusion

One of the mysteries of moral living is how to respond to cultural diversity. Scholars claim various theories that might help us explain the processes of cultural diversity, but they cannot calculate the moral value of unity or diversity. All we can know for certain about variety is that it gives us more options, both good and bad. Unity, on the other hand, gives us focus and integrity, but taken too far it can stifle cultural growth and even oppress people. One important moral issue that we face in a culturally diverse world is how to be responsible caretakers of this variety. What should we keep? What should we discard? Why? Who says so? These are difficult issues with political and cultural as well as technological implications. *Quis custodiet ipsos custodies?* asked the Romans. Who is to control the controller?[69]

Historically speaking, cultural traditions, especially religiously inspired habits of the heart, have contributed greatly to human diversity. Of course, religions can also limit diversity when they slip into moralistic tribalism or grievous fanaticism. Without voices of reason and moderation, religious faith can become as univocal and as instrumental as techno-correctness. At its best, however, religion represents a crucially important check on the moral value of our informational pursuits. Peter Cochrane, who runs British Telecommunications' (BT) version of Bell Labs, hires not only engineers but also economists, lab entomologists, and even theologians. Asked by a reporter what a theologian does at BT, Cochrane chuckled, "He sits in a corner and prays for success!"[70] Presumably, Cochrane was chiding the reporter, since prayer is only one way that faith can morally leaven our technological endeavors. Taken in by the prevailing informational orthodoxy, we too readily undervalue spiritual insights, moral wisdom, and the habits of the heart. As Cochrane later confirmed in personal correspondence, he seeks in technological projects "a more holistic view from a more holistic team."[71] Today, religious traditions provide some of the best ways of expanding the margins of our knowing beyond the bounds of techno-correctness.

Popular views of diversity today tend to embrace or discard differences on the basis of who stands to win or lose, who will make a profit, or whose power is greater. This approach to diversity has some merit, since there are real winners and losers in every society. But a diversity based on rights might not be as morally compelling as one anchored in mutual responsibilities. In the Christian tradition, for instance, the body of believers is inherently diverse. "The Church has strong members, and it also has weak ones," wrote St. Augustine. "It can't do without its strong members, and it can't do without its weak ones . . . because without both of them there is no Church."[72] Just as the church is responsible for the care of all its members, the information society needs to consider its responsibility to those people on the margins of high-tech life.

Today, we ought to consider how to maintain a cosmic diversity that addresses responsibility. Our instrumental instincts too easily lead us to lop off the technologically unproductive parts of humanity in our quest to reengineer a better world. Our informational endeavors will be more morally fruitful when they are shaped by respect for noninformational ways of knowing. If we do this, we will always discover extra capacity in the diversity of people's talents and skills, in the range of their experiences, and in the fabric of their particular ties to communities of moral discourse. Information technology without cosmic diversity is likely to be monotonous, uncreative, and even oppressive, whereas with cosmic diversity it will always be more interesting, rich, and liberating. In today's cybernetic mind-set, the value of virtue seems oddly anachronistic, but perhaps we need more moral and less technological relevancy. The past, too, is a source of moral richness from the margins.

Cosmic diversity can reveal not just our differences but also our common humanity. It admits that human knowing is not merely technical but also human and therefore moral. Cosmic diversity accepts differences in culture and personality but also seeks to identify truths and realities that transcend our differences. Our "opening up" to greater diversity provides not just more variety but also greater ways of conceiving our moral unity as human beings. Each of us is intimately connected through the commonness of our shared humanity, including our shared responsibilities.

Conceived as a moral quest for both unity and diversity, cosmic diversity carries deeply spiritual overtones. Colin E. Gunton contends that the traditional Christian doctrine of the Trinity—God in three Persons, the Father, Son, and Holy Spirit—reflects both diversity and unity in the creation. The Holy Spirit, he believes, represents richness and variety, not static homogeneity. God the Spirit is "the source of autonomy, not homogeneity," because by the Spirit's action "human beings are constituted in their uniqueness and particular networks of relationality."[73] When this diversity is displaced by reason or human will, he argues, the "disastrous inhumanities and irrationalisms of the modern age take hold. Particularity is drowned in homogeneity, or asserts itself as the denial of genuine and open human relations."[74] Gunton says that the human spirit is part of the unique ability of people to "transcend themselves, to think and act beyond the present and the place in which they are set."[75]

Cosmic diversity, like personality itself, is built into the creation. Such variety within unity intrinsically challenges monopolies of knowledge, including techno-correctness. Cosmic diversity presents us all with the fact that expert practices and instrumental techniques are invariably too narrow, too parochial, and too techno-centric; they need to "open up" to a wider vision. Informational work exists for humanity as much as humanity exists for such work.[76]

chapter seven

Nurturing Virtue
in Community

■ The idea of renewing community life seductively draws our attention in the information age. All people, says Milan Kundera, have "aspired to an idyll, to that garden where nightingales sing, to that realm of harmony where the world does not rise up as a stranger against man and man against other men."[1] Americans are particularly hopeful that technology will enable them to recapture Paradise Lost on earth.[2] They imagine cyberspace, like the western frontier in its day, as a location for re-creating community. Michael Dertouzos claims that networked computers "will rebuild the notion of community, this time among millions of people."[3] If so, what kind of community will it be? Will cyber-communities have the capacity to sustain moral discourse and nurture virtue?

Regardless of how well information technologies can foster community, they invariably alter the actual places where we dwell, work, and play. Langdon Winner says that the "issues that divide or unite people in society are settled not only in the institutions and practices of politics proper, but also, and less obviously, in tangible arrangements of steel and concrete, wires and semiconductors, nuts and bolts."[4] Information technologies are never community-neutral, since they always separate or join us by altering our patterns of social intercourse. Some technologies undoubtedly are better for building local community life, while others more appropriately support instrumental messaging systems that span the globe.

This chapter addresses one of the great paradoxes of our time. In Michele Willson's words, although we have more "technologically aided"

165

communication than ever, the individual in society is "feeling increasingly isolated and is searching for new ways to understand and experience meaningful togetherness."[5] Any attempt to renew community life with information technologies must consider the moral qualities of the resulting social relations. To the extent that our technological imaginations inspire us to build merely communities of efficiency and control, they lead us morally astray. Instead, we should aim for "beloved communities" that foster virtue over technique. Martin Luther King Jr. used the term "beloved community" to refer to the kind of community of justice, equality, and freedom that is in tune with both the ideals of American democracy and the shalom of the Hebrew Scriptures. He wrote that neither political nor economic power should be an end in life; instead, "that end or that objective is a truly brotherly society, the creation of the beloved community."[6] The term "beloved community" is used here to suggest that *technological* and *informational* ends are insufficient for the kinds of communities we as human beings are called to embrace. Cyber-technologies can assist us in our quest for community, but they cannot themselves sustain communities of virtue. More important than cyber-technologies are the communal traditions and customs that have long given us the means and the ends for moral lives of gratitude and responsibility.

The first section of this chapter contends that a community of virtue is above all a *dwelling place*. Online community ultimately lacks a real environment where people can be fully *neighborly* and *hospitable*. "Conquering space" with information technologies may actually weaken locales as meaningful settings for beloved communities. High-tech community that exists primarily "out there," on wires and radio waves or on beams of light, is too morally amorphous to sustain virtuous living. In the information age, we tend to think of local culture as merely tribal and parochial—which sometimes it is. Nevertheless, dwelling places are best suited to be the primary places of generosity, friendship, and other good pursuits. If we sincerely desire to be a grateful and responsible society, we will have to commit ourselves to renewing local community as much as we do to extending our messaging into the distant reaches of cyberspace.

The second section suggests that oral communication, especially conversation, is crucial for nurturing communities of virtue. Such *orality* is the primary means we have for enjoining each other in real-time relationships of trust, respect, and civility. When we can no longer speak meaningfully and listen carefully to one another, we cannot be virtuous people. Much of our cyber-messaging actually thwarts community by deflating the speech that binds us together. Cyberculture nurtures primarily superficial messaging and highly monologic discourses that lack the richness, equality, and spontaneity of conversation. Proximate speech is the primary "technology" that we use to build mutuality, trust, and a shared sense of the common good. Orality especially fosters *memory* and *hope*—two crucial characteristics of virtuous communities.

The third section addresses the importance of public communication in information societies. Information technologies tend to empower us as individual, private "users," not as participants in public associations. We envision the ideal Internet user as a libertine who freely surfs through cyberspace, publishes her or his own ruminations online, and engages in personal email and instant messaging. We do not think of ourselves online as part of a wider public—a coherent, common mind and heart—but rather as private individuals who join interest groups or participate in private commerce.

The conclusion addresses the difference between *communication* and *communion*. Too often we applaud technologies that enable us to exchange information (communication) without attending to those means of sharing that build intimacy and deepen our communion with God and each other. Communion and community are two aspects of the same mystery of living "in common" with others.

Dwelling in Neighborly Places

Writer Hope Lewis delightedly accepted her company's offer to become a telecommuter. Her employer's telecommuting program was designed for part-time employees, and because she was just returning to work from maternity leave, she gladly reduced her weekly hours to be able to spend more time at home with her family. "Telecommuting sounded ideal," Lewis recalled in 1997. In spite of all the technologies that connected her to a supervisor and colleagues, however, she felt cut off from the company while working at home. "I moved from the corporate suburban park, business attire and social environment of colleagues and friends to the isolation of my basement office," she says. Soon Lewis's new manager, who only grudgingly accepted her status as a telecommuter, paid little attention to her. Office politics worsened without Lewis being able to participate. She also found that her isolation at home decreased her motivation to do the work. After three years of telecommuting, she gladly accepted a severance package. "As a telecommuter," she concluded, "I lost my sense of importance as an employee and knew it was time to move on."[7]

Telecommuting works well in some situations, but it is hardly a panacea for employers or employees. Popular rhetoric about information technologies creates the illusion that we can build meaningful relationships purely in cyberspace, apart from any shared geographic location. Some technologists, for instance, advocate classroom-free "distance education" that will supposedly produce fertile communities of learning in cyberspace. One writer in the *New York Times Magazine* glowingly describes a new type of company "where everybody's a temp." Holographic videophones and 3-D fax machines, he says, suggest a "new stage in the dismantling of the traditional company. With each technological leap, we move closer to the reality of a truly virtual conglomerate that has no headquarters, no shipping and warehouse departments, no infrastructure at all—a company that is no more than the sum of its ever changing human parts."[8] Other observers suggest the possible resurgence of local life. Nicholas Negroponte predicts that a growing number of people will soon be free to live and work in the countryside. Most of us will enjoy "safer, saner, cleaner and more private lifestyles" in rural areas. After all, he claims, the digital world has "no center and therefore no periphery."[9] "Geography is dead," pronounces futurist Thornton May. "People will not spend time commuting. . . . By the year 2008, technology will have trivialized the concept of 'place.'"[10] Such prognostications make it sound as though we will all become happy telecommuters working and living in harmony with nature and others.

The scope of cyber-rhetoric about "conquering space," "the end of place," and "renewing community" is staggering. William J. Mitchell imagines cities with "new urban tissues" characterized by "live/work dwellings, twenty-four-hour neighborhoods, loose-knit, far-flung configurations of electronically mediated meeting places, flexible, decentralized production, marketing and distribution systems, and electronically summoned and delivered services."[11] "The world is going to become a smaller and much more efficient place," predicts Dinesh D'Souza.[12] The Information Marketplace, says Dertouzos, "can help us nurture our ethnic heritage, further reducing the need for a traditional, physically local nation."[13] Many advocates of cyber-community situate information technology *above* geographic space, as a kind of heavenly realm transcending the existing cultural variations marked by narrow terrestrial location. Their rhetoric points to a peaceful, worldwide community that is cohesive, intimate, and personal.

Others are not as enthusiastic about the cyber-revitalization of community. Paul Virilio says that new technologies are "de-localizing" us, thereby "unrooting" our lives. Instead of situating ourselves in the "here and now," he argues, we increasingly live in a "situation" of instantaneity, immediacy, and ubiquity.[14] Ivan Illich describes workers who "spend their days next to a telephone in an office and their nights garaged next to their cars."[15] In the information age, we go one step further, tethering people to their offices with cell phones and wireless laptop com-

puters. Carl Mitcham says that we now "live in a world in which the arti-
fice of our environment overwhelms the natural foundation or context
of the past."[16] We spend more and more time in front of technological
screens—such as computer monitors and television sets—and less and
less in face-to-face interaction with others.[17] Manuel Castells argues that
information technologies create "placeless space" and contends that
place is still a crucially important dimension of human culture.[18]

Critics of cyber-community rightly recognize that important cultural
practices and traditional forms of human interaction depend on proximity. Pubs, schools, coffee houses, parish churches, neighborhoods,
and the like are not residuals from lost eras. Who found "ordinary per-
ambulatory activities so burdensome as to be worth the cost to eliminate them?" wonders Theodore Roszak.[19] Humans do not merely *live*
somewhere; we also *dwell* in particular (vernacular) space that "hosts"
our shared concept of the good life. "At the end of the day, Irish people network in the pub, not on the Internet," says an Irish technical
director.[20]

Popular mythology celebrates our ability to conquer space through
information technologies, but it mistakenly imagines the results as a
return to bucolic forms of community. It naively holds two attractive
but contradictory sentiments: the craving to annihilate geographic bar-
riers and the longing to find our beloved community within a real
dwelling place. Consequently, we are pulled in opposite directions—
toward a deeply intimate dwelling, on the one hand, and toward a global
cosmopolitanism, on the other. We pretend to solve this dilemma by
equating globalization with community. Differences and commonali-
ties among people are both part of community life, whether local or
international. We can neither conquer these differences nor return to
old-fashioned communities that likely are little more than the fabrica-
tions of our nostalgic yearnings.

Like expeditioners throughout history, we hope to plant better communities in new parts of the world, including "cyber-place." As David
Gross points out, once the concept of "beginning anew" was accepted
in the seventeenth century, people began imagining life as a means of
starting over in a new place.[21] Today, manufacturing online communities is like creating gold-rush towns that come and go with the promises of the day. Such overnight communities, devoid of the time and
place of tradition, have no moral anchors. We can build up and tear
down online communities at will, depending on the market for membership. "We ceaselessly create communities out of need, desire, and
necessity but then continually try to escape from the authority of what
we have created. We are forever building a city on the hill and then
promptly planning to get out of town to avoid the authority and con-

straint of our creation," writes James W. Carey.[22] Alexis de Tocqueville wonders about the effects of coming and going on the nation's moral character. "Amidst the continual movement that reigns in the heart of a democratic society," he observes, "the bond that unites generations is relaxed or broken; each man easily loses track of the ideas of his ancestors or scarcely worries about them."[23] His description from the 1830s aptly describes today's information age as well.

Geographic proximity is not something for us to conquer as much as it is a necessary, fertile setting for cultivating communities of moral discourse that nurture virtue. Whereas our cross-geographic communication tends to be highly instrumental and self-interested, our intimate, localized relationships are likely to be more stable and virtuous. If we have a choice, each of us would rather receive a hug than an e-card.

The concept of *neighborhood*—the place *in* which and *of* which we are neighbors—perhaps best captures the fundamentally moral character of dwelling together. In America, we often consider our hometown to be a place of parochial vision and ethnocentric ways of life—which it can be. But a home can also be the place of greater personal freedom, where we do not have to meet the expectations of people who do not know us, who do not truly care about us, and who want to interact with us only because they have an instrumental purpose to fulfill—such as selling us something. "Expansion by personal understanding and judgment," writes John Dewey, "can be fulfilled only in the relations of personal intercourse in the local community."[24] This kind of neighborly place of humane dialogue and friendly intelligence is certainly idealistic. Nevertheless, it is more realistically approximated in real dwelling space than in cyberspace. It is a good ideal worth striving for. Neighbors do not have to agree on everything, but they generally do recognize the need to be mutually respectful and to pursue shared interests. To be neighbors is to recognize that we inhabit a shared locale and should pursue the common good as well as personal-private endeavors.

In a very real sense, human freedom is most palpable in the intimate relationships that grow among neighbors, not in the more promiscuous intimacies occurring throughout cyberspace. Eugene H. Peterson says that we "discover the meaning of the free life in acts of compassion and loving service, not in running after people who make big promises to us."[25] In short, we are most fully "empowered"—if we should even use such a well-worn phrase—when we can live virtuously in the knowledge that people are our neighbors, not just our business associates, professionals, politicians, clients, students, and the like.[26] Moral freedom comes from knowing others and recognizing them as neighbors. "The more local and settled the culture," writes Wendell Berry, "the better it stays put, the less the damage. It is the foreigner whose road of excess leads to a desert."[27]

Cyberculture tends to identify us as tourists roving across geographic space rather than as neighborly inhabitants of a particular place. Like earlier innovations in transportation, from the steamship to the loco-motive and airplane, cyber-technology makes it easier for us to move quickly from place to place without knowing the natives. Charles Kuralt once described the interstate highway system as a "wonderful thing" that enables people "to go from coast to coast without seeing anything or meeting anybody."[28] Now cyberspace offers the same kind of non-intimate tourism. If we become too mobile, however, we are likely to deny any obligations we should have toward distinct persons and par-ticular communities. Neighborliness obligates us to know whom we are talking with, whereas cyberspace accepts anonymity, voyeurism, and superficiality. "We have tremendous powers when it comes to innova-tion and commercialization of technologies," says one scholar of the area, "but we are remarkably weak in social ties."[29] This is especially true in Silicon Valley, where one study concludes that "there has been a tremendous decline in all forms of social connection."[30] Ironically, people who live in the most wired place in the world are also among the most socially isolated. Email and online chat technologies surely can help us to stay in contact with distant friends and family, but cyber-tech-nologies tend not to build community as much as they convert neigh-bors into tourists.

A dwelling place is not just for growing plants and erecting buildings but also for fostering neighborliness, where diverse friends share their lives. Neighborliness cannot be mandated by the laws of the land, the formalities of social standing, or the habits of technique. It is a form of voluntary association bound to the seemingly idiosyncratic realities of geography and culture. Instead of trying to build new communities by conquering space, we should be expanding neighborliness within geo-graphic space. Lewis Mumford reminds us, "To create organs for neigh-borly help and initiative, to meet face to face for personal assessment and vivid discussion, to take part in communal celebrations, not in vast anonymous masses, but in a circle of identifiable faces and persons, all these survivals of aboriginal village life are still necessary."[31] Informa-tion technologies can supplement this type of neighborliness, but they cannot substitute for it.

Locale is also the setting for *hospitality,* one of the most important neighborly traditions across many cultures. Acts of hospitality reflect some classical virtues, including the *courage* to open one's home to peo-ple who are different from us, the *love* that leads us to share what we have with others, and the *wisdom* to respect another's wishes and preferences.[32] Many different sentiments can lead us to be hospitable, but chief among them is our desire to treat others as we would like to be treated. Hospitality turns our own resources over to the service of someone else; it invites others to become our neighbors regardless of where they dwell. Hospitality thereby transforms homelessness into neighborliness. There is no "virtual" equivalent of hospitality, since it occurs in a place. Illich says that hospitality requires a "threshold" over which one can invite another. Communication technologies, he argues, tend to abolish the walls, doors, and tables that we need to practice hospitality. He says that we need to recover "a practice of hospitality . . . threshold, table, patience, listening." Such hospitality provides the "seedbeds for virtue and friendship" and hence the place for the rebirth of community.[33]

Whereas geographic proximity requires different groups to work together, cyberspace tends to bring together people who share one or more special interests. As Robert D. Putnam puts it in *Bowling Alone,* "Social networks based on computer-mediated communication can be organized by shared interests rather than shared space." He adds, "Real-world interactions often force us to deal with diversity, whereas the virtual world may be more homogeneous, not in demographic terms, but in terms of interest and outlook."[34] We can talk about cyberspace as a global village, as if it unifies the world into a community, but our actual uses of cyber-technology suggest that we select our online affiliations to maximize our own narrow interests, not to reach out beyond those interests. In the biblical account of the Good Samaritan, the Samaritan traveler faces a real dilemma—whether to help a Jew (Luke 10:25–37). The Jew is, after all, his "neighbor," in spite of their cultural differences. Forming communities around only our own interests is a way of avoiding the wider practice of neighborliness.

Historically speaking, the social institutions vested with the authority to nurture the habits of the heart were organized locally as places of neighborliness and hospitality. These included especially domiciles, schools, and houses of worship. Moreover, the voluntary associations that emerged in urban America, from the YMCA to halfway houses and Habitat for Humanity, directed compassion locally. Responsible international corporations take seriously their role as stewards of local communities, encouraging employees to be active citizens as well as productive workers. In the information age, we need to nurture local, nontechnological participation in public life, not just mediated involvement in distant endeavors. Carey writes, "The technology of the foot, the horse, and the megaphone offered as many and probably more genuine opportunities for democratic participation than are afforded by advanced computer systems despite the illusions of empowerment contained in the keyboards, plasma screens, and the imagined town meetings of 'interactive systems.'"[35] Clifford Stoll reminds us that an "obsession with computing tilts community activity. . . . There's no reason to improve the library, start a health clinic, or open a community college. Just bring in the Internet."[36]

Telecommuting and other modes of distance communication certainly have their places in modern social life. Nevertheless, living in proximate community is still the primary social means of cultivating virtue; families, schools, and churches, for instance, depend on such community. Dwelling in community creates a "surplus of love" called neighborliness.[37] We can then carry this surplus into the other institutions in which we are involved, including governments and businesses. Any technologies that weaken the primary nurturing institutions or dampen our ability to transfer the habits of the heart to the larger and more distant institutions are not truly community-building technologies. Stephen Doheny-Farina rightly argues that "we do not need electronic neighborhoods; we need geophysical neighborhoods, in all their integrity."[38] Robert K. Greenleaf suggests that "human service that requires love cannot be satisfactorily dispensed by specialized institutions that exist apart from community, that take the problem out of sight of the community."[39] Mediated relationships are not likely to be as virtue-nurturing as direct ones. As David F. Ford puts it, "One lesson is that wisdom is best learned face to face by apprenticeship to those who have themselves learned it the same way. Perhaps the ultimate privilege is to have wise parents, teachers, and friends—a wise community of the heart."[40]

Technologies that weaken subsidiary moral bonds also deflate community life. Some Web surfers like to think of themselves as "disembodied cybernauts" who freely traverse the world online.[41] But only the computer companies and Internet service providers really gain from such rhetoric.[42] Geographic proximity does more than any information technology to encourage us to know our neighbors and to be hospitable people. Locale is a gift that opens up the potential for meaningful relationships of mutuality and trust. "Local freedoms," writes Tocqueville, "which make many citizens put value on the affection of their neighbors and those close to them, therefore constantly bring men closer to one another, despite the instincts that separate them, and force them to aid each other."[43] So we need to watch our language, particularly our overly sanguine use of a term such as "cyber-community." Too often such fashionable lingo "disassociates the word from its multiple yet bound associations with the fellowship, not of abstract entities, but of fleshly ones."[44]

Conversing on Common Ground

A writer in *smartbusinessmag.com* describes a remarkable presentation at a technology trade show in Las Vegas. The presenter is Mark Lucente—"part David Copperfield, part high-tech soothsayer"—who dazzles the crowd with a demonstration of new technology that promises "natural interfaces to computer data." "Give me the world," Lucente calls out in godlike fashion to a wall-size screen projected in front of him. He spreads his arms in the shape of a circle and a large, spinning globe appears on the screen. "Make it this big," Lucente commands as he reduces the size of the ring formed with his arms and hands. The rotating globe responds by narrowing its circumference. The crowd gasps.[45] Lucente's technological innovations, the writer suggests, will one day help us make computers that are truly responsive to the complex movements of the human body. "Someday, indeed, the breakthroughs Lucente has pioneered might help seismologists model oil fields without touching a keyboard or online shoppers inspect merchandise that isn't really there."[46]

Since when is being somewhere merely a *problem?* If Lucente had not been *there*—in the room with his audience—his presentation would have fallen flat. Moreover, his capacity for live speech—his ability to "speak" a version of digital reality into existence with voice and body—was very likely more compelling than anything he could have done remotely. Lucente's physical showmanship required him to be there with others. The man who is solving the "problem of being there" is, himself, being there.[47] He is not a cyborg. Instead, he is a human person using the currency of presence and the power of speech to impress a live, in-the-flesh audience. "If Internet communications and interactive video systems are so effective, why do computer enthusiasts flock like lemmings to computer conventions?" asks Clifford Stoll.[48] Because we prefer to commune in person.

We are creatures of the spoken word, our native medium, and no humanly devised communication technology can improve on it. We can devise fast digital messaging systems such as email, but they invariably reduce the richness, conviviality, and even accuracy of oral dialogue. In one survey, 51 percent of office workers indicated that recipients of their email often misperceive the tone of their messages.[49] Even the cell phone, arguably the most natural and mobile means of audio communication apart from proximate speech, fails to deliver the visual cues that can be so important in interpreting what others mean to say. Cicely Berry warns that "computer technology threatens to dehumanize communication."[50] Oral communication takes patience, not efficiency. Speech-based community naturally gives our lives the kind of temporal coherence we need to cultivate virtue. This is why Clifford G. Christians correctly argues that technologies are legitimate only if they have some capacity to maintain cultural continuity.[51] Speech communities require duration as well as location, because only in and through time can they maintain their own integrity from generation to generation.

The contemporary hoopla about cyber-communication generally ignores the fundamentally oral nature of our createdness. We are created principally as speech agents, as conversationalists, not as keyboarders, uploaders, and downloaders. No matter how many new types and technologies of communication we fabricate, the most powerful and character-shaping forms of human discourse are always tied to our native *orality*—to our speaking and listening "in person" with each other. Derivative forms of human communication—such as writing, printing, and electronic messaging—are extensions of our basic ability to use language to interact orally with other people. Oral communication is the most natural form of human interaction; perhaps conversation is the basic template for all human interaction.[52] A facility for keyboarding or Web surfing cannot reasonably substitute for the abilities to speak carefully, listen wisely, and dialogue congenially.

Walter J. Ong explains how the spoken word carries more power than the written word to facilitate communication.[53] Sound, he argues, unites human beings more than any other medium. The "presence" of sound captures our ongoing activities, our sense of who we are, where we are, and what we are currently thinking, feeling, hoping, and fearing. When we speak, we invite another person to exist with us, to associate with us, to reciprocate in affirming mutual presence in real time. As we converse, we are able to commune with each other's inwardness, encountering the thoughts and sentiments we might otherwise merely carry around in our own minds or never even contemplate.[54] The spoken word, writes Ong, "is curiously reciprocating not only intentionally, in what it is meant to do (establish relationships with another), but also in the very medium in which it exists. Sound binds our interiors."[55] Speech is primary communication for human beings; it is our chief means of communion with one another. We incarnate ourselves and our communities over and over again through the presence of the spoken word.

Speech is certainly not a perfect form of communication, but all other means of communication display more severe limitations. Relationally speaking, there is no greater bandwidth than that available through open conversation. "Encounters with others in which no words are ever exchanged are hardly encounters at all," says Ong. "The written word alone will not do, for it is not sufficiently living and refreshing."[56] The more technological our communication becomes, the more it is like transferring information rather than participating in community. Digital forms of communication can supplement other modes, but if they erode our capacity for speech, they also weaken community life and diminish the corresponding habits of the heart. "Distance learning," writes Stoll, "offers all the information, all the facts, all the boredom of an ordinary classroom, with none of the inspiration, none of the commitment, and none of the joy. It's ideal for the student who equates information with education. Perfect for the school that wants to hustle students through with minimal human interaction."[57]

From a moral perspective, we should question any technological endeavor that reduces human interaction to impersonal technique. We are created not as monologic beings but as dialogic creatures whose communication is meant to be intimate and responsible.[58] Much of our moral bearing in life comes from our everyday rituals of conversation, through which we mutually attempt to build trust through dialogue. The discipline of listening to one another, of truly trying to empathize and sympathize, is part of what makes us human. Civility in public life depends on such intrinsically moral practices. So-called advanced forms of communication—from digitally delivered television programs to DVDs and online audio streaming—are not better for building communities of moral discourse. Five-hundred-channel digital television systems are great for delivering specialized programming to audiences and for segmenting audiences for advertisers, but they will never promote the forms of discourse that nurture virtuous character and build moral communities. Efficient messaging systems do not usually engender communal trust, respect, and mutuality. All other modes of human technological communication must be measured against the remarkable capacity of speech to foster communities of moral discourse. Although the power inherent in speech can be horribly misused, the sheer capacity for human expression and comprehension through orality is nevertheless one of the greatest gifts for building community and spreading virtue.

Learning to be virtuous speech agents, then, is crucial for building virtuous community—much more important than technological proficiency. A supervisor who fires an employee via email is not being merely expedient; he or she has abrogated the moral responsibilities that come with the gift of orality.[59] When companies route customers through layers of recorded telephone messages without giving them an opportunity to talk with a live person, they are denying the obligation toward mutuality and respect that we have inherited with orality. The examples of such irresponsible communication abound in the information age. A computer programmer's "idea of heaven," says Ellen Ullman, is not having to speak directly with others.[60] Partly because of the technologizing of our daily communication, we are losing the moral dimensions of speech and slipping into inhumane forms of monologic communication.

Human speech is the primary means for incarnating human community—for bringing it into existence in particular social bonds.[61] All other forms and modes of human communication, from motion pictures to printing, depend on this capacity for "wording" the world. We even gain our understanding of the meaning of images from our discourse about them. Humans have expanded wording into nonauditory modes of discourse, from printing to sign language. In the case of sign language among deaf people, the visual "words" and syntax are enormously complex, filled with subtleties of discourse that oral communicators can barely begin to grasp. Denied direct access to the power of spoken words, humans nevertheless have the linguistic ability to "word" their experiences collectively with others, to establish speech-like communities of moral discourse that similarly build trust, mutuality, and respect. Where speech is not possible, for whatever reason, we should fully embrace the alternative ways that people word their everyday worlds. Deaf people, for instance, have benefited significantly from Internet technologies that foster textual communication within their communities, but they also rely on the reading of lips and related bodily modes of expression. Non-oral communities invariably develop low-tech, embodied forms of interaction that imitate orality. Moreover, we can all learn from them how to develop non-oral capacities for communion with others.

Two aspects of orality in a high-tech world merit special attention—*hope* and *memory*.[62] Technologically mediated expressions of hope are nearly always abstractly instrumental; they direct our attention away from our own communities and focus it on some distant state of affairs. Such instrumental expressions of hope thereby tend toward a form of propaganda predicated on using technique to gain audiences' attention and to enjoin them to desire something—such as becoming more attractive or believing in an ideology. Advertising and movies are filled with such propagandistic expressions of hope—hope for cosmetic beauty, happy endings, and cleaner wash. Moral hope, on the other hand, comes not through rhetorical manipulation but through authentic dialogue nurtured in communities over time. It flows from the life of the community as members commune orally. Ong calls this kind of hope "arrested dialogue," an expression of mutuality and shared desire. "Hope," writes Ong, "is the difference between information encoded in machines and real knowledge in the consciousness of man."[63] Words enable us to share hope, like an invitation to riposte, to life with others.

Dialogue, in particular, can be the back and forth of emerging hope as participants build trust and mutuality even among their differences. Monologue, on the other hand, offers no opportunity to build shared hope, only a chance for the ego to express itself. One-way transmissions can signal the end of relationship, and hence of community.

Orality also engenders communal memory, which is crucial for maintaining communities of virtue through time. We do not recollect primarily by recording events in printed form and later rereading the historical documents. Nor do we recall well by putting information in electronic databases for subsequent access via computer. Human memory is above all the art of telling and retelling each other our shared stories about the past, present, and future. We "store" our narrative recollections in human memory primarily through the practices of speaking and hearing stories from past generations. We can use printed materials, professional storytellers, and databases to help us remember, but memory takes hold of our imaginations only as we ourselves repeatedly speak it into existence. This is why the Christian community emphasizes the preaching of the gospel as well as reading it and expressing it in visual practices such as liturgical dance and church architecture. Speech carries a kind of sacramental potential that enables us to re-invoke special meaning and significance into our understandings of our lives in relationship to others. Berry reminds us that "when a community loses its memory, its members no longer know one another. How can they know one another if they have forgotten or have never learned one another's stories? If they do not know one another's stories, how can they know whether or not to trust one another?"[64] Speaking and hearing our stories are the primary ways of reminding ourselves who we are, especially why and how we should be both grateful and responsible.

Oddly enough, in our world of abundant messaging, we are losing both our memories and our communities. As information technology mediates the world for us, we have less direct association with others, and we consequently lose our own sense of interdependence. We find that associating with others increasingly becomes a time-consuming matter of the will rather than a natural result of custom. Consequently, we have to make more of an effort to associate with others. For many people, especially the shy or socially awkward, cyberspace requires less effort to meet others, although the resulting relationships are less likely to become genuinely deep and lasting. Our speech in the cyber-era is not as spontaneous, lively, and sustained as it should be, perhaps because we rely too much on technological crutches, such as sending someone an email message or leaving them a telephone message rather than speaking to them in person. John L. Locke says that we are witnessing the "de-voicing of society."[65] Machines give us the power to "flit around the universe," but they also can cause our communities to "grow more fragile, airy, and ephemeral even as our connections multiply."[66] In order to live morally coherent lives, we need what Edward M. Hallowell calls the "sense of purpose and meaning in support" that can emerge only from long-term affiliations with others.[67] That meaning and purpose must be cultivated continually through speaking our memories to each other.

The Getty Center's Information Institute once convened a symposium on preserving digital information and published the proceedings in a book titled *Time and Bits: Managing Digital Continuity.*[68] By the time the book came out, however, the Institute was defunct, many of the Web sites mentioned in the proceedings no longer existed, and an online forum initiated by the conference was gone. The community of people formed around this shared study of digital memory was now only a distant recollection. High-tech modes of remembering make us dangerously dependent on machines that will one day obliviate digitally recorded memories.

An organic community, living in both location and duration, should depend more on speech than on any messaging technology to nurture lasting habits of the heart. All forms of communication can help us build community life, but our wording is the most crucial of all. When our informational pursuits lead us to squander the gift of orality, they threaten the communities of moral discourse we need to live in good communion with each other. Among other things, through speech we carry on our virtuous traditions from generation to generation, thereby challenging monopolies of instrumental communication, including commercial and political propaganda. "The great challenge of the present era," says Václav Havel, "is to seek out forms of democracy that suit the present times while they revive the very face-to-face contact that marked the birth of democracy."[69] We could make the same claims for all social institutions, from business to education. No fancy technologies that promise to relieve us of the burden of being somewhere are adequate substitutes for conversation, let alone for communities of hospitality and neighborliness. Being in real time and place speaks volumes, as Lucente demonstrated in his own presentation.

Communing in Public Life

In his book *The Control Revolution,* Andrew L. Shapiro addresses the ways in which digital technologies shift power in society from large organizations to individuals. "This is one of the true marvels of interactive technology," he writes, "the instant ability to spread your unexpurgated words—a piece of yourself, really—to the four corners of the Earth. Even in the rush of millennial tidings, the singularity of this achievement cannot be overlooked. It is a privilege that would stir envy in the hearts of history's most powerful rulers and statesmen, not to mention fear." He envisions a "vast transformation in who governs information, experience, and resources." Shapiro sees long-standing social hierarchies "coming undone," traditional gatekeepers "being bypassed," and power "devolving down to 'end users.'" The upshot of the new information technologies, he concludes, is the "ability to put individuals in charge."[70]

Shapiro's vision of individuals spreading bits of themselves around the world is somewhat overblown, but it nevertheless captures the prevailing individualism in cyberculture. For all the rhetoric about cybercommunity, the Internet is less a forum for shared public life than an arena for individuals to express their egos and find information in tune with their personal needs and desires. In addition, most so-called cybercommunities are organized around specialized interests, not public life. They are instrumental, not traditional or even organic communities. Cyberspace generally fosters *libertinism* and *pseudo-communal consumerism* over real community.

As David Gross suggests, the growing influence of one-way messaging in society is "drying up" the "public sphere founded on dialogue and discourse."[71] The Internet is not as one-way as radio, television, and the press, but neither is it as dialogic as speech. Live "chat" (really "texting"), email, and message-posting technologies enable a low degree of dialogue, but they are not as discourse-friendly as actual conversation. Online interactions are more disjointed, stilted, and mechanical than in-person discussions. Although we can easily compose and then post or transmit messages in cyberspace, we cannot dialogue very well online. The richest online dialogue might eventually result from some type of audio-video technology similar to existing video-telephone equipment. But even this type of technology would not be nearly as helpful for building community life as it would be for instrumental purposes, such as conducting a business meeting or providing customer service. Putnam argues that computer-based communication lacks the "social cues and social communications" that facilitate consensus-forming and solidarity; it "depersonalizes" human communication and therefore also makes misunderstanding and misrepresentation more likely.[72]

We fool ourselves into believing that information technologies will patch together our disintegrating social fabric. The opposite is actually the case: These technologies tend to divert our attention away from real community life, including the kind of public life we need for democratic participation in our political futures. Today, many local communities, struggling to restore their own disintegrating social institutions, are no longer able to pick up the moral slack caused partly by the commodification and technologizing of culture. We misguidedly respond to these communal deficiencies by trying to equip people to become "end users," or consumers of messaging technologies. Cyberspace gives these users smorgasbords of special-interest groups to join and greater consumer options. Instead of renewing community, these ever expanding cybernetic systems tend to band people together in like-minded or similarly interested groups. They equip us with new means of pursuing our own interests more than they nurture communities of diverse people who nevertheless seek shared lives and common ends.

C. A. Bowers wonders whether computers, in particular, introduce individualistic ways of knowing that are inherently incompatible with more communal ways of knowing. Bowers believes that the cultural forms that guide information processing—the interpretive sentiments, ideas, and metaphors we adopt along with computerization—validate instrumental and individualistic ways of knowing while marginalizing alternatives. Informational forms of thought "amplify the Western view of the individual as autonomous in matters of rational judgment and moral decision making"; "reinforce the Western way of experiencing time, which involves a linear sense of movement into the future and away from the past"; and "amplify the cultural orientation that represents moral values as subjectively determined," while marginalizing "the way other cultures pass on their moral norms through narrative and ceremony."[73] If Bowers is correct, information technologies, as presently constituted, retard our ability to make noninstrumental, nonindividualistic sense of the world. They are not liberating us for community as much as ensnaring us in informational ways of knowing and non-dialogic means of messaging.

Informational technologies carry instrumental biases in favor of individualism and against shared moral understanding. We imagine that the Internet is a fantastic technology because it gives the individual more choices of information and enables him or her to send and receive messages with other individuals more quickly. If the individual's interests are more important than shared interests, digital messaging seems like a dream come true. *I* have more choices. *I* have more processing power at my disposal. *I* can tell the world how *I* feel about anything in the universe. Contrasted with earlier mass media, such as television and magazines, the Internet apparently gives *me* much more of a voice in society.

As individuals, however, what can we really accomplish with these efficient messaging instruments? Will we listen more attentively to each other? Will we have a better or deeper sense of our obligations to others? Are we more likely to be charitable, friendly, civil, and just? Is it possible that we will have a clearer vision of the need for shalom in the world? Where in this individualistic cyber-world is the moral fabric, the less selfish "us"? Implicit within our understanding of cyberspace is the metaphor of the libertine Web surfer, a selfish bandit grabbing all the digital gusto he or she can. It should not surprise us, then, that the Internet has probably generated more antisocial communication than any earlier media. Make no mistake about it, the Internet fosters individualistic anarchy, and this is precisely the personal "right" that so many cyber-gurus ultimately are defending—the freedom to be able to say whatever one desires before a worldwide audience, and sometimes even to say so anonymously. Cyberspace empowers us to become more efficient libertines, scurrying along the digital trails in search of anything that we desire, dropping our two cents worth like mouse pellets along the way. Even though we recognize that we are increasingly dependent on others, especially experts, to make our way through contemporary life, we have little sense of "belonging to a large whole."[74] For many people, the real lure of cyberspace is personal expression, not mutuality.

This is why online communities are far more individualistic than communal. They tend to be collections of people who want to be able to express themselves, not those who want to listen to others or work toward shared understandings. Even when their members enjoy the same special interest—such as a professional activity, avocational pursuit, or technical expertise—they generally do not try through dialogue to become more than the sum of their preexisting selves. This kind of online individualism bypasses such crucial virtues as empathy, reciprocity, and humility. The individualism of cyberspace is symbolized in the person sitting alone before a computer, deciding what sites to visit and how to interpret the incoming messages. In this myopic social model, he or she needs nothing but network connections, because the individual is supposedly sufficient for moral awareness and virtuous character.

Because online groups usually lack shared mores, however, they often become outposts of uncivil rhetoric. Cyberspace is riddled with a libertinism that, in the name of free expression, masquerades as democratic discourse. One of the earliest and best-informed chroniclers of the Internet, Ed Krol, laments the decline in online civility and community. The most significant online transformation, he says, is the shift from "being a collaborative interpersonal tool to an information service." In his view, databases, junk email, and corporate messaging now define the Web. "The sense of community and decorum" has disappeared, he laments. "I had always hoped that people would be refreshed that the online community was so much more stable than the real world and it would continue." Instead, he says, people buy a modem and "feel they have the right to be uncivil. I guess I like a cybervillage and what we have now is a cybercity, with all the problems of the city."[75] Krol's sobering comments capture the unfulfilled dreams of online community as well as the libertinism that plagues cyberspace.

If online community is all about creating digital soapboxes, we are in deep moral trouble. Francis Fukuyama points out that we should have learned as a society by now that there "are serious problems with a culture of unbridled individualism, in which the breaking of rules becomes, in a sense, the only remaining rule." He adds that we must accept the fact that "moral values and social rules are not simply arbitrary constraints on individual choice but the precondition for any kind of cooperative enterprise."[76] The online world is not reinstating such values and rules as much as further eroding them. Cyberspace simply fails to advance our capacity for dialogue, cooperation, and consensus. On the contrary, it appeals to the individual ego.

We are reaching a point at which commercial organizations are engineering online "community" in order to further their private interests. "Usually the driving reason for a business to start an online community is that they want to generate repeat business on their Web sites," says Amy Jo Kim in her paper entitled "Ritual Reality: Social Engineering in Cyberspace." She says such manufactured community is a means of getting people who use the same consumer products to help each other online so that the company does not have to spend so much on customer support.[77] One toy company boasts these features of its online community: "a toy registry, a selection of gift wrap, a list of 'hot' toys, customer product reviews, optional new product notifications, a birthday club, and a selection called 'the community' that provide[s] articles on parenting and offers a chat room for parents and teachers."[78] This kind of "community" might be good for commerce, but it is hardly the kind of community that will nurture virtue. High-tech CEO Jeff Shuman speaks of the need to "monetize" an online community by tying it to a business model.[79] As most of the earlier, more indigenous experiments with online communities have dissolved, these types of commercial enclaves have become the norm. Goals such as retaining customer loyalty or building site traffic for advertisers have eclipsed purposes such as pursuing mutually good ends and engendering civil discourse. Many online communities today are merely privately controlled and organized around consumer lifestyles for largely pecuniary purposes.

In spite of all our rhetoric about cyber-community, cyberspace usually substitutes consumption for conversation. "E-community" is increasingly a vehicle for e-commerce. Now we can buy online what we want, when we want it, without waiting for local stores to receive it. We do not have to be satisfied with inadequate inventories or poor product selections at local shops. We do not have to pay hefty prices to support local businesses. We do not even have to talk to anyone at any store, let alone actually know a merchant, pharmacist, grocer, or bookstore proprietor. All we need is a computer and a credit card. In *The One-to-One Future: Building Relationships One Customer at a Time,* Don Peppers and Martha Rogers tell us that massive corporations can operate online as if they were local shops. The new technologies, they say, enable "even the mass marketer . . . to assume the role of small proprietor, doing business again with individuals, one at a time."[80] Who are they kidding? Online companies' employees are not friends with customers. Cyber-transactions and database processes are hardly social "relationships." E-commerce furthers the kinds of depersonalized business transactions championed by chain stores and fast-food restaurants, not the types of relationships that local merchants have with customers who are also their neighbors.[81]

Instead of renewing our disintegrating communities and softening our libertine messaging, much of cyberspace provides some of the most efficient forms of consumerism and marketing imaginable. Information technologies produce ever more impersonal but efficient markets that give businesses and technicians more power over traditional culture. Bill Gates, imagining the prospects for the media with broadband technology, says that "the market mechanism for culture" will "work much more efficiently than it does now. The match between buyers and sellers—what you want to read, what you want to learn, whom you want to spend time with—will be far more precise and customized."[82] Thanks to digital personalization, we supposedly will all get to consume what we want, when we want it. But this "personal" form of communication actually depersonalizes interaction and substitutes database access for dialogue, since no one needs to know anyone else in the entire marketing and messaging system.

Regardless of the rhetoric about cyberspace democratizing human communication, cyber-technologies lend themselves to the goals of discrimination and injustice. In a cover story titled "Why Service Stinks," *Business Week* cited companies' use of databases to distinguish between customers who deserve good service and those who do not. Information technology enables companies to "push their customers—especially low-margin ones—toward self service." Often "self service" means automated phone systems instead of live operators and Internet-based purchasing instead of storefront help. Automated voice-messaging phone systems become digital processing systems that enable organizations to rid themselves of unwanted communication. In other words, information technologies make it possible for organizations to discriminate more effectively against costly customers who want to return a product, get it repaired, or seek assistance using it.[83] This type of one-to-one "community" is really only a highly discriminatory form of machine marketing.[84]

Long before the Web emerged as a commercial medium, unchecked individualism was already becoming the center of American culture. In the age of cyberspace, people tend to refer ever more to themselves—to their own personal views, likes, and interests.[85] Cyberculture, for all its rhetoric about community, has become one of the frontiers of such private individualism. Internet companies do not sell only access to the Internet; they peddle the means for each individual to extend his or her ego across geographic space, without any concomitant obligations. The Internet is a marketplace for the self, not a community for virtue. Information technologies, in particular, replace cultural knowing with informational consumption, thereby encouraging the growth of impersonal messaging markets over shared ways of moral knowing. Jeremy Rifkin says that in a "cyberspace economy," the "commodification of goods and services becomes secondary to the commodification of human relationships."[86] We need to remind ourselves that the "free market is a good servant but a bad master." Without moral grounding, Lesslie Newbigin warns, what "is experienced as freedom by a minority is experienced as bondage by a majority."[87] The information revolution extends modern rationalization and commercialization to cyberspace, all the while tickling our egos and encouraging us to join consumption communities.

As human beings, we are not designed for libertinism and commercialism as much as for responsibility in community. But such community cannot survive the ravages of libertinism and consumerism without shared habits of the heart. "Only by the voluntary nurturing in ourselves of freely accepted and serene self-restraint can mankind rise above the world stream of materialism," says Aleksandr I. Solzhenitsyn.[88] Cyberspace cannot sustain the kind of public domain necessary as a precondition for maintaining a republic. As people select their online information, says Cass Sunstein, they limit their own access to a diverse range of speakers as well as to "particular institutions, and practices, against which they seek to launch objections."[89] Cyberculture tends to reject the possibility of the very thing that it most needs to foster community: an overarching moral vision predicated on personal responsibilities, framed by shared obligations, and forged through civil dialogue. No compilation of online interest groups or socially engineered consumption communities is a substitute for such community. In fact, moral vision grows out of a community that accepts responsibility for a place and time, not out of lone tourists traveling through cyberspace in hopes of getting the best deal on the latest product or advocating their two cents worth. Instant messaging and online plebiscites without an ennobling moral vision are poor substitutes for real communities of moral discourse.

Conclusion

Eugene H. Peterson says that words can be grouped into two categories: those used for *communication* and those used for *communion*. The latter group would include words that help us tell stories, nurture intimacies, and build trust. These terms "do not define as much as deepen mystery—entering into the ambiguities, pushing past the safely known into the risky unknown."[90] The language of communication, on the other hand, is best used for instrumental purposes, such as buying and selling stocks, directing traffic, and teaching mathematics. Each category of words has its own rightful place in human affairs. Every profession needs to make sure that it uses the right kind of language in a given situation. For example, if pastors "approach people as masters of communication," says Peterson, "they will be as out of place as a whore at a wedding. We are not here to sell intimacy. We are here to be intimate."[91]

Most of the rhetoric about cyber-community wrongly assumes that we can deeply commune with one another using only the instrumental techniques of communication. As argued throughout this chapter, the most virtue-cultivating forms of human communion ultimately occur *across* generational time and *within* geographic space. Any community that adopts information technologies must face the historical fact that *duration* and *location* are two of the nutrients in the type of soil that grows morally verdant culture. The gift of speech enables us to commune together in real communities of moral discourse that equip us with responsible practices such as hospitality and neighborliness. If we lose these kinds of shared, morally infused practices, we will destroy community as well as virtue. Berry suggests that if any community hopes to last long, it must "exert a sort of centripetal force, holding local soil and local memory in place. Practically speaking, human society has no work more important than this."[92] Archbishop Charles J. Chaput rightly argues that "hostility for the organic" in high-tech culture should trouble us. Enchanted by technology, we come to feel as though the "body isn't good enough. Nature isn't good enough. And pretty soon the human person won't be good enough."[93] If we hold up messaging machines as our standard, surely our communion with one another will atrophy.

Living in community requires far more than mastering cyber-technologies. If we live too fully in accelerating cyberspace, we become high-tech nomads, lost in non-intimate existence, deprived of the potential virtues cultivated primarily within proximate community. As experts debate the impact of information technologies on social life, they frequently focus too narrowly on whether individuals feel lonely or alienated rather than on the larger issues of whether people are engaged in life-giving communities of moral discourse.[94] In the age of information, we find it increasingly difficult to attend to what is important in life, including our speech communities, where memory and hope are crucial for everyone's well-being. We fill up our personal lives with incessant messaging and profuse information, creating the illusion that our work and play are significant. We even fold our communal life into private activities, such as consuming endless information that is produced and marketed by experts. As a result of our harried lives, we lack what Gabriel Marcel calls *disponibilité*, a facility for making ourselves available to others.[95] We forget that community is, among other things, the arena in which we give ourselves to one another, simply because it is the right thing for neighbors and friends to do.

Dialogue is an act of making ourselves available for community. "In the multitudinous contacts of social life," writes Paul Tournier, "how often do we . . . commit our inmost selves in . . . dialogue?" We can "chat endlessly, engage in abstruse intellectual arguments, read whole libraries . . . , travel the world over [even online!], be a dilettante collector of all sorts of impressions, react like an automaton to every caprice of sentiment, without ever really encountering another person or discovering oneself by taking up a position with regard to him."[96] Real community, says Jean Bethke Elshtain, "implicates us in a world of others who bind us to them as well as to time and space."[97] Time-honoring customs of the spoken word strongly resist frenetic and impersonal messaging. To be morally wise in the information age, we still have to practice sufficient modes of communion. All of the most virtue-producing human activities, from parenting to teaching, mentoring to praying, are anchored in such oral customs. Nurtured in virtuous community, speech can better avoid the abstractions of the market and the superficialities of busyness and embrace people as beings of inherent value who reside in real time and space.

When he toured the United States in the 1830s, Alexis de Tocqueville recognized that the most conducive forms of moral virtue emanated from the country's local communities of faith. Without such religious influence on Americans' habits of the heart, individualism could destroy the moral fabric of democracy. To the extent that information technologies promote purely instrumental, individualistic, and commercial forms of messaging, cyberspace is not an ally to virtuous community.

To the degree that we can revive organic forms of community marked by neighborliness, we can protect cyberspace from the ravages of heartless egos run amok. Of all institutions, religious fellowships have been among the most important for maintaining such organic forms of association as avenues for moral discourse.

chapter eight

Sojourning with Heart

■ A cartoon in the *New Yorker* depicts four men sitting in a circle, neck-deep in the sulfuric waters of hell. The devil, pitchfork in hand, watches from a nearby hilltop. One of the men says to the others, "It's an amazing coincidence, isn't it, that we all served on the same board of directors?"[1] Like those directors, we sometimes lose our moral bearings. In retrospect, even our successes often seem inflated. Taking a break from our busyness gives us an opportunity to reflect on the moral fabric of our lives.

This book has illuminated some of the implications of our growing dependence on information technology. Today, we are so enamored with cyber-innovation that we often fail to perceive the deeper moral issues at stake. Informationism, in particular, clouds our moral vision. We face a "techno-moral crisis"—a crisis not just of ethical values but also of concrete responsibilities. Too often our informational exploits lack any overarching vision of goodness and rightness. We celebrate our ability to transmit messages quickly across geographic space while ignoring their impact on the quality of our personal lives as well as our social institutions. Unless we employ information technology more responsibly, we will become cyber-savvy people who have little heart for virtue.

The cyber-frontier is one place where our passions and consciences are fighting each other for control. From a purely secular-rational view, the story of information technologies demonstrates the human ability to invent powerful means of collecting, storing, and disseminating vast quantities of information. From the view of revealed religion, however, the tale is mixed. In addition to the practical benefits of information technology, the accompanying informationism breeds arrogance, impatience, and foolishness instead of nurturing the habits of the heart.[2] In short, our cyber-progress fosters moral chaos.

This concluding chapter suggests six callings that will help us to live virtuously in the information society. They have long served people who value the habits of the heart. Each one is suggestive rather than definitive, since I, too, am lost in the digital miasma. After we first *admit the lightness of our digital being*, we should *distrust the prevailing techno-magic* that promises us unrealistic benefits from cyber-technologies. We should also *de-technologize our religious traditions* by ridding them of excessive technique and renewing their virtue-nurturing practices. Thankfully accepting our inheritance of the created world, we should *responsibly serve God and neighbor. Inviting friendship* is one of the most fitting means of cultivating moral relationships. Finally, we should *sojourn with heart* through life.

Admitting the Lightness of Our Digital Being

Psychiatrist Robert Coles recalls conversations he had during the 1970s with Dorothy Day, the leader of the Catholic Worker Movement. As they discussed "secular life," Day recalled how busyness affected her worldview. "I get so busy doing the things I want to do, love doing, that I forget to ask myself the why of it all; and I forget to ask myself what *might* be, what *ought* be, because I'm in the midst of doing, doing." She later thanked God for "giving us a mind that can turn to Him, to ask 'why' and 'wherefore' as well as spend itself to exhaustion getting things done."[3]

The age of information is indeed an era of doing, doing. It is not so much a time of reflection as a period of incessant movement. Paul Virilio describes our condition as an "instant transmission sickness" that turns our memories into "junkshops—great dumps of images of all kinds and origins, used and shop-soiled symbols, piled up any old how."[4] We surf on one new digital wave of experiences after another, quickly discarding each one in favor of the next. Cyberculture seduces us into this constant motion, keeping us occupied with the emerging present. If faster messaging truly saves us time, however, we hardly feel the discretionary benefits. Information technology seems to give us greater time only for more technology and more information. The resulting busyness, stress, and incoherence render our lives unimportant and superficial. Our lives begin reflecting the tenor of cyber-industry, where "what you are doing now will be meaningless tomorrow."[5]

Seduced by high-tech optimism, we imagine significant payoffs down the information pike—perhaps higher income, elevated social status, greater happiness, or more impressive mastery of technique. But all the while we are losing some of the deeper meaning that we cannot derive merely from information technology. Our narrow focus on improving our instrumental skills weakens our moral and spiritual practices. The more fully we embrace information technologies as routes to joy and happiness, the more vacuous our lives become.

We are being stripped not only of venerable habits and customs but also of perspectives and people for moral reference. Sven Birkerts says, "We see no real leaders, no larger figures of wisdom. Not a brave new world at all, but a fearful one."[6] Seduced by the rhetoric of the digital sublime, we lose the nontechnical reference points we need to identify ourselves as responsible caretakers of the creation. Our cyber-routines are not meaningful enough to give our identities more than a modicum of moral weight.

The relentless motion of cyberspace produces an online diaspora, where people experiencing the lightness of digital being gather. Some spend hours online, trying to reach anyone who will care about them, however superficially. Cyberspace often attracts such people who do not have a coherent and meaningful existence in the offline world. Many lonely, rootless individuals seek solace online, particularly when they cannot find it in person. Although a digital "place" cannot possibly provide the levels of neighborliness and hospitality we need for community, some of those surfing the cyber-diaspora do find temporary comfort there.

The noise of knee-jerk criticism also contributes to the lightness of our digital being. In cyberculture, people are slow to reflect and quick to vent. George Steiner argues that today we live in a "perpetual hum of aesthetic commentary, of on-the-minute judgements, of pre-packaged pontifications."[7] Pseudo-experts are ready twenty-four hours a day to tell us how we should think and feel about practically everything. Such asynchronous commentary never ceases, relentlessly diverting our attention to causes, opinions, and scandals. This criticism deflates our spirits with caustic comments and hasty invectives. Everyone has opinions, but few people seem to have any wisdom.

The noise of digital messaging eclipses solitude and suffocates reflection. Digital messaging offers us no peace to contemplate our direction in life. We are replicating the age-old human problem of restlessness in the new test tubes of cyberspace. "In a certain sense all of us are running," wrote Søren Kierkegaard, long before cyberspace. "We are running after money, status, pleasure. We run with gossip, rumors, foul talk, with lies, fiction, and trivialities. We run now to the east and now to the west, panting on our activistic errands. But we are not running on the racetrack."[8] Today, we run through cyberspace. The "preternatural resonance of cyberspace invited cacophony rather than clarity," says Albert Borgmann.[9]

Our flighty messaging renders our lives morally unfocused. In a technological society, we get used to chasing "fugitive visions, themselves without a past and without a future, and without any substance even in the present," says Jacques Ellul.[10] Because we demand instant information, writes Aleksandr I. Solzhenitsyn, the public media must resort to "guesswork, rumors, and suppositions to fill in the voids."[11] We desire this hasty messaging even though we know it confuses and confounds us. We seem to have "mastered" every communication technique, observes Walker Percy, but now our poets and artists are telling us that we are isolated from each other and unable to commune with one another except on the most superficial levels.[12] Facile messaging is no solution for incoherent living.

Every so often, however, we catch glimmers of the lightness of our digital being—its hollowness, superficiality, and temporality. For a few moments we sense that there must be something more significant and longer lasting, something that resonates with our souls. We begin asking the kinds of root questions that Dorothy Day considered when her busyness subsided. What is the meaning of my life? To whom am I responsible? How can I connect more intimately with others?

The lightness of our digital being is a moral and spiritual crisis evident partly in our inability to use information technology responsibly for nobler purposes. This is why Wendell Berry sounds like a radical when he writes, "I do not see that computers are bringing us one step nearer to anything that does matter to me: peace, economic justice, ecological health, political honesty, family and community stability, good work."[13] Berry might be right or wrong about computers, but he is responsibly trying to avoid the lightness of digital being, to hang on to purpose and significance, and ultimately to hope. Ivan Illich describes the lightness among his students, who chase after a "new kind of text," "a printout which has no anchor, which can make no claim to be either a metaphor, or an original from the author's hand. Like the signals from a phantom schooner, its digital strings form arbitrary font-shapes on the screen, ghosts which appear and then vanish." Now books, too, he says are little more than a "metaphor pointing toward information."[14] Lost in the miasma of evaporating information, we cannot help but feel the lightness of digital being.

Distrusting the Prevailing Techno-Magic

Jim Reardon loved the freebies he got online. He thrived during the 1990s, when new dot-coms were giving away products and services to entice people to their sites. His home office included a free color printer and scanner, free Internet access, free voice mail, free subscriptions to *Wired* and other magazines, free digital photo prints—even a free lava lamp. Two years later, with the fall of the dot-coms, Reardon was down on his freeloading luck. "The Internet used to be a little like a 1968 Haight-Ashbury commune, where essentially everything was free," remarks an Internet executive about the days when Reardon hit the online jackpot. "Now," he adds, "it's becoming more like Manhattan in 2001, where you have to pay for the things you most want to do."[15]

The free ride in cyberspace has come to an end. The days of cyber-prosperity succumbed to market devaluations, layoffs, and bankruptcies. Many of the promises associated with the Internet were never fulfilled. Education was not revolutionized. The dream of digital democracy now seems like a fairy tale. "Frictionless competition" is an empty slogan. Many of the dot-com "pure plays"—started as new Internet businesses without brick and mortar backgrounds—lost market share to some of the older, more established corporate empires that not too long ago were labeled the dinosaurs of the New Economy. Digital promises are evaporating. Web guru Jakob Nielsen declares, "Last year's business model was: How can we separate the investors from their money? This year's business model is: How can we separate the customers from their money?"[16] This is progress?

The digital revolution was so oversold that eventually it had to underperform. Like earlier technological heartthrobs—radio, television, cable, and satellites—the new digital stars are more hype than reality. Techno-gurus and symbol brokers promised a grand revolution but delivered far less. Instead of gaining more free time, we suddenly seem shackled to email and cell phones. Expecting to be able to find online all the information we could ever want, we are swimming in polluted search engines, oceans of digital trivia, and a rising tide of misinformation. Spam artists fill our email boxes with links to trash, including invitations to orgiastic bliss.

Nevertheless, informationists still admonish us not to lose hope. Supposedly new, more powerful technologies will soon replace the "old" ones. Who are they kidding? All new information technologies also carry the potential to further unravel our communities and dampen our habits of the heart. Every informational advance both binds us and divides us, levels us and differentiates us. Wisdom consists partly of knowing how we are being separated and fragmented, and partly of knowing what to do about it. We need more meaning, not more information.

In the midst of streams of technological hyperbole, we have a responsibility as caretakers of creation to be skeptical. We should ask the tough questions rather than accept the prevailing cyber-shibboleths. Virilio reminds us that "never has any progress in technique been achieved without addressing its specific negative aspects."[17] This is particularly true in the early years of new technologies, when we make all kinds of decisions that will bind us to particular uses, understandings, and institutions. Langdon Winner writes, "By far the greatest latitude of choice exists the very first time a particular instrument, system or technique is introduced."[18]

Perhaps cyberspace is little more than another means of organizing messages and distributing information. Tom Wolfe overstates the case only moderately when he says that the Web "does one thing. It speeds up the retrieval and dissemination of information, messages, and images, partly eliminating such chores as going outdoors to the mailbox to picking up the phone to get a hold of your stockbroker or some buddies to shoot the breeze with."[19] Albert Borgmann similarly argues that the past and future will be much more closely connected than cyberculture can envision. The "information revolution," he writes, "if it stays on its present trajectory, will devolve into an institution as helpful and necessary as the telephone and as distracting and dispensable as television with an unhappily slippery slope between its cultural top and bottom."[20] Historical perspective can dissipate our triumphalist rhetoric. Humankind's technological exploits have never lived up to early hype—except in the minds of the gurus who make a living peddling their techno-magic.

Questioning technological prognostications is not merely a matter of addressing annoying glitches and short-term inefficiencies. We also have to examine deeper moral issues, such as moderation, wisdom, humility, and authenticity. When we do this, we discover a mixed story: Particular technological means lead us to both humane and inhumane ends. Extirpating all the evil from our informational endeavors is impossible, since we cannot remove all of it from either human hearts or social institutions. The dominant evil impulse in our cyber-pursuits is usually the drive to rule others. This urge seizes human hearts and minds, corrupting our high-tech practices. St. Augustine saw the urge to dominate *(libido dominandi)* as one of the crucial aspects of human nature. He believed that it was nothing less than the ongoing manifestation of the devil's first pride and the cause of Adam's fall.[21] Distrust of the techno-magicians, then, should be common sense in a broken world in which people desire power to lord over others. We should be able to laugh at the folly of one high-tech genius who proclaims, "Since we are going to be gods, we might as well start acting like ones."[22]

If we challenge the prevailing deference to technology, we will discover how deeply informationism has infected our hearts as well as our minds. When Berry published an article about why he would not buy a computer—why he did not need a machine that would enable him to work with greater speed, ease, and quantity, because these are not his writing standards—he "scratched the skin of a technological funda-mentalism that . . . wishes to monopolize a whole society and, there-fore, cannot tolerate the smallest differences of opinion."[23] Berry says his critics "repeat, like a chorus of toads, the notes sounded by their leaders in industry. . . . The past was gloomy, drudgery-ridden, servile, meaningless, and slow. The present, thanks only to purchasable prod-ucts, is meaningful, bright, lively, centralized, and fast. The future, thanks only to more purchasable products, is going to be even better. Thus consumers become salesmen, and the world is made safer for cor-porations."[24] Regardless of whether we fully agree with Berry, he is doing his part to challenge responsibly the prevailing techno-magic.

Euphoria over information technology is a secular faith that deserves heretics. Virilio rightly contends that rationality and science in the mod-ern world create a *deus ex machina* (a machine-god) that negates the transcendent God of revealed religion. When we question the existence of this techno-savior, we will be labeled traitors to the cause of material progress.[25] We are nevertheless morally obligated to hold the futurists accountable for their prophetic tales about the impending benefits of new devices. As Eugene H. Peterson observes, the myth of progress is the most common form of secular eschatology in America today. This myth "takes the materials of the present and projects them into the future, enlarging them in the process under the assumption that the future has some magical growth hormone in it."[26] High-tech hype uses quasi-spiritual language to spin heavenly predictions about cyberspace. Surely we ought to question such secular eschatology.

Questioning the techno-magic is a means of challenging long-stand-ing myths about the salvific power of humanly fabricated devices. As Carl Mitcham shows, such rhetoric extends back to the ancient Greek notion of a technologist as a grammarian or rhetorician.[27] Humans have long used spiritual language and evocative prose to convey the appar-ent power of technology—even to the point of creating an emotionally charged rhetoric of technology.[28] This fanatical conviction dangerously incites blind but incontestable allegiance to technological innovation. Václav Havel cautions us that fanatical attempts to "organize a 'heaven on earth' inevitably lead to an earthly hell."[29] Although the gospel of tech-nological progress brings fame and fortune to many peddlers of cyber-prophecy, we should be skeptical. "If all the mythos of cyberculture can do is mimic the religious quest for 'eternal life' in the absurd techno-logical guise of a bad science-fiction plot," writes Thomas S. Valovic, "then that is a poor offering indeed."[30]

The gospel of techno-magic falsely assumes that what people need most is more information and greater cyber-expertise.[31] Cyberspace is a marvelous innovation, but it solves few of our deepest problems, most of which are cultural, political, or spiritual. As the Hebrew and Christian traditions remind us, humankind is fundamentally flawed. We are prone to chase after false gods and then blame the poor results on someone else. From at least Babel forward we have churned through new techniques in the hope of making a name for ourselves. We tend to wear the clothing of technological power rather than the garments of personal humility.

Today, cyber-technique runs through modern culture like an enormous combine, gathering the easy fixes and technological wizardry while discarding ancient wisdom. We have transformed technique into a metaphysic—the new lord of our lives. Unless we see this idol for what it is, we will become its servants. Distrusting high-tech idols is a noble task and a cosmic responsibility. By together distrusting the prevailing techno-magic, we can resist the unchallenged momentum of emerging technologies while engaging a more profound and lasting reality.[32]

De-technologizing Our Religious Traditions

Saved from a potentially crippling political revolution in the 1770s, Americans have since embraced one technological revolution after another. No nation on earth has been so quick to discover, adopt, and celebrate new technologies, from the most practical eggbeaters and vacuum cleaners to atom smashers and rockets to Mars. The sheer pace and magnitude of technological development in America would seem to be enough to destroy all traces of preindustrial life, but some traditions nevertheless survive. As Lewis Mumford suggests, "traditional pieties" counterbalance technology.[33] Religious practices can yet soften the impact of technological innovations by maintaining noninstrumental practices, moral convictions, and communities of virtue.[34] Although two hundred years of technological changes have rattled local and national institutions and diluted secular as well as religious communities, religious traditions still supply many of the "pieties" needed for the habits of the heart. As long as we continue to de-technologize such traditions of their excess rationalism and instrumentalism, they can continue to serve us well as locations for moral discourse and virtuous character. If we fail to continually de-technologize our religions, they, too, will become worldly monuments to technique.[35]

History suggests that technology and democracy need a third partner—religious tradition. In David Gross's words, the "otherness of a tradition" gives us some critical leverage against the forces of modernity by equipping us with moral understandings and cosmic perspectives.[36] Religious traditions can provide a cogent diagnosis of our condition and a higher calling for our lives. They offer us nonmaterial hopes and non-instrumental practices as counterweights to market forces and high-tech innovations. Virilio suggests that we should be "atheists" of modern technology while simultaneously holding on to revealed truth. We should accept no humanly devised idols as substitutes for God, no Tower of Babel for the heavenly city. "My fetish image," he says, "is that of the battle of Jacob and the angel. Jacob is a believer, he meets the angel of God, but to remain a free man, he is obliged to do battle. This is the great figure. It is necessary to obey—but also to resist."[37] By continually renewing our religious traditions in the midst of our informational explorations, we can resist technological idolatry while obeying a higher calling.

De-technologizing our religious traditions renews the habits of our hearts. Religious traditions can help us to hear the voices of gratitude and responsibility, focus our hearts and minds on virtues, and subdue the power of technique within society. As long as it does not succumb to the heresy of informationism, revealed religion can remind us that no technological future is inevitable—regardless of what the gurus claim. John Huey in *Fortune* tells us to "embrace" the New Economy, "for it will transform our lives and the way we work more profoundly than we can imagine—and nothing is going to stop it."[38] On the contrary, religious wisdom reminds us that we are always in the midst of creating a conditional future. It helps us to remember that we are responsible today for maintaining the traditions that will usher in a good tomorrow. "Each generation exercises power over its successors: and each, in so far as it modifies the environment bequeathed to it and rebels against tradition, resists and limits the power of its predecessors," writes C. S. Lewis.[39] He further argues, the religious person should seek godly wisdom, self-discipline, and virtue, not the power of technique.

Contemplation—sustained reflection on higher things and devotion to God—is one important way of de-technologizing religion in the information society. Ellul says that the person absorbed by modern communication media "falls prey to these ways of acquiring information" and is "profoundly incapable of meditation and reflection."[40] Contemplative practices reject the ultimate authority of secular-rational information by sustaining ways of life that are less instrumental, more communal, and more virtuous than those of the wider technological society. The self-discipline of organizing our days around worship and prayer, for example, is fundamentally at odds with the frenetic and chaotic lives of people in the information society. Contemplative ways of life are not anti-technological as much as pro-community, pro-wisdom, and pro-faithfulness. They remind us all how important noninstrumental, non-informational thought and practice are for responsible living. Contemplation can help us de-technologize our religious practices by helping us embrace nontechnological ways of being, knowing, and doing.

Religious contemplation is not meant solely as the vocation of monastic persons.[41] While some individuals join monastic communities that are intentionally set apart from mainstream society, the practices and purposes of contemplation are important elements of religious life. Contemplative persons and communities regularly reflect on their lives, mindful that God is watching them and that their actions are part of their witness to the world. Their awareness of the presence of the Creator leads them to spiritual observances, such as prayer and sacrament, that might otherwise be discarded for their apparent lack of instrumental payoff. Contemplation also keeps people mindful of the human tendency to fall prey to technological pride. Living contemplatively is one way of regularly reminding ourselves that we are not God and that we will not become more intimate with God merely by tracking the latest information about God.

Religious contemplation also reminds us to integrate the *means* of life with inherently good *ends* for life. A contemplative life directs us to a moral telos that we can never fully reach but which is inherently good. We then seek informational moderation, for instance, because it is intrinsically worthy of our hearts' desires, not because we will necessarily gain any self-benefit. James M. Houston argues that "*techne* is the Trojan horse in the City of God."[42] He wonders if the techniques for counseling, the tools for Bible study, the means of organizing church life themselves tend to become a "technocratic religion."[43] If we are not careful, even prayer can become just another instrumental technology to employ when everyday modes of control do not work. Prayer slips into machine logic, a means for manipulating God and neighbor to produce our desired results. Contemplation helps us to prevent the technologizing of religion by rebinding our means to virtuous ends.

De-technologizing religious tradition does not require the rejection of technology per se. Often saying no to instrumental techniques is also a means of saying yes to virtuous practices. Each religious tradition must identify its own intrinsic ways of relating culture to information technology. The anti-technology stances of "plain people" such as the Amish, Old Order Mennonites, and Old German Baptist Brethren are not so much naive rejections of modernity as they are claims about the inherent value of older, more communal, and less rational ways of life.[44] Berry suggests that the Amish are "the truest geniuses of technology, for they understand the necessity of limiting it, and they know how to limit it."[45] But all religions need to define and then live within their own technological limits. The Shakers, for instance, were not anti-technological. Their moderation did not stop them from inventing washing machines with powered agitators, from being the first group to package and sell seeds, from devising a wrinkle-free fabric, a revolving oven, a pea sheller, and a technology that cored and quartered apples. The Shakers were technological geniuses who embraced particular technologies that they figured would save them time and energy that they could then devote to worship.[46] They recognized the limits of what technology could contribute to community and worship, but they also seized opportunities commensurate with their religious convictions as a community. They refused to abandon God for mere rationalism and scientism, recognizing that to do so would produce a religion of technology devoid of revelation.[47]

In an interview with *Time* in late 1996, Bill Gates remarked about the apparent inefficiency of religion: "Just in terms of allocation of time resources, religion is not very efficient. . . . There's a lot more I could be doing on a Sunday morning."[48] But religious endeavors are meant to nurture faith, not to increase our utility, as if people were mere tools. As long as we do not let them become overly technological endeavors, faith traditions can help us to live virtuously. In the Christian tradition, for example, the Holy Spirit is "neg-entropic energy" (i.e., energy that produces ordered openness in systems, as opposed to the disorder of closed systems, which is entropic).[49] "Hauling in truckloads of rationalism and technology from the world," says Peterson, will not make us more "spiritual."[50] De-technologizing religion is one way of holding on to wisdom and renewing our moral practices. Our quarrel with unmoderated instrumental logic should grow out of our love for eternal goodness. Only then can we faithfully counterbalance the authority of cyber-technique with the goodness of virtue in every area of life.

Serving Responsibly

Information technology facilitates our messaging, but it cannot make us more responsible messengers. Responsibility is a matter of the heart, not of machines. Responsible persons and institutions are conscientious caretakers of what they have inherited from past generations. Instead of merely deferring to the experts, responsible caretakers accept their own inherent obligations as human beings to serve others.

In the Hebrew and Christian traditions, all persons receive special standing as stewards of creation. Our identity as human beings springs immediately from our createdness, from our nature, not from who we *want* to be or how others *decide* to value us. We are created with a capacity for responsibility in order that we might be responsible. Unlike the other creatures, we inherit the responsibility of caring for everything on the earth. Professional offices, such as job titles and earned degrees, are subsidiary to our overarching obligations as God-created stewards of the world.

These traditions challenge the ways we reduce each other to beings with only professional-technical value. God designs in all people a moral value beyond measure. "What is man that you are mindful of him?" asks King David (Ps. 8:4). "You made him a little lower than the angels; you crowned him with glory and honor" (Heb. 2:7). This remarkable endorsement of the intrinsic value of each person says absolutely nothing about our instrumental abilities. Instead, it grants all of us a place "above" the creation as its rightful stewards. *Who* we are transcends *what* we are able to accomplish. Our primary title is *caretaker,* not technician or information worker. In this cosmic sense, our value as persons has nothing to do with technique. While cyberculture is enamored with technical skill, revealed religion focuses instead on our intrinsic obligation to serve others responsibly. As David F. Ford contends, we all inherit "the committed, focused, and therefore 'binding' freedom to do what is right."[51] Technical skill without this responsibility corrupts our calling as caretakers.

Responsible serving is the ministry of all people by virtue of their createdness. The word "ministry" comes from *minus,* which means "less."[52] A responsible person *empties* himself or herself on behalf of another. This, too, challenges technocratic supremacy, where gaining is the goal. The information society grants control to managers and technicians, but it fails to hold them accountable for what they give in return. Revealed religion suggests that serving is not so much the *domain* of the privileged as it is the *dominion* of responsible persons. A giving servant seeks to be responsible, not successful. A servant hears the call to responsibility, listens to those being served, and then ministers to them.

Our unique settings in life, then, provide each of us with arenas in which we can serve responsibly. Our *calling* as God-created beings is neither to distance ourselves from the world nor to gain control over it—the former is apathy and the latter is arrogance. Most high-tech innovations today are aimed at building successful companies, beating competitors to market, and managing organizations. None of these are inherently evil activities. Yet if we undertake them without any cognizance of our overarching responsibility to serve the world, they are not particularly virtuous. When we divorce our high-tech endeavors from the goal of serving others responsibly, we become amoral technicians. Berry calls professors, for instance, to "become people of experience rather than experts" and asks them to "apply their learning to the small problems of ordinary people and to recommend means and methods not

profitable to the suppliers of 'purchased inputs.'"[53] Every occupation
faces similar struggles between expert control and sacrificial service.

Serving others responsibly requires us to discern the gap between the
way things are in the world and the way they should be. Do we care
about how local schools employ computers and cyberspace on behalf
of our children? Are our libraries adequately serving patrons who might
not be able to afford their own access to the Internet and to informational databases? Serving responsibly requires the "reconciliation of
knowledge (moral and scientific), circumstance, and technology." The
responsible servant discerns and then reconciles.[54] Any kind of entrepreneurial success, says Martin H. Krieger, must be justified in terms
of the reconciliation it provides.[55] By serving others responsibly, we carry
God's love into the world, holding high the banner of shalom for the
world to see. The opposite of such love is not hatred but indifference.[56]

Inviting Friendship

In Peterson's *The Message*, in which he paraphrases the New Testament Greek in everyday American English, Jesus Christ says, "Live in
me. Make your home in me just as I do in you" (John 15:4). Jesus uses
an agricultural metaphor to get at the substance of such togetherness.
"I am the Vine, you are the branches. When you are joined with me and
I with you, the relation is intimate and organic, the harvest is sure to be
abundant" (John 15:5). "Make yourself at home in my love," Jesus urges
(John 15:9). Then he offers one of the greatest directives ever spoken:
"Love one another the way I loved you. This is the very best way to love.
Put your life on the line for your friends. You are my friends" (John
15:12).

At the heart of the Hebrew and Christian traditions is the mystery of
friendship with God and neighbor. In the information age, friendships
are no less important than they were in Jesus' time on earth. They may
now be even more critical as natural ways of morally leavening our overly
instrumental and impersonal relationships. Jesus paints a picture of
"intimate and organic" friendships that transcend self-interest with a
moral logic of mutual self-sacrifice. The gospel of Jesus Christ holds
that he made us his friends by dying on the cross for us. Now, we are to
befriend others by putting our lives "on the line" for them. This kind of
invitation to deep friendship undermines selfish logic and challenges us
to cultivate noninstrumental intimacies grounded in love rather than
technique.

Few human relationships form moral bonds more strongly than do
friendships. Generally speaking, our friends are the people we like and

know well, the ones who are "available" for us. They listen to us when others will not. They confide in us, as we do in them. Friends continue the relationship even when there is no instrumental reason to do so. Unlike purely professional or economic associations, friendships do not require people to attain technical expertise, to share a proprietary view of the world, or to exchange goods and services. They usually reveal our character—for good and for bad—and give opportunities to learn to be more virtuous. Whereas even familial bonds are formally inscribed by law, friendships are voluntary associations held together purely by mutual consent. For all these reasons, friendship is one of the most satisfying human endeavors, an "intimate and organic" way of associating that fits us naturally as human beings.

Friendship depends on virtue. It is far more than a sentimental emotion or a long-standing relationship between persons. Friendship results when people cultivate a habitual facility for doing right and being good with others. As friendship embodies virtue, it undergirds other forms of social relations, from politics to business and education.[57] People who do not desire to live virtuously in friendships, for instance, will not likely make good citizens or business associates.[58] One test of the moral quality of a social institution is whether its members are also friends. Do they associate only by professional demand or legal necessity, or also by friendship? Do they care about one another as more than a means to instrumental ends? In his oration on people's desire to break into the "Inner Ring" of status, pride, and ambition, C. S. Lewis suggests instead that people seek the "real" inner ring of friendship.[59] Friendships are crucial for the common good.

Anything that dissolves friendship usually weakens virtuous character as well. Extreme individualism, for instance, destroys friendship by encouraging us to live selfishly. Instrumentalism promotes "I-It" relationships in which people treat others as "things" to use for their own selfish purposes.[60] Friendships, on the other hand, are inherently mutual associations in which the friends' own interests become somewhat identical. One way of assessing the value of information technologies is considering how well they nurture friendships as opposed to superficial or instrumental relationships. But even more important may be the deleterious impact of our informational habits on our everyday, in-person friendships. The same technologies that can help us to "stay in touch" with friends can scatter and devalue our friendships.

The flourishing of friendship in modern society depends far more on the spread of virtue than on access to information technology. We can sometimes find potential new friends online, and we can also exchange messages with existing friends through email, but virtuous friendships themselves are not fully sustainable merely through digital messaging.

In-person media, from voice to touch and eye, are the natural ways to practice friendship. The moral qualities of friendship become embodied in proximate conversations, in the habits of intimate, unthreatening dialogue. Ivan Illich calls these "disciplined, self-denying, careful, tasteful friendships" through which we can rediscover the good.[61] Historically speaking, local social institutions such as the family, school, and church implicitly encouraged virtuousness and thereby promoted friendships. The best friendships are ongoing, in-person invitations to be mutually virtuous people.

Marva J. Dawn reminds us that it is difficult in our society to "embrace people instead of things, to cherish time rather than space." Our "technologically efficient and materially exploitative culture," she says, values instrumental activities over personal relationships. Therefore, she argues, we must maintain friendly practices that soften technicism and materialism.[62] Dawn believes that the tradition of Sabbath-keeping is one way of voluntarily dedicating time to friendships. Such relationships "stand against the technologization of our culture," engendering organic communities of friends.[63] In cyberculture, friendships need safe times and places protected from frenzied messaging and information overload.

The decisive significance of friendship in the information society leads us back to the importance of community. Friendship ultimately softens radical individualism and bolsters community. In the Christian tradition, for instance, the acquisition of virtue is collective, not individual. People discover the good life as they associate virtuously.[64] The church itself is meant to be a faithful fellowship of virtue-seeking people who value friendship and cultivate shared moral bonds. Historically, the church described the deepest form of friendship as love. Houston says that such love is a "fellowship of doing good to each other, redeeming each other, reconciling ourselves with each other, loving each other, sharing with each other, sacrificially assuring and building up each other to grow together in community."[65] This kind of deep friendship cannot be lived purely through time-conquering communication technologies that tend to dehumanize our relationships, dissolve local community, and weaken neighborly love.

Most mysterious of all, friendships can direct us to the Creator. Palladius (363–431)[66] observed, "If you have seen your brother, you have seen God."[67] Human friendship whispers divine relationship to us, since the intimate bonds of virtuous friendship reflect some of the characteristics of divine companionship. Both types of associations depend on beings that have personality. In the Hebrew and Christian traditions, the Garden of Eden was where the God-human and human-human friendships began and thrived. Before the fall into sin, Eden was the dwelling place where human beings treated each person as a "thou" made in the divine image. This idea of a garden of friendship symbolizes rich, untarnished community life, the place of shalom. "Eden" even connotes delight and embodies the ideas of luxury, joy, and erotic rapture.[68] Heaven is the place for the new city that will include not only the friendships of the garden but all the good intimacies known and enjoyed by God.[69] To live with the Creator in heaven is to be an everlasting friend of God.

Religious communities form some of the richest friendships. To become a friend within a religious tradition is to associate with some of its current adherents in the ongoing conversations and practices that may extend back millennia.[70] A tradition can provide the "moral particularities" from which we can acquire virtuous customs.[71] Alasdair MacIntyre concludes *After Virtue* by calling for the "construction of local forms of community within which civility and the intellectual and moral life can be sustained through the new dark ages which are already upon us."[72] We cannot create such moral bonds out of nothing; invariably, we must grow them in the soil of existing traditions and their extant friendships, such as parishes, congregations, and fellowships. In the Christian tradition, a person's primary legacy should be that he or she was a faithful friend of both God and neighbor.

Our habits of the heart, then, nurture friendships within communities in which we dwell. Robert Bellah and his colleagues emphasize the importance of community in America as an antidote to the tendencies toward selfish individualism. They suggest that communities are constituted largely out of their histories and their shared narratives.[73] Alexis de Tocqueville, too, saw that Americans love to associate with one another. He observed in the 1830s a new nation filled with voluntary associations, including religious groups. "Americans use associations to give fêtes, to found seminaries, to build inns, to raise churches, to distribute books, to send missionaries to the antipodes; in this manner they create hospitals, prisons, schools," he wrote.[74]

Without such friendly associations, we can lose ourselves in individual pursuits that, while often good in and of themselves, do not cultivate virtue. The habits of the heart grow the strongest through the organic friendships that constitute community life. Religious communities generally are the most powerful moral agents because of their high regard for establishing cross-generational friendships that maintain eternal goodness. As we become friends with those in a living religious tradition, we cultivate some of the strongest moral bonds, learn some of the greatest goods, and become friendly persons of virtuous character. Tocqueville suggests that religious associations cultivate citizens who are "regulated, temperate, moderate, farsighted, masters of themselves; and if it does not lead directly to virtue through the will, it brings them near to it insensibly through habits."[75] Our use of information technologies alone cannot sustain such virtuous associations.

Sojourning with Heart

The decline of the technology sector of the American economy in 2000 shook the confidence of thousands of information workers who wondered if the New Economy was merely a one-time, short-term bonanza. In the preceding years, many of them had been working so intensively that their labor had become their lives. As the economy cooled down and the value of technology stocks plummeted, some began asking themselves if their lives were truly good. One owner of a New York–based online recruiting firm hoped to sell her business in order to move to South Carolina and raise money for a village in Guatemala. "I feel like I've gone from the lottery ticket to starting all over again," she told a reporter. "It's a good time to rethink life." She hoped to relocate to "Normalville" and perhaps even "get married and have kids."[76] For many, the high-tech slump was an opportunity to overcome the lightness of digital being by searching for deeper meaning and purpose.

Americans' love of technology has always been a romance with new beginnings. Joseph Sittler says that Americans transmuted the frontier "from a fact of national history into a point of view in the mind." When Americans reach a point where something in life is intolerable, unsatisfactory, or too restricting, they simply move on to a new beginning. On the one hand, this frontier mentality displays some remarkable traits. "To uproot the thousand continuities of one's life and settle in a wilderness required courage, decisiveness, resolution, ingenuity, and huge output of activity," writes Sittler. On the other hand, repeatedly starting anew does not equip Americans with the wisdom needed to address the anxieties and confusion that eventually result from each new adventure. "The realities of 'limit' and 'boundary,' the spirit-educating forces that operate when one cannot move on, or start anew, but must come to terms with life where it is and where it is bound to remain—these forces have not deeply entered into the American national consciousness," concludes Sittler.[77]

Endless series of fresh starts create dislocations and discontinuity. If life is all about pursuing only "product innovations" and "self-discoveries," we will be consigned to the chaos of change without the stability of telos. In the words of theologian Emil Brunner, our means will not be "hallowed" by the most worthy end.[78] New beginnings too easily focus on ever changing identities and intimacies with no respect for intrinsic meaning or greater moral purpose. The information society constantly revises reality and updates experience so that the transformations themselves become our sole bearings.[79] Our only viable metaphors for living become essentially technological: endless "new releases" of the self. Self-improvement and social progress are merely motions, not worthy destinations. They find meaning in innovation rather than virtue. Running after change, we become techno-evangelists, surfing after the latest fads with no clear route or destination. Some people might call this freedom, but it is the freedom of the unattached and restless tourist, not the contemplative freedom of the sojourner.

Ivan Illich suggests that in the Western world the idea of leaving home and seeking self-discovery "on the road" became one of the chief metaphors for living. "Pilgrims and crusaders, traveling masons and mill mechanics, beggars and relic thieves, minstrels and wandering scholars—all of these take to the road by the end of the twelfth century," writes Illich.[80] Some of these characters undoubtedly were evil or at least noncommittal tourists for whom life on the road was merely an opportunity to avoid responsibility. For others, such as the pilgrims, traveling was a sojourn from everyday routines and toward a spiritual home.

Today, our love of new information and novel information technologies can transform us into mere "thieves and beggars," but it can also prod us to contemplate the meaning of our short lives. In the midst of our busyness, we might recognize that we are not merely tourists but sojourners in the larger flow of history, perhaps even eternity. In our sojourns, we do not understand all the complexities, mysteries, and absurdities of life, but we nevertheless seek to travel in the right direction. We recognize that the current world is not fully home; it is not a perfect fit for the shalom we desire. Nevertheless, this world is the place where our journey occurs. Here we discover where we are from as well as evidence of the things to come. We sojourn in a "now" that is informed by wisdom from the past and directed by desires for a good future.

Morally speaking, we have no reasonable option other than to sojourn simultaneously in the past, the present, and the future. In the past, we find the wisdom of tradition, the origins of the habits of the heart. In the present, we try to discern a realistic understanding of our situation—where we are at in the journey. Finally, we share a hope for an eternal future that we can barely perceive through the shadows of time. But we do know that this future is more than information or technology. Probably no one ever died wishing that he or she had more information. Instead, one dies usually hoping to journey to a place where hearts are full and souls are at rest. We desire this future because it is good and right. It fits perfectly the longings of our hearts. Every time we taste shalom in this world we are reminded of the ultimate telos. In the Christian tradition, for instance, the believer sojourns through creation and fall and eventually to eternal redemption, where the sojourn does not end but is instead fulfilled in the new heavens and the new earth.

One of our most fundamental choices in the information age is whether to approach life superficially as tourists or more intimately as sojourners. The diversions of cyberculture lure us to become rootless tourists hopping from gizmo to gizmo and message to message in search of novel experiences and temporary satisfactions. We jockey through life itself as if we were surfing through cyberspace. Enchanted by the technological future and engulfed in the informational present, we constantly "upgrade" our activities and cart our memories to the junkyard, like deleting files on a computer. After all, there are new people to meet, uncharted places to visit, and novel activities to try.

Change can be a good thing, but not when it is severed from virtue. In the life of the cyber-tourist, virtue has little soil in which to grow. Instead of taking the time to pursue moral wisdom, the tourist dips into fashionable self-help literature and celebrates trendy information technologies. Havel describes this tourism: "Yet though we live, find pleasure, think, suffer, meet, part, pass each other by in various ways, that fatal lack of focus or perspective makes everything around us and within us somehow unstable, disconnected, confused." He depicts such an existence in his play *The Mountain Hotel,* in which people latch on to illusory values.[81] For the tourist, there is no eternal reality, only experience. Nor is there any tradition, only nostalgia. Present diversions and amazing prognostications keep the tourist busy. Meanwhile, the inner echo of the tourist's heart grows ever dimmer.

Sojourners live in the same technological world as the tourists, but they perceive reality differently. For the sojourner, the short journey of life, although not fully home, has purpose and direction, even if they are not entirely clear. Informed by the wisdom of earlier travelers, the sojourner discovers guiding truths that serve as maps for the journey. As Havel puts it, the sojourner repeatedly poses the "primordial questions" in order to examine the direction he or she is going.[82] Who are we? Why were we created? What is good and worthy of our attention? How shall we then live? Hoping to leave this world a better place as a worthy inheritance to future generations, the sojourner seeks virtue. As the Hebrew prophet Micah puts it, the sojourner seeks to act justly, love mercy, and walk humbly with God (Micah 6:8).

Ultimately, cyber-tourists live by the promises of technique, whereas virtuous sojourners live by the promises of faith. Information technology offers a future that looks rosy, until we arrive there. Tourists can employ the most efficient travel agents and learn the secrets of online searches for the best travel deals but never know how to get to peace and joy. In this sense, the information age is also the era of past futures, foretold glories of information revolutions that never fully materialized. For the tourist, such high-tech hope is nothing more than an infatuation with human cleverness, with digital magic that people conjure up as if they were well-networked Rasputins. Instead of announcing, "Welcome!" or "You've got mail," the software ought to shout, "Abracadabra!" to remind us of the way that technology charms us. The sojourner forgoes such magic in favor of greater wisdom. Recognizing that we are stewards of the God-created world, the sojourner tries humbly to obey God rather than play God. His or her faith grows every time the sojourner participates in something that is truly good and right. Virtuous pursuits are part of the sojourner's preparation for the eternal feast of shalom that we only sample here on earth.

If we live as techno-tourists, our primary legacy is technique. If instead we are heartful sojourners, embracing both gratitude and responsibility, we will leave behind a far richer legacy of virtue as a witness to future generations. Our gratitude and the resulting responsibility are both gifts from the past and gifts for the future. They cut through the fog of informational life and open our hearts to faithfulness. As Solzhenitsyn puts it, modernity has "trampled upon" us. "No one on earth has any other way left but—upward."[83]

Conclusion

We love to celebrate the latest technological innovations, hoping that they will give us greater control over our destinies. In this sense, our current fascination with digital messaging systems and informational storage and retrieval devices is not essentially new. Human beings have always acclaimed their own technical inventions; the veneration of technique is as old as the human race. Just as the Babylonians tried to make a name for themselves by constructing the Tower of Babel, today we build silicon testaments to our expertise. We love to presume that our newest contraptions will equip us to engineer a better world. We thereby display an extraordinary capacity for collective self-delusion, because the same machines that appear to give us a greater command of life are harder and harder for us to control. Havel writes that as "soon as man began considering himself the source of the highest meaning in the world and the measure of everything, the world began to lose its human dimension, and man began to lose control of it."[84]

Therefore, we need again to reconcile our embellishments of technology with the reality of what it means to be human. In spite of all of the changes in human culture and society over the millennia, human nature remains essentially the same. There is no such thing as incontrovertible human progress. We certainly are capable of improving our material conditions, but developing our spiritual and moral natures is not so simple. Human beings are not mere mechanical or electronic systems awaiting the latest innovation.

Instead of loading our days willy-nilly with digital messaging, we should address more honestly the underlying truth of human nature: that we are neither beasts nor angels. Although we are talented creatures who can accomplish much, we also must strive continuously to rid ourselves of arrogance and to get ourselves back on the path to virtue. No matter how grandly we pursue technique, we will not be able to amend the fundamental truth that it takes greater character to achieve good rather than bad.[85] We are free to declare progress, but we will discover—if we listen to the pace and tenor of our high-tech lives—that we are growing increasingly hurried and anxious. Our infatuation with new information technologies is not leading us to peace and truth; instead, it is diverting our attention from eternal verities about the human condition, such as our original sin and our tendency to idolize the latest technology. We cannot become more virtuous unless we are honest with ourselves about our own tendencies and limitations.

To regain a moral footing in contemporary life, we must dig deeper than information and knowledge, to the traditions that carry virtue from generation to generation. We will have to invest as much time and energy in the habits of our hearts as we do in our high-tech practices. Otherwise we will lose track of the crucial links to the past that can illuminate the path to goodness.

Notes

Introduction

1. Po Bronson, *The Nudist on the Late Shift: And Other True Tales of Silicon Valley* (New York: Broadway Books, 1999), 191–92.

2. Ibid., 187–88.

3. Nat Goldhaber, "About Time," *newmedia.com*, September 1998, 22.

4. George Gilder, *Telecosm: How Infinite Bandwidth Will Revolutionize Our World* (New York: The Free Press, 2000), 4.

5. David F. Noble, *The Religion of Technology: The Divinity of Man and the Spirit of Invention* (New York: Knopf, 1997).

6. Langdon Winner says that computer enthusiasts "employ the metaphor of revolution for one purpose only—to suggest a drastic upheaval, one that people ought to welcome as good news. It never occurs to them to investigate the idea or its meaning any further" (Langdon Winner, *The Whale and the Reactor: A Search for Limits in an Age of High Technology* [Chicago: University of Chicago Press, 1986], 101).

7. See, for example, Arthur Kroker and Michael A. Weinstein, *Data Trash: The Theory of the Virtual Class* (New York: St. Martin's Press, 1994); Paul Virilio, *The Information Bomb* (London: Verso, 2000); Stephen L. Talbott, *The Future Does Not Compute: Transcending the Machines in Our Midst* (Sebastopol, Calif.: O'Reilly & Associates, 1995); Stephen Bertman, *Cultural Amnesia: America's Future and the Crisis of Memory* (Westport, Conn.: Praeger, 2000); Stephen Bertman, *Hyperculture: The Human Cost of Speed* (Westport, Conn.: Praeger, 1998); Neil Postman, *Technopoly: The Surrender of Culture to Technology* (New York: Vintage Books, 1992); C. A. Bowers, *Let Them Eat Data: How Computers Affect Education, Cultural Diversity, and the Prospects of Ecological Sustainability* (Athens, Ga.: University of Georgia Press, 2000); Clifford Stoll, *High-Tech Heretic* (New York: Anchor Books, 1999); Thomas S. Valovic, *Digital Mythologies: The Hidden Complexities of the Internet* (New Brunswick, N.J.: Rutgers University Press, 2000); and Albert Borgmann, *Holding On to Reality: The Nature of Information at the Turn of the Millennium* (Chicago: University of Chicago Press, 1999). For specifically Christian critiques, see Douglas Groothuis, *The Soul in Cyberspace* (Grand Rapids: Baker, 1997); David Lochhead, *Shifting Realities: Information Technology and the Church* (Geneva: WCC Publications, 1997); and Gene Edward Veith Jr. and Christopher L. Stamper, *Christians in a .com World: Getting Connected without Being Consumed* (Wheaton: Crossway Books, 2000).

8. Sven Birkerts, *The Gutenberg Elegies: The Fate of Reading in an Electronic Age* (New York: Fawcett Columbine, 1994), 211.

9. Alexis de Tocqueville, *Democracy in America*, ed. and trans. Harvey C. Mansfield and Delba Winthrop (Chicago: University of Chicago Press, 2000), 275.

10. Ibid., 500.

11. Michael Wolff, *Burn Rate: How I Survived the Gold Rush Years on the Internet* (New York: Simon & Schuster, 1998), 268.

12. J. Budziszewski, "The Future of the End of Democracy," *Findings* 1, no. 2 (2001): 5.

13. Jacques Ellul, *The Technological Society* (New York: Vintage Books, 1964), xxv.

14. *Business Week*, 18 June 2001, cover.

15. Danny Hillis, "Disney's Wizards," interview by Katie Hafron, *Newsweek*, 11 August 1997, 49–50.

16. Doug Guthrie, "'Consider Yourself Deleted,' Son Tells Mom," *Grand Rapids (Mich.) Press*, 26 April 2001. Cited 26 April 2001. Online: http://gr.mlive.com/news/index.ssf?/news/stories/20010426g3koetje2105805.frm.

17. Richard Pyle, "In a Word, High-tech Mumbo Jumbo Finds a Home," *Grand Rapids (Mich.) Press*, 16 September 2001, p. E7. Langdon Winner puts it this way: "As we compare our own minds to the operations of a computer, we acknowledge that an understanding of technical devices has somehow merged with the most intimate levels of self-understanding" (Winner, *Whale and the Reactor*, ix).

18. Dinty W. Moore, *The Emperor's Virtual Clothes: The Naked Truth about Internet Culture* (Chapel Hill: Algonquin Books of Chapel Hill, 1995), 184.

19. Aleksandr I. Solzhenitsyn, *A World Split Apart: Commencement Address Delivered at Harvard University* (New York: Harper & Row, 1978), 51.

20. G. Pascal Zachary, "The Right Mix: Global Growth Attains a New, Higher Level That Could Be Lasting," *Wall Street Journal*, 13 March 1997, p. A1. For one review of the military roots of cyber-technologies, see Manuel Castells, *The Rise of the Network Society* (Malden, Mass.: Blackwell Publishers, 1996), 59–60. For an assessment of deregulation, see Jeremy Rifkin, *The Age of Access: The New Culture of Hypercapitalism, Where All of Life Is a Paid-for Experience* (New York: Putnam, 2000), 10.

21. The conflicts between a global economy and local cultures produce all kinds of legal and ethical issues. See Deborah G. Johnson, "Global Economy, Local Ethics," *Beyond Computing*, June 1998, 12–13.

22. As Jeremy Rifkin puts it, we are witnessing the "absorption of the cultural sphere into the commercial sphere" (Rifkin, *Age of Access*, 11).

23. Michelle Conlin, "Workers, Surf at Your Own Risk," *Business Week*, 12 June 2000. Cited 19 September 2001. Online: http://www.businessweek.com/2000/00_24/b3685257.htm.

24. Cees J. Hamelink, *The Ethics of Cyberspace* (London: Sage Publications, 2000), 26–27.

25. Robert Kuttner, *Everything for Sale: The Virtues and Limits of Markets* (New York: Knopf, 1997).

26. Langdon Winner, "Cybertarian Myths and Prospects for Community," n.p. [cited 13 October 2001]. Online: http://www.rpi.edu/~winner/cyberlib2.html.

27. Václav Havel, *The Art of the Impossible: Politics as Morality in Practice, Speeches, and Writings, 1990–1996*, trans. Paul Wilson (New York: Fromm International, 1998), 91.

28. Ibid., 226.

29. Daniel J. Boorstin, *The Americans: The Democratic Experience* (New York: Vintage Books, 1973), 89–164.

Chapter 1

1. Solzhenitsyn, *A World Split Apart*, 39, 1.

2. Quoted in Cynthia Crossen, "How to Sell How-to Books," *Wall Street Journal*, 14 March 2001, p. B1.

3. Quoted in ibid.

4. Mary E. Boone, *Leadership and the Computer: Top Executives Reveal How They Personally Use Computers to Communicate, Coach, Convince, and Compete* (Rocklin, Calif.: Prima Publishing, 1993), 6.

5. My use of the term *informationism* is different from Manuel Castells's use of *informationalism,* which is essentially an information-based form of capitalism. Nevertheless, I agree with much of his assessment of the "ethical foundation of informationalism" as the "corporate ethos of accumulation" and the "renewed appeal of consumerism" (Castells, *Rise of the Network Society,* 198).

6. To illustrate knowledge *about* versus knowledge *of,* Borgmann writes, "I know of Death Valley; I know that it is arid and contains the lowest point in the United States. But, I must confess, I do not know it. I know of Toni Morrison; I know that she wrote *Tar Baby* and received the Nobel Prize. But, I regret to say, I do not know her" (Borgmann, *Holding On to Reality,* 14).

7. John Dodge, "Philanthropy Hasn't Clicked Much with Internet Firms," *Wall Street Journal Interactive Edition,* n.p. [cited 26 October 1999]. Online: http//interactive .wsj.com/archive/retrieve.cgi?id=SB940862276266783080.djm&template=printing.tpml. Furthermore, a survey conducted by the Social Capital Community Benchmark reported residents of Silicon Valley ranked 31 percent lower than national respondents in charitable giving as a percent of household income ("Valley Residents Network but Don't Connect," n.p. [cited 1 March 2001]. Online: http://www.siliconvalley.com/ docs/news /valley/social030101.htm and http://www.cfsv.org).

8. Dodge, "Philanthropy Hasn't Clicked."

9. "Nightlife, Culture Embrace Geek Chic: But Philanthropy, Civics Shortchanged," *Crain's New York Business,* 29 November–5 December 1999, 40, retrieved via Wilson SelectPlus.

10. B. Keith Fulton, quoted in Dodge, "Philanthropy Hasn't Clicked." James Fallows says that this lack of giving is "one indication" of new millionaires' "continued financial youth" (James Fallows, "Counting Young Net Money," *The Industry Standard,* 30 August–6 September 1999, 24). Older technology companies are far better stewards of their wealth. See Betsey Streisan, "The New Philanthropy," *U.S. News & World Report,* 11 June 2001, 40–42.

11. Quoted in "Nightlife, Culture."

12. One *New York Times* reporter said that Seattle's "geekocracy of high technology is not known for sharing, and grateful-but-skeptical Seattleites often point out the string attached to gifts" (Carey Goldburg, "Computer Age Millionaires Redefine Philanthropy," *New York Times,* 6 July 1997, sec. 1, pp. 1, 9). Software engineer Paulina Borsook writes, "In Silicon Valley and its regional outposts . . . it's not even a joke, not even an embarrassment, that there's so little corporate philanthropy. . . . High-tech employees rank among the lowest of any industry sector for giving to charity" (Paulina Borsook, "Cyberselfish," *Mother Jones,* July/August 1996, 56–60, retrieved via WilsonSelectPlus).

13. William Gibson, who coined the term *cyberspace* in his 1984 novel *Neuromancer,* says that the "cyberpunk hard guys of '90s science fiction . . . already have a certain nostalgic romance about them. These information highwaymen were so heroically attuned to the new technology that they laid themselves open to its very cutting edge. They became it; they took it within themselves" (William Gibson, "Will We Plug Chips into Our Brains?" *Time,* 19 June 2000, 21).

14. Wolff, *Burn Rate,* 268.

15. Ibid., 45, 76, 130.

16. The real genius of our age, says George Steiner, is journalism. Journalistic knowing "articulates an epistemology and ethics of spurious temporality" (George Steiner, *Real Presences* [Chicago: University of Chicago Press, 1989], 26).

17. Theodore Roszak, preface to *The Cult of Information: A Neo-Luddite Treatise on High Tech, Artificial Intelligence, and the True Art of Thinking,* 2d ed. (Berkeley: University of California Press, 1994), xiii.

18. Inigo Thomas, "The Breaking News Epidemic," 18 October 2001, n.p. [cited 22 October 2001]. Online: http://slate.msn.com/idea/01/10/18/idea.asp.

19. Apparently some companies even look to science fiction writers to gain an understanding of the future. See Elizabeth Wiese, "Firms Look to Sci-fi Writers for Advice," *USA Today*, 22 July 1998. Cited 26 September 2001. Online: http://www.usatoday.com/life/enter/books/b550.htm.

20. Joel Stratte-McClure, "You Ain't Seen Nothing Yet," *Continental*, April 2001, 45.

21. James M. Houston, *I Believe in the Creator* (Grand Rapids: Eerdmans, 1980), 120–21.

22. David Gross, *The Past in Ruins: Tradition and the Critique of Modernity* (Amherst, Mass.: University of Massachusetts Press, 1992), 4.

23. Terry Mattingly, "Looking for a New God? A Fresh Creed?" *Terry Mattingly's Religion Column*, 28 February 2001. Cited 28 February 2001. Online: http://www.gospel com.net/tmattingly/2001/col/col.02.28.2001.html.

24. "SelectSmart.com" n.p. [cited 6 May 2001]. Online: http://www.selectsmart.com/RELIGION/.

25. Lewis Mumford, *The Transformations of Man* (New York: Collier Books, 1962), 118.

26. Although "distant places have become instantly accessible to us," writes Michael Roemer, "we can hardly call our relationship to them 'intimate'" (Michael Roemer, *Telling Stories: Postmodernism and the Invalidation of Traditional Narrative* [Lanham, Md.: Lowman and Littlefield, 1995], 355).

27. Jerzy Kosinski, "A Nation of Videots," interview by David Sohn, in *Television: The Critical View*, ed. Horace Newcomb, 3d ed. (New York: Oxford University Press, 1979), 351–66.

28. James M. Houston, *The Heart's Desire: Satisfying the Hunger of the Soul* (Colorado Springs: NavPress, 1996), 100.

29. Ibid., 106.

30. Tocqueville, *Democracy in America*, 482, 483, 487.

31. Ibid., 487.

32. Mark Slouka, *War of the Worlds: Cyberspace and the High-Tech Assault on Reality* (New York: Basic Books, 1995), 22.

33. Frederick Buechner writes that "to know is to participate in, to become imbued with, for better or worse to be affected by. When you really know a person or a language or a job, the knowledge becomes a part of who you are" (Frederick Buechner, *Whistling in the Dark: An ABC Theologized* [San Francisco: Harper & Row, 1988], 71). Hebrew wisdom equates "knowing" with both emotional and physical intimacy, especially sexual intimacy. The Hebrew term for intimacy *(yedia* or *yadah)* means "knowledge." Genesis 4:1 says, "And Adam *knew* Eve his wife; and she conceived" (KJV, emphasis added).

34. Richard P. Cimino and Don Lattin, *Shopping for Faith: American Religion in the New Millenium* (San Francisco: Jossey-Bass, 1998), 58.

35. Tyler Chin, "Browsing for a Second Opinion," *Grand Rapids (Mich.) Press*, 31 May 2001, p. B3.

36. Gregory J. Millman, *The Day Traders: The Untold Story of the Extreme Investors and How They Changed Wall Street Forever* (New York: Times Business, 1999), 32.

37. Amey Stone, "The Darwinism of Day Trading," *Business Week*, 23 May 2001. Cited 7 November 2001. Online: http://www.businessweek.com/technology/content/may2001/tc20010523_908.htm.

38. David Futrelle, "Day-Traders Are Here to Stay: The Demise of the Day-Trader Has Been Greatly Exaggerated," *Money*, 1 March 2001, 133, retrieved via General Reference Center Gold.

39. Ibid.

40. Mayer Offman, "The Rabbi of Day Trading," interview by Stephen B. Shepard, *Business Week*, 4 December 2000, 150.

41. Jim Collins, "Shareflipping Cheats Shareholders of Real Value," *USA Today*, 24 February 2000, p. 15A.

42. Margaret C. Whitman, "A Talk with Meg Whitman," *Business Week*, 19 March 2001, 99.

43. Denise Caruso, "Digital Commerce," *New York Times*, 3 January 2000, p. C4.

44. Described in Jodie Allen, "Whatever," *New Republic*, 5 June 2000, 6.

45. Peter Drucker, quoted in Robert Lezner and Stephen S. Johnson, "Seeing Things as They Really Are," *Forbes*, 10 March 1997, 125.

46. Ibid.

47. To read more about the online pornography industry, see Frederick S. Lane III, *Obscene Profits: The Entrepreneurs of Pornography in the Cyber Age* (New York: Routledge, 2000); and David Lake, "Is Porn Still the Web's Great Test Bed?" *The Industry Standard*, 15 November 1999, 172.

48. See, for example, Deb Levine, *The Joy of Cybersex: A Guide for Creative Lovers* (New York: Ballantine Books, 1998); Susan Rabin and Barbara Lagowski, *Cyberflirt: How to Attract Anyone, Anywhere on the World Wide Web* (New York: Plume, 1999); Cathy Winks and Anne Semans, *The Woman's Guide to Sex on the Web* (New York: HarperCollins, 1999); and Lisa Skriloff and Jodi Gould, *Men Are from Cyberspace: The Single Woman's Guide to Flirting, Dating, and Finding Love Online* (New York: St. Martin's Press, 1997).

49. Quoted in Donald A. Yerxa and Karl W. Giberson, "Vegetables Don't Have a History: A Conversation with Historian John Lukacs," *Books & Culture*, July/August 2000. Cited 7 April 2001. Online: http://www.christianitytoday.com/bc/2000/004/6.14.html.

50. Joel Deane, "Waiting for the Political E-revolution," *ZDNet*, 17 August 2000. Cited 11 June 2001. Online: http://www.zdnet.com/zdnn/stories/comment/0,5859,2616851,00.html.

51. Ibid. See also "The Center for Democracy and Technology," n.p. [cited 20 September 2001]. Online: http://www.cdt.org/mission; "The Center for Digital Democracy," n.p. [cited 20 September 2001]. Online: http://www.democraticmedia.org/; "The Direct Democracy Meeting Place," n.p. [cited 20 September 2001]. Online: http://www.mts.net/~kolar/DD; and "Digital Democracy: A Fifty State Report on Computerizing Campaign Finance Disclosure," n.p. [cited 20 September 2001]. Online: http://www.opensecrets.org/pubs/digdem.

52. Virilio, *Information Bomb*, 109. Robert D. Putnam says, "Some of the allegedly greater democracy in cyberspace is based more on hope and hype than on careful research. The political culture of the Internet . . . is astringently libertarian, and in some respects cyberspace represents a Hobbesian state of nature, not a Lockean one" (Robert D. Putnam, *Bowling Alone: The Collapse and Revival of American Community* [New York: Simon & Schuster, 2000], 173). Armand Mattelart says that we create messianic discourses about the democratic virtues of technology (Armand Mattelart, *Networking the World, 1794–2000* [Minneapolis: University of Minnesota Press, 2000]).

53. John Kozlowicz, "Arizona Democrats Vote Online—What Do You Think?" online posting, 11 March 2000, n.p. [cited 11 June 2000]. Online: http://web1.uww.edu/wcb/schools/400/890/kozlowij/1/forums/forum2/messages/128.html.

54. Alan Zuckerman, quoted in Jack McCarthy, "Arizona Democrats Will Vote Online," *PC World.com*, 16 December 1999. Cited 11 June 2001. Online: http://www.pcworld.com/news/article/0,aid,14403,00.asp.

55. "Dogonvillage.com's Get-Out-the-Vote Efforts a Hit in Arizona," n.p. [cited 11 June 2001]. Online: http://www.dogonvillage.com/az.

56. Robert K. Greenleaf says that an "informational gap" plagues modern decision making. We always face a gap, he believes, between the "solid information in hand and what is needed to make a wise decision" (Robert K. Greenleaf, *Servant Leadership* [New York: Paulist Press, 1977], 23).

57. Jean Bethke Elshtain, preface to *Who Are We? Critical Reflections and Hopeful Possibilities* (Grand Rapids: Eerdmans, 2000), xii.

58. Michelle Kessler, "IBM Faces Lawsuit over Nazi's Use of Technology," *USA Today,* 13 February 2001, p. 3B.

59. Theodore Caplow, Louis Hicks, and Ben J. Wattenberg, *The First Measured Century: An Illustrated Guide to Trends in America, 1900–2000* (Washington, D.C.: AEI Press, 2001), xii.

60. Boorstin, *Americans*, 165–244.

61. Quoted in Amber Veverka, "Digital Disciple," *Grand Rapids (Mich.) Press*, 19 November 1997, p. A9.

62. Ferris Research, "Quantifying Email Productivity Gains," 21 January 2000, n.p. [cited 19 September 2001]. Online: http://www.ferris.com/rep/20000121/email_productiv ity.xls and http://www.ferris.com/rep/20000121/SM.html.

63. Don Steinberg, "Money from Nothing," *SmartBusinessMag.com*, April 2001, 70.

64. Quoted in Special Advertising Section, *Business Week*, 2 March 1998, 149.

65. Keith H. Hammonds, "The Optimists Have It Right," *Business Week*, 31 August 1998, 146.

66. Susan Breidenbach, "MBA-Ware: Forecasting Smarts in a Box," *Investor's Business Daily*, 25 April 1997, pp. A1, A11.

67. Greenleaf, *Servant Leadership*, 140.

68. Max DePree, *Leadership Is an Art* (New York: Doubleday, 1987), 47.

69. Erik Davis, *Techgnosis: Myth, Magic + Mysticism in the Age of Information* (New York: Harmony Books, 1998), 89.

70. See "Editorial," *Media Development* 48, no. 1 (2001): 2.

71. Norbert Weiner, *The Human Use of Human Beings: Cybernetics and Society* (Garden City, N.J.: Double Anchor Books, 1954), 16.

72. Quoted in Roszak, *Cult of Information*, 9.

73. Weiner, *Human Use of Human Beings*, 32.

74. Roszak, *Cult of Information*, 11.

75. Ibid.

76. Ibid., 12–13.

77. See Virilio, *Information Bomb*, 143.

78. B. F. Skinner, *Walden Two* (New York: Macmillan, 1948), 291.

79. Stoll, *High-Tech Heretic*, 16.

80. James R. Beniger, *The Control Revolution: Technological and Economic Origins of the Information Society* (Cambridge: Harvard University Press, 1990), 8.

81. C. S. Lewis, "The Inner Ring" (memorial oration at King's College, London, 1994), in C. S. Lewis, *The Weight of Glory and Other Addresses* (Grand Rapids: Eerdmans, 1977), 61. Cited 25 October 2001. Online: http://www.hu.mtu.edu/~dsulliva/classes/lewis/ inner_ring.htm.

82. The cybernetic model is not neutral. It "entails a particular concept of mind, of reason, of knowledge and skill, and it forecloses alternative conceptions. It privileges mechanistic over holistic thinking; cognition over intuition; calculative over deliberative rationality" (Kevin Robins and Frank Webster, *Times of Technoculture: From the Information Society to the Virtual Life* [London: Routledge, 1999], 181).

83. Peter L. Bernstein, *Against the Gods: The Remarkable Story of Risk* (New York: Wiley, 1998).

84. Edward Yourdon, *Rise and Resurrection of the American Programmer* (Upper Saddle River, N.J.: Yourdon Press, 1998), 133.

85. Mark J. P. Wolf, *Abstracting Reality: Art, Communication, and Cognition in the Digital Age* (Lanham, Md.: University Press of America, 2000), 22.

86. Lukacs, "Vegetables Don't Have a History."

87. Ellen Ullman, *Close to the Machine: Technophilia and Its Discontents* (San Francisco: City Lights, 1997), 24.

88. John Seely Brown and Paul Duguid, *The Social Life of Information* (Boston: Harvard Business School Press, 2000), 1.

89. Peter Kreeft, *Back to Virtue: Traditional Moral Wisdom for Modern Moral Confusion* (San Francisco: Ignatius Press, 1992), 27.

90. Clifford G. Christians, "Justice and the Global Media," *Studies in Christian Ethics* 13, no. 1 (2000): 83.

91. Quoted in Declan McCullagh, "Kurzweil: Rooting for the Machine," *Wired*, 3 November 2000. Cited 6 November 2000. Online: http://www.wired.com/news/print/0,1294,39967,00.html.

92. George Dyson, *Darwin among the Machines: The Evolution of Global Intelligence* (New York: Perseus Books, 1998).

93. Neil Gross, "21 Ideas for the 21st Century," *Business Week*, 30 August 1999, 134.

94. Christopher Lasch, "Technology and Its Critics: The Degradation of the Practical Arts," in *Technological Change and the Transformation of America*, ed. Steven E. Goldberg and Charles R. Strain (Carbondale, Ill.: Southern Illinois University Press, 1987), 84.

95. Quoted in Carlos Oliveira, "Global Algorithm 1.7: The Silence of the Lambs: Paul Virilio in Conversation," trans. Patrice Riemens, *CTHEORY*, 2 September 1995, n.p. [cited 7 April 2001]. Online: http://www.ctheory.com/global/gal07.html.

96. Václav Havel, *Open Letters: Selected Writings 1965–1990*, ed. Paul Wilson (New York: Vintage Books, 1992), 153.

97. Jacques Ellul, *Presence of the Kingdom*, 2d ed. (Colorado Springs: Helmers & Howard, 1989), 87.

98. Recognizing our plight, some organizations are beginning to "de-automate" and "de-engineer" informational systems in the hopes of balancing technique with distinctly humane practices (Bernard Wysocki, "Some Firms Let Down by Costly Computers, Opt to De-Engineer," *Wall Street Journal*, 30 April 1998, pp. A1, A6). Steve Talbott says that "with our technologies in hand, we are given the freedom to construct a hellish, counter-human, machine-like society, or else a more humane society in which the machine, by being held in its place, reflects back to us our own inner powers of mastery" (Steve Talbott, "The Trouble with Ubiquitous Technology Pushers [part 2]," n.p. [cited 15 October 2001]. Online: http://www.oreilly.com/~stevet/netfuture/2000/Jan2700_101.html).

99. Quoted in "Information Explosion Takes Places in Ethical Void," *Grand Rapids (Mich.) Press*, 7 November 1999, p. A16.

Chapter 2

1. Denis Diderot, "Encyclopédie," in *Encyclopédie III*, ed. J. Lough and J. Proust (Paris: Hermann, 1976), 234–35.

2. John Willinsky, *Technologies for Knowing: A Proposal for the Human Sciences* (Boston: Beacon Press, 1999), 30.

3. Lisa Guernsey, "Seek—But on the Web, You Might Not Find," *New York Times on the Web*, 8 July 1999, n.p. [cited 12 July 1999]. Online: http://www.nytimes.com/library/tech/99/07/circuits/articles/08geek.html.

4. *The Oxford Dictionary of Modern Greek (Greek-English)*, comp. J. T. Pring (Oxford: Clarendon Press, 1965), 155.

5. Jorge Luis Borges, "The Library of Babel," *Ficciones* (New York: Grove Press, 1962), 79.

6. Ibid., 80–81, 83, 84, 86, 87.

7. "The library is the symbol of the chaos of the universe," says Jaime Alazraki. It is a "labyrinth ordered according to laws which are incomprehensible to human intelligence and which are consequently, undecipherable" (Jaime Alazraki, *Jorge Luis Borges* [New York: Columbia University Press, 1971], 12). Also see Dominic Gates, "The Library of Babel: The Dream of Cyberspace as a Universal Library," *PreText Magazine*. Cited 25 June 2001. Online: http://pretext.com/oct97/features/story1.htm; Christopher Rollason, "Borges' 'Library of Babel' and the Internet," n.p. [cited 20 June 2001]. Online: http://www.themod ernword.com/borges/borges_papers_rollason2.html; and Douglas Wolk, "Webmaster Borges," *salon.com*, 6 December 1999, n.p. [cited 20 June 2001]. Online: http://www.salon .com/books/feature/1999/12/06/borges/print.html.

8. Robert D. Hormats, "The Technologies of Freedom," *Wall Street Journal*, 22 December 1999, p. A18.

9. This is the argument of David Hall, a professor of American religious history at Harvard Divinity School. Karen J. Winkler, "How and What Did People of Past Ages Read? Researchers Encounter a Host of Scholarly Puzzles," *Chronicle of Higher Education*, 14 July 1993, p. A8.

10. Richard Saul Wurman, *Information Anxiety* (New York: Doubleday, 1989), 32.

11. Lexis Nexis Corporate Communications (corpcomm@lexisnexis.com), email to author, 22 September 2001.

12. Wurman, *Information Anxiety*, 32.

13. A company called Alexa has been trying to collect Web content and make it available online even after material has been removed by its original publishers. After the tragic events of September 11, 2001, when terrorists commandeered jet planes and steered them into the World Trade Center and the Pentagon, Alexa began archiving memorial Web sites, survivor registries, news articles and government materials about the topic. By October 11, 2001, the site already included five terabytes of information. "Internet Archive Wayback Machine: World Trade Center–Pentagon Terrorists Attacks, 2001," n.p. [cited 22 October 2001]. Online: http://web.archive.org.

14. Gilder, *Telecosm*, 2.

15. Ibid., 73.

16. Eugene H. Peterson, *Subversive Spirituality* (Grand Rapids: Eerdmans, 1997), 163.

17. Gilder, *Telecosm*, 263, 2, 3, 4, 264.

18. George Gilder, *Microcosm: The Quantum Revolution in Economics and Technology* (New York: Simon & Schuster, 1989), 17.

19. George Gilder, quoted in "Briefings: Quick Tips to Help You Use Schwab More Effectively," *On Investing*, fall 2000, 62.

20. Gilder, *Telecosm*, 261.

21. Ibid., 263. Dinesh D'Souza sees informational abundance as the result of the social value inherent in capitalism. In his view, capitalism best advances society by rewarding people who truly serve others. "Success is defined as the ability to serve the needs and desires of others," he writes, "and the most successful entrepreneurs are those who do this best. . . . More than any social type, except perhaps the clergy, the Capitalist is, in his everyday conduct, oriented to the task of helping and serving others" (Dinesh D'Souza, *The Virtue of Prosperity: Finding Values in an Age of Techno-Affluence* [New York: The Free Press, 2000], 263).

22. Andrew Piper, "The Invisible World Order," *The Atlantic Online*, 29 July 1998. Cited 23 March 2001. Online: http://www.theatlantic.com/unbound/digicult/dc980729.htm.

23. Quoted in Tara Brabazon, "He Lies like a Rug: Digitising Memory," *Media Development* 48, no. 1 (2001): 20.

24. Steven Levy, "Search for Tomorrow," *Newsweek*, 28 October 1996, 88.

25. Michele Willson, "Community in the Abstract: A Political and Ethical Dilemma?" in *Virtual Politics: Identity and Community in Cyberspace*, ed. David Holmes (London: Sage Publications, 1997), 147.

26. Rifkin, *Age of Access*, 6.

27. Orrin E. Klapp calls this a "meaning lag"—a rapid accumulation and distribution of information beyond our ability to make sense of it (Orin E. Klapp, *Essays on the Quality of Life in the Information Society* [New York: Greenwood Press, 1986], 105–15).

28. Ivan Illich, *Tools for Conviviality*, ed. Ruth Nanda Anshen (New York: Harper & Row, 1973), 9.

29. Carol Hymowitz reports in the *Wall Street Journal* about business managers who believe that the "worst casualty of this overload is time to do the deep thinking that managers need to come up with new ideas and ponder decisions." Struggling to keep up with the ongoing influx of messages, leaders have little peace and quiet for "big-picture thinking," she says (Carol Hymowitz, "Taking Time to Focus on the Big Picture Despite Flood of Data," *Wall Street Journal*, 27 February 2001, p. B1).

30. Kevin Kelly, quoted in John Brockman, *Digerati: Encounters with the Cyber Elite* (San Francisco: HardWired, 1996), 160.

31. "The End," n.p. [cited 13 June 2001]. Online: http://www.cdsusa.com/.

32. "Well now home entertainment was my baby's wish / So I hopped into town for a satellite dish / I tied it to the top of my Japanese car / I came home and I pointed it out into the stars / A message came back from the great beyond / There's fifty-seven channels and nothin' on" (Bruce Springsteen, "Human Touch," Sony, 1992).

33. Phillip J. Longman, "American Gridlock," *U.S. News & World Report*, 28 May 2001, 16, 18, 17.

34. Ibid., 18–19, 22.

35. Talbott, *Future Does Not Compute*, 11.

36. Samuel Beckett, *Waiting for Godot* (New York: Grove Press, 1954), 29.

37. T. S. Eliot, *The Complete Poems and Plays: 1909–1950* (New York: Harcourt, Brace & World, 1962), 96.

38. Madeleine L'Engle, *The Rock That Is Higher* (Wheaton: Harold Shaw, 1993), 135.

39. Amy Harmon, "The Search for Intelligent Life on the Internet," *New York Times on the Web*, 23 September 2001, n.p. [cited 24 September 2001]. Online: http:// www.nytimes.com/2001/09/23/weekinreview/23HARM.html.

40. Putnam, *Bowling Alone*, 173.

41. Terry Mattingly, "Rumors, Visions Abound," *Grand Rapids (Mich.) Press*, 13 October 2001, p. B4.

42. Houston, *I Believe in the Creator*, 161.

43. Walter Benjamin, "The Work of Art in the Age of Mechanical Reproduction," in *Illuminations*, ed. Hannah Arendt (New York: Schocken Books, 1979), 217–51.

44. Darryl Brown, "We've Got Porn," *Christianity Today*, 12 June 2000, 32–33, retrieved via WilsonSelectPlus. See also Dom Serafini, "Webcasting: The New Frontier?" *Video Age International*, October 1998, 1–3.

45. Robert D. Putnam makes a similar argument particularly with regard to consumer interests. Putnam, *Bowling Alone*, 177.

46. Andrew L. Shapiro makes a strong case for the ways that the Internet, in particular, is fragmenting our common, public lives and even eclipsing our sense of the need for such a public life (Andrew L. Shapiro, *The Control Revolution: How the Internet Is Putting*

Individuals in Charge and Changing the World We Know [New York: PublicAffairs, 1999]). Also see Cass Sunstein, *republic.com* (Princeton, N.J.: Princeton University Press, 2001).

47. St. Anselm, "Meditation on Human Redemption," *Anselm of Canterbury: Volume One*, ed. and trans. Jasper Hopkins and Herbert Richardson (Toronto: The Edwin Mellen Press, 1974), 137.

48. Václav Havel, *Letters to Olga: June 1979–September 1982*, trans. Paul Wilson (New York: Henry Holt and Company, 1989), 8–9.

49. James W. Carey calls *Letters to Olga* "one of the great political documents of our time." He also cites Stanislaw Baranczak, who says that the book is one of the "great articulations of human freedom" (James W. Carey, "A Republic: If You Can Keep It," in *James Carey: A Critical Reader*, ed. Eve Stryker Munson and Catherine A. Warren (Minneapolis: University of Minnesota Press, 1997), 213.

50. Peter Steiner, *New Yorker*, 5 July 1993, 61.

51. I am not equating "shared understanding" with "agreement." We ought not to confuse the moral obligation to strive for mutual understanding with another moral obligation to respect the persons with whom we disagree. Democratic discourse is premised on both the value of opposing ideas and the value of dialogue as a means to understanding such ideas even if we do not hold them ourselves.

52. Mike France, "Journalism's Online Credibility Gap," *Business Week*, 11 October 1999, 122.

53. Wolff, *Burn Rate*, 253.

54. Peterson, *Subversive Spirituality*, 178.

55. Janet H. Murray, *Hamlet on the Holodeck: The Future of Narrative in Cyberspace* (New York: The Free Press, 1997), 274–75. The medium, she says, is the "most capacious ever invented," enabling us to "move around the narrative world, shifting from one perspective to another one at our own initiative" (283).

56. Richard A. Lanham, *The Electronic Word: Democracy, Technology, and the Arts* (Chicago: University of Chicago Press, 1993), 133.

57. Castells, *Rise of the Network Society*, 476.

58. For an examination of American temporariness, see William Leach, *A Country of Exiles: The Destruction of Place in America* (New York: Pantheon, 1999). Thomas S. Valovic argues that impermanence and immediacy become values to cultivate, creating a culture marked by a "sense of permanent impermanence" (Valovic, *Digital Mythologies*, 61).

59. C. A. Bowers, *Educating for an Ecologically Sustainable Culture: Rethinking Moral Education, Creativity, Intelligence, and Other Modern Orthodoxies* (New York: State University of New York Press, 1995), 27.

60. Jakob Nielsen, "Usability Makes the Web Click," interview by Katherine Mieszkowski, *Fast Company*, October 1998, 56.

61. Linton Weeks, "The No-Book Report: Skim It and Weep," *Washington Post*, 14 May 2001, C01. Cited 15 May 2001. Online: http://washingtonpost.com/ac2/wp=dyn/A23370-2001May13.

62. Veronis Suhler, "Communications Industry Forecast," *Industry Spending Projections 2000–2004*, 14th edition, July 2000, 37. Cited 29 October 2001. Online: http://www.veronissuhler.com/publications/forecast/2000CIFSample.pdf.

63. *Where the Heart Is* (Los Angeles: Twentieth Century Fox, 2000), motion picture.

64. Rodney Clapp, *Border Crossings: Christian Trespasses on Popular Culture and Public Affairs* (Grand Rapids: Brazos Press, 2000), 146.

65. Pope John Paul II, *Centesimus Annus* no. 36. Cited 7 November 2001. Online: http://www.vatican.va/holy_father/john_paul_ii/encyclicals/documents/hf_jp-ii_enc_01051991_centesimus-annus_en.html.

66. NUA Internet Surveys, "How Many Online?" August 2001, n.p. [cited 7 November 2001]. Online: http://www.nua.com/surveys/how_many_online/index.html. According to Nielsen/NetRatings, the figure is actually a bit lower. See Nielsen/NetRatings, "429 Million People Worldwide Have Internet Access, According to Nielsen/NetRatings," 11 June 2001, n.p. [cited 7 November 2001]. Online: http://www.eratings.com/news/20010611.htm.

67. Brabazon, "He Lies like a Rug," 19.

68. Virilio, *Information Bomb*, 72.

69. Stoll, *High-Tech Heretic*, 143.

70. Thomas S. Valovic makes a similar argument in *Digital Mythologies*, 52–53.

71. Henry Adams, *The Education of Henry Adams*, ed. Irab Nadel (Oxford: Oxford University Press, 1999), 196.

72. Dorothy C. Bass, *Receiving the Day: Christian Practices for Opening the Gift of Time* (San Francisco: Jossey-Bass, 2001), 102.

Chapter 3

1. Elaine St. James, "(Keep It) Simple," interview by Michael Warshaw, *Fast Company*, June/July 1998, 156–59.

2. Ibid., 156.

3. John F. Kasson, "The Invention of the Past: Technology, History, and Nostalgia," in *Technological Change*, 50.

4. Eugene H. Peterson writes that "returning to Square One is not only the return to a realization of God, but also listening to what God says. God *said.* Did you listen? Do you listen? Listening is linked, not only lexically *(akouo* and *hupakouo),* but spiritually to obedience, to response" (Peterson, *Subversive Spirituality,* 23).

5. Garry Wills, *Saint Augustine* (New York: Viking, 1999), 74.

6. John Steinbeck, *Sweet Thursday* (London: Penguin Books, 2000), 22.

7. Quoted in Ruth Conway, *Choices at the Heart of Technology: A Christian Perspective* (Harrisburg, Pa.: Trinity Press, 1999), 21.

8. Greenleaf, *Servant Leadership*, 218.

9. See Nicholas Woltertorff, *Until Justice and Peace Embrace: The Kuyper Lectures for 1981 Delivered at the Free University of Amsterdam* (Grand Rapids: Eerdmans, 1983).

10. A vocation, writes novelist Frederick Buechner, "is the place where your deep gladness and the world's deep hunger meet" (Frederick Buechner, *Wishful Thinking: A Seeker's ABC* [San Francisco: HarperSanFrancisco, 1993], 119).

11. Wendell Berry, *What Are People For?* (New York: North Point Press, 1990).

12. James W. Carey, *Communication as Culture: Essays on Media and Society* (Boston: Unwin Hyman, 1989), 2.

13. One of the more compelling aspects of the Hebrew and Christian traditions, in my view, is the fact that they both affirm the "fallenness" of human beings who are incapable of knowing all truth and building heaven on earth.

14. The idea of a cyber-church, for instance, confuses messaging with community. See Steve Hewitt, "Can There Be a REAL Internet Church?" *Christian Computing Magazine,* September 1998. Cited 15 October 2001. Online: http://www.gospelcom.net/ccmag/members/articles/covr0998.shtml.

15. Jaroslav Pelikan, *The Vindication of Tradition* (New Haven: Yale University Press, 1984), 65.

16. Gross, *Past in Ruins*, 8.

17. G. K. Chesterton, *Orthodoxy: The Romance of Faith* (New York: Image Books, 1990), 48.

18. Hans-Georg Gadamer, cited in Gross, *Past in Ruins*, 106.

19. Quoted in ibid., 102.

20. Ibid., 10.

21. Dietrich Bonhoeffer, *Ethics* (New York: Macmillan, 1962), 33.

22. Roszak, *Cult of Information*, 91.

23. Steiner, *Real Presences*, 7.

24. Martin H. Krieger, *Entrepreneurial Vocations: Learning from the Callings of Augustine, Moses, Mothers, Antigone, Oedipus, and Prospero* (Atlanta: Scholars Press, 1996), 123.

25. Frederick Buechner describes wisdom as "not only a matter of the mind but of the intuition and heart, like a woman's wisdom. It is born out of suffering as a woman bears a child" (Buechner, *Whistling in the Dark*, 112).

26. Blaise Pascal, *Pensées: Thoughts on Religion and Other Subjects*, ed. H. S. Thayer, trans. William Finlayson Trotter (New York: Washington Square Press, 1965), 80.

27. See Ronald F. Thiemann, "Public Religion: Bane or Blessing for Democracy," in *Obligations of Citizenship and Demands of Faith: Religious Accommodation in Pluralist Democracies*, ed. Nancy L. Rosenblum (Princeton, N.J.: Princeton University Press, 2000), 75–76. Of course, religious fanaticism has led to untold terror and carnage through the ages, but "pure reason" without the leavening of religion has resulted in some of the worst "killing fields" in history. See William McGurn, "Holy Terror: A Critique of Pure Reason," *Wall Street Journal*, 15 October 1999, p. W17.

28. Tocqueville, *Democracy in America*, 278–79.

29. David F. Ford, *The Shape of Living: Spiritual Directions for Everyday Life* (Grand Rapids: Baker, 1997), 97.

30. Hillel Schwartz, "Beyond Tone and Decibel: The History of Noise," *Chronicle of Higher Education*, 9 January 1998, p. B8.

31. Putnam, *Bowling Alone*, 174.

32. Houston, *I Believe in the Creator*, 124.

33. Thomas Merton, *A Vow of Conversation: Journals 1964–1965*, ed. Naomi Burton Stone (New York: Farrar, Straus & Giroux, 1988), 51.

34. Anthony de Mello, *Taking Flight* (New York: Doubleday Image Books, 1988), 27. The same concept is usually attributed to Quakerism.

35. Havel, *Open Letters*, 235.

36. Peterson, *Subversive Spirituality*, 23.

37. Esther de Waal, *A Life Giving Way: A Commentary on the Rule of St. Benedict* (Collegeville, Minn.: The Liturgical Press, 1995), 48.

38. Thomas Merton says, "The truth is formed in silence and work and suffering, with which we *become* true. But we interfere with God's work by talking too much about ourselves—even telling Him what we ought to do—advising Him how to make us perfect and listening for His voice to answer us with approval" (Patrick Hart and Jonathan Montaldo, eds., *The Intimate Merton: His Life from His Journals* [San Francisco: HarperSanFrancisco, 1999], 106).

39. Nicholas Wolterstorff, *Divine Discourse* (Cambridge: Cambridge University Press, 1995).

40. Robert Coles, *The Secular Mind* (Princeton, N.J.: Princeton University Press, 1999), 4.

41. Solzhenitsyn, *A World Split Apart*, 51.

42. Walker Percy, *The Message in the Bottle: How Queer Man Is, How Queer Language Is, and What One Has to Do with the Other* (New York: Picador USA, 2000), 242.

43. Elshtain, *Who Are We?* 4.

44. Alasdair MacIntyre, *After Virtue: A Study in Moral Theory* (Notre Dame: University of Notre Dame Press, 1984), 219.

45. Roszak, *Cult of Information*, 97.

46. Cornel West, *The Cornel West Reader* (Washington, D.C.: Basic Books, 1999), 295.

47. David Gross, *Lost Time: On Remembering and Forgetting in Late Modern Culture* (Boston: University of Massachusetts Press, 2000).

48. Houston, *Heart's Desire,* 22. St. Augustine found the three vital aspects of human beings to be memory, intellect, and will. He found parallels between these and the three parts of the Trinity. Wills, *Saint Augustine,* 97.

49. Pascal, *Pensées,* 107.

50. It is interesting to note that the hymn sung at funerals in the Eastern Orthodox tradition is "Memory Eternal," reminding all believers of their hope to be held in the memory of the Holy Trinity.

51. See Tom Standage, *The Victorian Internet: The Remarkable Story of the Telegraph and the 19th Century's Online Pioneer* (New York: Penguin Putnam, 1999).

52. Peterson, *Subversive Spirituality,* 154.

53. Ibid., 154–55.

54. Eugene H. Peterson, *Christ Plays in Ten Thousand Places: The 1998 J. J. Thiessen Lectures* (Winnipeg: CMBC Publications, 1999), 51.

55. Havel, *Art of the Impossible,* 137.

56. Søren Kierkegaard, *Provocations: Spiritual Writings of Kierkegaard,* ed. Charles E. Moore (Farmington, Pa.: The Plough Publishing House, 1999), 394.

57. For a more in-depth discussion of institutional caring, see Greenleaf, *Servant Leadership,* 243.

58. Vinoth Ramachandra, *Science and Technology in Christian Perspective* (Singapore: Graduates' Christian Fellowship, 1991), 44.

59. Illich, *Tools for Conviviality.*

60. Keith Regan, "Report: Four Web Sites Control Half of Surfing Time," *E-Commerce Times,* 4 June 2001. Cited 5 June 2001. Online: http://www.ecommercetimes.com/perl/printer/10222/.

61. Bonnie A. Nardi and Vicki L. O'Day, *Information Ecologies: Using Technology with Heart* (Cambridge: MIT Press, 2000).

62. Quoted in Max DePree, *Leading without Power: Finding Hope in Serving Community* (San Francisco: Jossey-Bass, 1997), 107.

63. James Roland, "Kat's Fight," *Manatee (Fla.) Herald Tribune,* 29 April 2001, pp. 1E, 8E.

64. MacIntyre, *After Virtue,* 218.

65. Mumford, *Transformations of Man,* 106.

66. Castells, *Rise of the Network Society,* 477.

67. Walker Percy, *Signposts in a Strange Land* (New York: Picador USA, 1991), 309.

68. Mumford, *Transformations of Man,* 108–9.

69. Dallas Willard, *The Divine Conspiracy: Rediscovering Our Hidden Life in God* (San Francisco: HarperSanFrancisco, 1966), 145.

70. Elshtain, *Who Are We?* 6.

71. Solzhenitsyn, *A World Split Apart,* 59.

Chapter 4

1. Toni Locy, "Case Raises Questions about FBI's Internal Security," *USA Today,* 21 February 2001, p. 4A.

2. Quoted in ibid.

3. Quoted in ibid.

4. Duncan Campbell, "How the Plotters Slipped US Net," *The Guardian,* 27 September 2001. Cited 25 October 2001. Online: http://www.guardian.co.uk/waronterror/story/0,1361,558371,00.html.

5. Quoted in *The 365 Stupidest Things Ever Said Page-a-Day Calendar* (New York: Workman Publishing, 1997).

6. For an explanation of how the virus destroyed files and caused other problems, see Kristen Philiposki, "How the Slimy Worm Works," *Wired*, 4 May 2000. Cited 15 October 2001. Online: http://www.wired.com/news/technology/0,1282,36129-2,00.html.

7. Mark Landler, "A Filipino Linked to 'Love Bug' Talks about His License to Hack," *New York Times on the Web*, 21 October 2000, n.p. [cited 25 October 2000]. Online: http://www.nytimes.com/2000/10/21/technology/21VIRU.html.

8. It is becoming easier and easier to write a virus. Instructions are even located online. After he turned himself in to authorities, a Dutch citizen who designed the Anna Kournikova virus said that he was not a competent programmer. Donna Howell, "Virus Writing Is Now Infectious," *Investor's Business Daily*, 20 February 2001, p. A6.

9. This fact reported by McAfee Corporation of Sunnyvale, California. Ibid.

10. Eugene Peterson, *Where Your Treasure Is* (Grand Rapids: Eerdmans, 1985), 124–25.

11. Landler, "Filipino Linked."

12. Havel, *Art of the Impossible*, 81.

13. Richard Power, "Shining Light on Cybercrime," interview by M. J. Zuckerman, *USA Today*, 23 October 2000, p. 3D.

14. Carrie Kirby, "Cyber Sleuths," *San Francisco Chronicle*, 26 February 2001, pp. B1, B3.

15. Mike France, "The Litigation Machine," *Business Week*, 29 January 2001, 117–23.

16. John Schwartz, "Chief Privacy Officers Forge Evolving Corporate Roles," *New York Times on the Web*, 12 February 2001, n.p. [cited 13 February 2001]. Online: http://partners.nytimes.com/2001/02/12technology/12PRIV.html.

17. Julie Schmidt, "High Tech Job Hopping," *USA Today Tech Report*, 21 August 1998. Cited 24 August 1998. Online: http://www.usatoday.com/life/cyber/tech/ctd317.htm.

18. Quentin Hardy, "Technology Boom Allows the Wizards of Silicon Valley Unusual Freedom," *Wall Street Journal Interactive Edition*, n.p. [cited 29 September 1998]. Online: http://interactive.wsj.com/articles/SB907021501829664000.htm.

19. Quoted in Conway, *Choices at the Heart of Technology*, 21.

20. This semi-public Web site, whose Web address is itself obscene, publishes unvarnished criticisms easily rated R if they were in the movies. Some of the language has been banned from American broadcasting. The anger boils among burned-out and misled information workers.

21. See Katie Hafner, "Lessons in the School of Cut and Paste," *New York Times*, 28 June 2001, pp. D1, D6.

22. Conlin, "Workers, Surf." See also Ariana Eunjung Cha, "Pirating of Software Rampant on Campus," *Washington Post*, 24 November 2000, p. A01. Cited 25 September 2001. Online: http://www.washingtonpost.com/ac2/wp-dyn?pagename=article&node=&contentId=A48671-2000Nov21.

23. Conlin, "Workers, Surf."

24. "Silence Is Golden," *Newsweek*, 20 July 1998, 8.

25. Conlin, "Workers, Surf." See also Deborah Branscum, "bigbrother@the.office.com: Your Boss Can Track Every Click You Make," *Newsweek*, 27 April 1998, 78.

26. For a report on employers monitoring employees' email, see Lisa Guernsey, "You've Got Inappropriate Mail," *New York Times*, 5 April 2000, pp. C1, C10.

27. Conlin, "Workers, Surf."

28. See also John Yaukey, "Firms Crack Down on E-mail," *USA Today Online*, 28 June 2000, n.p. [cited 20 September 2001]. Online: http://www.usatoday.com/life/cyber/tech/cti164.htm.

29. Conlin, "Workers, Surf."

30. Within the hacker community, however, damage and fraud are not acceptable practices. Hackers often help to catch crackers. Brendan I. Koerner, "Who Are Hackers, Anyway?" *U.S. News & World Report,* 14 June 1999, 53.

31. For more information on the hacker ethic, see Stephen Levy, *Hackers: Heroes of the Computer Revolution* (New York: Doubleday, 1984); and Douglas Thomas, "Finding a New Term: From 'Hacking' to 'Cybercrime,'" *Online Journalism Review,* 22 February 2000, n.p. [cited 24 September 2001]. Online: http://ojr.usc.edu/content/story.cfm?request=335.

32. Bernard Wysocki Jr., "Companies Let Down by Computers Opt to 'De-Engineer' after Clashes," *Wall Street Journal,* 30 April 1998, pp. A1, A6.

33. Jayson Blair, "Billions Will Be Spent on Replacing Technology," *New York Times on the Web,* n.p. [cited 20 September 2001]. Online: http://www.nytimes.com/2001/09/20/nyregion/20COMP.html.

34. It takes about 700 chemical compounds to make a computer and nearly half of them are hazardous. Santa Clara County in California has over 150 groundwater contamination sites and more so-called Superfund sites than any other U.S. county. From 1986 to 1997, the domestic production of printing and writing paper rose by one-third. In the United States, we "retire" some twenty million computers annually, one in six of which ends up in landfills. Massachusetts estimates that by 1999 discarded televisions and computers already accounted for 75,000 tons of waste per year. B. J. Bergman, "The Hidden Life of Computers," *Sierra* 84, no. 4 (July/August 1999): 32–33, retrieved via Wilson SelectPlus.

35. Examining the role of new technologies in industrial production, Jeffrey Madrick concludes, "For all this Jeffersonian appeal, however, flexible production and distribution have not yet produced the gigantic gains in productivity that mass production provided when it was first adopted" (Jeffrey Madrick, *The End of Affluence: The Causes and Consequences of America's Economic Dilemma* [New York: Random House, 1997], 102). See also Andrew Leonard, "Do Computers Boost Productivity?" *Salon.com,* n.p. [cited 26 September 2001]. Online: http://www.salon.com/21st/feature/1998/04/24feature.html.

36. "Your Call Cannot Be Completed," *U.S. News & World Report,* 10 February 1997, 4.

37. Farhad Manjoo, "Paper Still Rules Paperless World," *Wired,* 23 October 2001. Cited 24 October 2001. Online: http://www.wired.com/news/print/0,1294,47785,00.html.

38. After the terrorist attacks on the World Trade Center and the Pentagon in 2001, the average weekly Web traffic to news sites from home and office computers jumped as high as 400 percent. Melinda Patterson Grenier, "Traffic to Online News Outlets Remains Higher after Attacks," *Wall Street Journal Interactive Edition,* 23 October 2001, n.p. [cited 25 October 2001]. Online: http://interactive.wfj.com/archive/retrieve.cgi?id=SB100379 0109165860720.djm. Also see Melinda Patterson Grenier, "Record Number of Office Workers Used Web Broadcasts Last Month," *Wall Street Journal Interactive Edition,* n.p. [cited 15 October 2001]. Online: http://interactive.wsj.com/archive/retrieve.cgi?id=SB1002819 156270229840.djm; and Andrea Orr, "News, Nostradamus, Knock Out Sex in Cybersearches," n.p. [cited 20 September 2001]. Online: http://news.excite.com/news/r/010919/20/net-attack-internet-dc.

39. Stephen Roach, quoted in Anthony B. Perkins and Michael C. Perkins, *The Internet Bubble: The Overvalued World of High-Tech Stocks—and What You Need to Know to Avoid the Coming Shakeout* (New York: HarperCollins, 2001), 178.

40. It appears that terrorists have accessed the Internet at public libraries to conduct their criminal endeavors. See Walter S. Mosberg, "Internet Becomes Key Topic in Fight against Terrorism," *Wall Street Journal Interactive Edition,* 4 October 2001, n.p. [cited 16 October 2001]. Online: http://ptech.wsj.com/archive/print-ptech-20011004.html.

41. Vinoth Ramachandra, *Gods That Fail: Modern Idolatry and Christian Mission* (Downers Grove, Ill.: InterVarsity Press, 1996), 112.

42. James Der Derian, "Future War: A Discussion with Paul Virilio," *Virtual Y2K*, Brown University, n.p. [cited 7 April 2001]. Online: http://www.brown.edu/Departments/Watson _Institute/programs/gs/VirtualY2K/futurewar.html.

43. Ibid.

44. Ibid.

45. This is, of course, what happened when terrorists flew jet airliners into the World Trade Center and the Pentagon. Stephen King says these "crazos" used nothing more than knives and box cutters "to keep people off balance long enough to accomplish their goals." For less than one hundred dollars' worth of "technology," these "cut-rate, low-tech, stealth guerillas" worked "under the radar of American 'intelligence'" (Stephen King, "The Weapon," *New York Times on the Web*, n.p. [cited 23 September 2001]. Online: http://www .nytimes.com/2001/09/23/magazine/23ELEMENTS.5.html).

46. Kenneth Burke, *The Rhetoric of Religion: Studies in Logology* (Berkeley: University of California Press, 1970), 273–316.

47. Ibid., 275.

48. Tom Wolfe, "Digibabble, Fairy Dust, and the Human Anthill," *Forbes ASAP*, 4 October, 1999, 218.

49. Havel, *Art of the Impossible*, 91.

50. Paulina Borsook, author of *Cyberselfish: A Critical Romp through the Terribly Libertarian Culture of High Tech*, says that the high-tech community empowers a "religion" whose main tenets are "Technology is the solution to all human problems," "The market is the true test of everything," and "Money is the highest good" (Paulina Borsook, "Silicon Values," *Christianity Today*, 6 August 2001, 42–43). My concept of the mythos of the digital sublime is adapted from James W. Carey's excellent work. See especially Carey, *Communication as Culture*, 113–41; and Robert Lewis Shayon and Nash Cox, eds., *Religion, Television, and the Information Superhighway* (Philadelphia: Waymark Press, 1994).

51. Havel, *Art of the Impossible*, 19.

52. Ibid., 30–31.

53. Ibid., 49.

54. Esther de Waal, *Living with Contradiction: Reflections on the Rule of St. Benedict* (San Francisco: HarperSanFrancisco, 1989), 96.

55. C. S. Lewis, *The Abolition of Man* (Nashville: Broadman & Holman, 1996), 84.

56. Charles E. Moore, introduction to Kierkegaard, *Provocations*, xxii.

57. Ibid., 19.

58. Ibid., 399.

59. Wendell Berry, *The Unsettling of America: Culture and Agriculture* (San Francisco: Sierra Club Books, 1977), 213.

60. David Lyon, *The Silicon Society* (Grand Rapids: Eerdmans, 1986), 117.

61. Tampering with computers for a cause, called "hackivism," is becoming more common. Donna Howell, "Virus Writing Is Now Infectious," p. A6.

62. Robert McAfee Brown, *Creative Dislocation: The Movement of Grace* (Nashville: Abingdon, 1980), 144.

63. Alison Linn, "Former 'Amazonian' Takes Hit One-Man Show on the Road," *Manatee (Fla.) Herald Tribune*, 17 April 2001, pp. D1, D7.

64. Ibid.

65. Harry Boonstra, "Can Satire Be Religious?" in *The Christian Imagination: Essays on Literature and the Arts*, ed. Leland Ryken (Grand Rapids: Baker, 1981), 235.

66. Havel, *Art of the Impossible*, 57.

67. Percy, *Signposts in a Strange Land*, 182.

68. Brown, *Creative Dislocation,* 134.

69. Ibid., 135.

70. Dave Barry, *Dave Barry in Cyberspace* (New York: Crown Publishers, 1996).

71. West, *Cornel West Reader,* 299.

72. Dennis Miller, *Ranting Again* (New York: Doubleday, 1998).

73. Lisa Guerney, "Researchers Bring Voice Recognition to Palmtops," *New York Times on the Web,* 11 October 2001, n.p. [cited 12 October 2001]. Online: http://www.nytimes.com/2001/10/11/technology/circuits/11VOIC.html.

74. Havel, *Open Letters,* 309.

75. Louise Wilson, "Cyberwar, God, and Television: Interview with Paul Virilio," *CTHEORY,* 21 October 1994, n.p. [cited 7 April 2001]. Online: http://www.ctheory.com/article/a020.html.

76. Barry, *Dave Barry in Cyberspace,* 79.

77. Miller, *Ranting Again,* 60.

78. Robert Lemos, "Should the Government Get Its Own Net?" *ZDNet News,* 11 October 2001. Cited 12 October 2001. Online: http://news.excite.com/news/zd/011011/07/should-the-government.

79. Barry, *Dave Barry in Cyberspace,* 124.

80. "Washington Flooded with E-Mail," *Reuters/CNET,* n.p. [cited 18 March 2001]. Online: http://news.cnet.com/news/0-1005-200-5173083.html?tag=lh.

81. Helen Dewar, "Lawmakers Want Their Mail Back," *Washington Post,* 28 October 2001. Cited 7 November 2001. Online: http://www.washingtonpost.com/wp-dyn/articles/A60233-2010ct27.html.

82. Donald P. McNeil, Douglas A. Morrison, and Henri J. M. Nouwen, *Compassion: A Reflection on the Christian Life* (Garden City, N.J.: Doubleday & Company, 1982), 100.

83. Scott Adams, "An Interview with Dilbert Creator: Scott Adams," interview by Becky Garrison, *The Door Magazine,* May/June 2000, 2.

84. Ibid., 4.

85. Ibid., 5.

86. He addresses this theme especially in Scott Adams, *The Dilbert Future: Thriving on Stupidity in the Twenty-first Century* (New York: HarperBusiness, 1997).

87. Houston, *I Believe in the Creator,* 219.

88. Quoted in ibid., 221.

89. Flannery O'Connor, *Mystery and Manners* (New York: Farrar, Straus & Giroux, 1969), 167.

90. Barry, *Dave Barry in Cyberspace,* 205.

91. Miller, *Ranting Again,* 61–62.

92. James W. Carey, "Afterword: The Culture in Question," in *James Carey,* 316.

93. Ibid.

94. Quoted in *"It's Not a Bug, It's a Feature!" Computer Wit and Wisdon,* compiled by David Lubar (Reading, Mass.: Addison-Wesley, 1995), 202.

95. Archbishop Charles J. Chaput, "Deus ex Machina: How to Think about Technology," *Crisis* 16 (October 1998): 19.

96. See Archbishop Charles J. Chaput, "Fools with Tools Are Still Fools," *Nuntium* (June 1998). Cited 26 October 2001. Online: http://www.archden.org/archbishop/docs/foolswithtools.htm.

Chapter 5

1. Michael Lewis, "Faking It: The Internet Revolution Has Nothing to Do with the Nasdaq," *New York Times on the Web,* 15 July 2001, n.p. [cited 18 July 2001]. Online: http://www.nytimes.com/2001/07/15/magazine/15INTERNET.html.

2. Ibid.

3. Lisa Rogak, *Pretzel Logic* (Grafton, N.H.: William Hull Publishing, 1999).

4. Sherry Turkle, *Life on the Screen* (New York: Simon & Schuster, 1997); Richard Holeton, *Composing Cyberspace: Identity, Community, and Knowledge in the Electronic Age* (Boston: McGraw Hill, 1998); and Indra Sinha and Andra Sinha, *The Cybergypsies: A True Tale of Lust, War, and Betrayal on the Electronic Frontier* (New York: Scribner, 1999).

5. Lanham, *Electronic Word*, 25.

6. Daniel Chandler, "Personal Home Pages and the Construction of Identities on the Web," 18 August 1998, n.p. [cited 23 April 2001]. Online: http://www.aber.ac.uk/media/Doc uments/short/webident.html.

7. Quoted in Bowers, *Let Them Eat Data*, 31.

8. Julia Scher, "All Me, All the Time," *Chronicle of Higher Education*, 15 December 2000, B4. Cited 21 December 2001. Online: http://chronicle.com/free/v47/il6/16b00402.htm; and Paul Kaihla, "The Tao of the Net," *eCompany Now*, 6 February 2001. Cited 21 December 2001. Online: http://www.business2.com/articles/web/0,1653,9432,FF.html.

9. Quoted in Cynthia Drake, "Diary an Open Book Online," *Grand Rapids (Mich.) Press*, 29 June 2001, pp. J1, J10. Also see David D. Kirkpatrick, "Dear Internet Diary: It Rained All Day and Now I'm So Sad," *Wall Street Journal*, 24 April 1997, pp. B2, B3.

10. Davis, *Techgnosis*, 4.

11. Derrick de Kerckhove, introduction to *The Skin of Culture: Investigating the New Electronic Reality* (Toronto: Somerville House Publishing, 1995), xx.

12. Kenneth J. Gergen, *The Saturated Self: Dilemmas of Identity in Contemporary Life* (New York: Basic Books, 1991), 3.

13. Jonathan D. Salant, "Airlines Will Let You Surf on Board," *Grand Rapids (Mich.) Press*, 14 June 2001, p. A3.

14. Milan Kundera, *The Book of Laughter and Forgetting* (New York: HarperPerennial, 1999) 147.

15. Robins and Webster, *Times of Technoculture*, 62.

16. Wolfe, "Digibabble," 216.

17. James W. Carey, "Marshall McLuhan: Geneology and Legacy," *Canadian Journal of Communication* 23 (1998): 2. Cited 18 November 2000. Online: http://www.cjc-online.ca/ ~cjc/BackIssues/23.3/carey.art.html.

18. Jacques Barzun, *Teacher in America* (Indianapolis: Liberty Fund, 1981), 437.

19. James C. Cooper and Kathleen Madigan, "Are We Talking Ourselves into a Recession?" *Business Week*, 8 January 2001, 31.

20. Quoted in Ken Auletta, "The Last Sure Thing," *New Yorker*, 9 November 1998, 47.

21. Quoted in Bill Holstein, "A Chat with Andy Grove," *U.S. News & World Report*, 22 May 2000, 56.

22. Scott Stossel, "Soul of the New Economy," *The Atlantic Online: Crosscurrents*, 8 June 2000, n.p. [cited 23 March 2001]. Online: http://www.theatlantic.com/unbound/cross currents/cc2000-06-08.htm.

23. James W. Carey describes these professional communicators as "symbol brokers" who translate "the attitudes, knowledge, and concerns of one speech community into alternative but suasive and understandable terms for another community" (James W. Carey, "The Communications Revolution," in *James Carey*, 132).

24. Lanham, *Electronic Word*, 227.

25. James W. Carey, "The Chicago School and the History of Mass Communication Research," in *James Carey*, 26.

26. Of course, such technological optimism is not limited to American soil; it also emerges in other industrialized areas. For a remarkable example from France, see Pierre

Lévy, *Collective Intelligence: Mankind's Emerging World in Cyberspace* (New York: Plenum Trade, 1997).

27. Pontifical Council for Social Communications, *Aetatis Novae,* 1992, n.p. [cited 28 October 2001]. Online: http://www.vatican.va/roman_curia/pontifical_councils/pccs/doc uments/rc_pc_pccs_doc_22021992_aetatis_en.html.

28. Yourdon, *Rise and Resurrection,* 262.

29. Roszak, *Cult of Information,* 31.

30. Wills, *Saint Augustine,* 45.

31. Wolff, *Burn Rate,* 11.

32. Valovic, *Digital Mythologies,* 15, 139, 140, 142.

33. Quoted in ibid., 144.

34. Ellul, *Presence of the Kingdom,* 84. Langdon Winner uses the term *mythinformation* to refer to the "almost religious conviction that a widespread adoption of computers and communication systems along with easy access to electronic information will automatically produce a better world for human living" (Winner, *Whale and the Reactor,* 105).

35. Ramachandra, *Gods That Fail,* 112.

36. Ibid.

37. John Perry Barlow, interviewed in "After the Media Class," *New Perspectives Quarterly* 12 (spring 1995): 42.

38. Thomas S. Valovic describes the "logical disconnect at work in the stories about and descriptions of the Internet in popular media." He suggests that the media had "gotten caught up in the Internet craze" and endlessly repeated the myths. The media "seemed to be involuntarily parroting the newly minted conventional wisdom without any deeper analysis or questioning" (Valovic, *Digital Mythologies,* ix).

39. Perkins and Perkins, *Internet Bubble.*

40. Ibid., 66.

41. Ibid., 130.

42. See, for example, David Shenk, *Data Smog: Surviving the Information Glut* (San Francisco: HarperSanFrancisco, 1998); Clifford Stoll, *Silicon Snake Oil: Second Thoughts on the Information Superhighway* (New York: Doubleday, 1995); and Talbott, *Future Does Not Compute.*

43. Paul Virilio, quoted in Bruno Guisaani, "Eurobytes," *New York Times on the Web,* 9 December 1997, n.p. [cited 20 June 2001]. Online: http://www.nytimes.com/library/ cyber/euro/120997euro.html.

44. Perkins and Perkins, *Internet Bubble.*

45. Ibid., 9.

46. Anthony B. Perkins and Michael C. Perkins say that "marketing and infrastructure are the two biggest expenses for an online business." They also note that "one-third of AOL's marketing revenues came from money-losing Web companies that used the proceeds from their public stock offerings to fund their promotional efforts" (Perkins and Perkins, *Internet Bubble,* 159, 165).

47. Of course, when the dot-coms became "dot-bombs" in 2000 and 2001, the advertising agencies suffered severe revenue losses. See Stuart Elliott, "Amid Jingles and Slogans, A Sober Mood," *New York Times,* 27 July 2001, pp. C1, C6.

48. Greg Farrell, "Dot-coms Eye Superbowl," *USA Today,* 29 November 1999. Cited 25 October 2001. Online: http://www.usatoday.com/life/cyber/tech/ctg766.htm.

49. Langdon Winner writes that the "techniques of advertising have become a customary way of altering people's ends to suit the structure of available means" (Winner, *Whale and the Reactor,* 48).

50. It also appears that Wall Street analysts were less than objective in their assessments of technology companies, partly because the analysts' own firms also provided

investment banking services to some of the same technology companies. See Marcia Vickers, "The Fall of the Analyst," *Business Week*, 11 December 2000, 108–10; and Gretchen Morgenson, "How Did So Many Get It So Wrong?" *New York Times on the Web*, 31 December 2000, n.p. [cited 6 January 2001]. Online: http://www.nytimes.com/2000/12/31/business/31ANAL.html.

51. Stephen Manes, "The Age of Almost Information," *PC World*, September 1999, 308.

52. Bronson, *Nudist on the Late Shift*.

53. Wolff, *Burn Rate*, 151.

54. See Erich Luening, "Online Ad Revenues Soar," *CNET*, 7 October 1997, n.p. [cited 30 October 2001]. Online: http://news.cnet.com/news/0-1003-200-322823.html; "'97 Web Ad Revenue Estimated at $597 Million," *InternetNews.com*, 29 January 1998, n.p. [cited 30 October 2001]. Online: http://www.internetnews.com/IAR/article/0,,12_1071.html.

55. Hillary Rosen, "Testimony before the House Judiciary Committee, Subcommittee on Courts and Intellectual Property," 15 June 2000. Cited 27 June 2001. Online: http://www.house.gov/judiciary/rose0615.htm.

56. Peter G. W. Keen, "The Future of IS: Elites and Free Agents," *Computerworld*, 20 October 1997, 87.

57. John Shoch, quoted in Perkins and Perkins, *Internet Bubble*, 180.

58. Pam Alexander, quoted in Katherine Mieszowski, "The Power of Public Relations," *Fast Company*, April/May 1998, 192.

59. Kim S. Nash, "The Hype Masters," *Computerworld*, 16 November 1998, 93.

60. Jeffrey R. Young, "MIT's Media Lab, a Media Darling, Seeks Global Role and New Missions," *Chronicle of Higher Education*, 12 October 2001, pp. A41, A42, A43.

61. Such techno-optimism is particularly American. "America's national creed is optimism," declares Jeffrey Madrick (Madrick, *End of Affluence*, 93). We assume that progress is inevitable, that each generation of new technologies will improve on previous ones. So the mythos of the digital sublime is an easy sell in the United States, where we proclaim the "end of the old" and the beginning of everything that is surely revolutionary, not just new. On the rise of "endism" in the rhetoric of the mythos, see Brown and Duguid, *Social Life of Information*, 16–17, 32–33. They rightly suggest that the "myth" of information is more powerful than information itself.

62. Steve Hamm, review of *The Difference between God and Larry Ellison*, by Mike Wilson, *Business Week*, 8 December 1997, 19.

63. Ibid.

64. Quoted in Bowers, *Educating for an Ecologically Sustainable Culture*, 152.

65. Anne Kates Smith, "Trading in False Tips Exacts a Price," *U.S. News & World Report*, 3 February 2001, 40.

66. Tocqueville, *Democracy in America*, 501.

67. Quoted in Virilio, *Information Bomb*, 26.

68. Kierkegaard, *Provocations*, 395.

69. Houston, *Heart's Desire*, 107.

70. St. Francis, *The Wisdom of St. Francis and His Companions*, comp. Stephen Clissold (New York: New Directions, 1978), 25.

71. Havel, *Art of the Impossible*, 100.

72. Quoted in *Augustine of Hippo: Selected Writings*, trans. Mary T. Clark (New York: Paulist Press, 1984), 240–41.

73. Kierkegaard, *Provocations*, 318.

74. Ibid., 350.

75. Gergen, *Saturated Self*, 202.

76. Ralph Frammolino and P. J. Huffstutter, "Porn Lures Hollywood Techs, Dot-commers," *Los Angeles Times*, 23 April 2001, pp. 1A, 4A.

77. Havel, *Open Letters*, 95.

78. Ibid., 145.

79. St. Augustine, *Confessions*, trans. Henry Chadwick (Oxford: Oxford University Press, 1991), 156.

80. For an excellent summary of Augustine's views on rhetoric, see George A. Kennedy, *Classical Rhetoric and Its Christian and Secular Tradition from Ancient to Modern Times* (Chapel Hill: University of North Carolina Press, 1980), 153–60.

81. Chip Scanlan, "Hello Sweetheart, Get Me My Urban Jungle Pack!" 21 March 2001, n.p. [cited 24 April 2001]. Online: http://www.poynter.org/centerpiece/032101.htm.

82. See, for example, Jonathan Alter, "Something in the Coffee," *Newsweek*, 13 July 1998, 66.

83. Valovic, *Digital Mythologies*, 161, 61.

84. Michael Oreskes, "Navigating a Minefield," *AJR Newslink*, November 1999. Cited 4 December 1999. Online: http://ajr.newslink.org/ajroresnov99.html.

85. Harold Adams Innis, *The Bias of Communication* (Toronto: University of Toronto Press, 1981), 82.

86. Steve Lohr, "New Economy," *New York Times*, 8 October 2001, p. C3.

87. For the connection between New Age religion and cyber-rhetoric, see Christopher Ziguras, "The Technologization of the Sacred: Virtual Reality and the New Age," in *Virtual Politics: Identity and Community in Cyberspace*, ed. David Holmes (London: Sage Publications, 2000).

Chapter 6

1. Anthony Walton, "Technology versus African-Americans," *The Atlantic Monthly*, January 1999, 16, 17. Also see John T. Barber and Alice A. Tait, eds., *The Information Society and the Black Community* (Westport, Conn.: Praeger, 2001).

2. Walton, "Technology versus African-Americans," 16.

3. Quoted in "A Web Hotshot," *BusinessWeek e.biz*, 19 March 2001, 28–34.

4. Quoted in John Riha, "Media Watchdog," *World Traveler*, December 1999, 8–14, 67. In spite of all of *Brill*'s hoopla, the magazine died in the fall of 2001. Matthew Rose, "Brill's Media Empire Ends in Collapse; Will Shut Magazine, Unload Inside.com," *Wall Street Journal Interactive Edition*, n.p. [cited 16 October 2001]. Online: http://www.interactive.wsj.com/archive/retrieve.cgi?id=SB1001709655524236360.djm.

5. Michelle Jeffers and Scott Lajoie, "Unleash the Talking Heads," *Forbes ASAP*, 23 August 1999, 101.

6. Ibid., 104.

7. Ibid.

8. Anonymous, "Confessions of a Ghost," *INC*, 20th Anniversary Issue, 1999, 149–52.

9. Gil Amelio, "My Tough Luck," interview by Joseph E. Maglitta, *Computerworld*, 27 July 1998, 75–76.

10. Tia O'Brien, "One Tough Selling Job," *PC Week*, 20 January 1997, A1; Cordell Koland, "Mac Evangelist Takes Acius toward Software Promised Land," *The Business Journal* 5, no. 41 (1988): 3.

11. See Susan Gregory Thomas, Leonard Wiener, and David Brindley, "Why Bill Gates and Steve Jobs Made Up," *U.S. News & World Report*, 18 August 1997, 19–20. Sean Silverthorne, "Steve Jobs 'Interim CEO'—Now and Forever?" *ZDNet*, 16 September 1997. Cited 19 September 2001. Online: http://www.zdnet.com/zdnn/content/zdnn/0916/zdnn0002.html.

12. Even Tom Peters, coauthor of the phenomenally popular *In Search of Excellence*, eventually confessed that he had no idea what he was doing when he wrote the book and

that he even "faked the data." See Tom Peters, "Tom Peters's True Confessions," *Fast Company*, November 2001, 78.

13. Gilder claims that he is not a futurist because he is merely addressing existing technological developments, but his rhetoric is nevertheless futuristic. He imagines a future world based on his understandings of current technologies. "Futurists falter because they belittle the power of religious paradigms, deeming them either too literal or too fantastic," writes Gilder (Gilder, *Telecosm*, 3). On the contrary, I would suggest that futurists are secular religionists whose faith is in technology, progress, and sometimes individualism.

14. Ibid., 10, 11.

15. Bronson, *Nudist on the Late Shift*, 168, 183.

16. Quoted in D'Souza, *Virtue of Prosperity*, 30.

17. Quoted in Bowers, *Let Them Eat Data*, 48.

18. Quoted in Valovic, *Digital Mythologies*, 15.

19. Linton Weeks, review of *Drudge Manifesto*, by Matt Drudge, *Manatee (Fla.) Herald Tribune*, 8 October 2000, pp. 4E, 5E.

20. Jerry Useem, "Burger Flippers, Contingent Workers, Change Agents! How Yesterday's Economic Catastrophe Becomes Today's Opportunity, Courtesy of Our Ever Flexible Pundits," *Business 2.0*, December 2001, 127.

21. Berry, *Unsettling of America*, 18.

22. Harvey C. Mansfield and Delba Winthrop, introduction to Tocqueville, *Democracy in America*, lxvii.

23. Mumford, *Transformations of Man*, 114.

24. Bowers, *Let Them Eat Data*, 74.

25. Berry, *Unsettling of America*, 21.

26. Ibid.

27. Michael L. Kent, "Managerial Rhetoric as the Metaphor for the World Wide Web," *Critical Studies in Media Communication* 18 (September 2001): 3, 359–75.

28. Berry, *Unsettling of America*, 21.

29. Bowers, *Let Them Eat Data*, 106.

30. Percy, *Signposts in a Strange Land*, 210.

31. Havel, *Letters to Olga*, 224.

32. Ibid., 360–61.

33. Thomas E. Weber, "For Those Who Scoff at Internet Commerce, Here's a Hot Market," *Wall Street Journal*, 20 May 1997, pp. A1, A8.

34. Peter F. Drucker, *Post-Capitalist Society* (New York: HarperCollins, 1993).

35. Charles Handy, *The Age of Unreason* (Boston: Harvard Business School Press, 1989), 153.

36. Ibid., 154.

37. Greenleaf, *Servant Leadership*, 136.

38. Birkerts, *Gutenberg Elegies*, 194.

39. See Eric Schlosser, *Fast Food Nation: The Dark Side of the All-American Meal* (Boston: Houghton Mifflin, 2001), 67–75.

40. Jonah Goldberg, "In the Issue," *National Review Online*, 19 June 2000, n.p. [cited 5 June 2000]. Online: http://www.nationalreview.com/19jun00/goldberg/061900.html.

41. Peterson, *Subversive Spirituality*, 59.

42. Of seventy Internet executives' backgrounds checked, twenty-seven were found to have problems. Caroline Daniel, "Skeletons in Dotcom Closets," *Financial Times.com*, 23 October 2000, n.p. [cited 24 October 2000]. Online: http://news.ft.com/ft/gx.cgi/ftc?pagename=View&c=Article&ci=FT3Ke16MOED&liv.

43. Quoted in Paul O'Brian, "New Toys for Boys," online posting, *Forum* 97, n.p. [cited 25 March 2001]. Online: http://www.dmc.dit.ie/fourm97/paul.html.

44. David Hillel Gelernter, quoted in Brockman, *Digerati*, 110.

45. Quoted in ibid., 109.

46. Quoted in ibid., 106.

47. David S. Bennahum, *Extra Life: Coming of Age in Cyberspace* (New York: Basic Books, 1998), 6.

48. Jeremy Rifkin suggests that the shift from industrial production to cultural capitalism is "being accompanied by an equally significant shift from the work ethic to the play ethic." Rifkin, *Age of Access*, 7.

49. Douglas Coupland, *Microserfs* (New York: Regan Books, 1996), 311.

50. Paulina Borsook, "Cyberselfish," *Mother Jones*, July/August 1996. Cited 21 June 2001. Online: http://www.mojones.com/mother_jones/JA96/borsook.html.

51. Bill Lessard and Steve Baldwin, *NetSlaves: True Tales of Working the Web* (New York: McGraw-Hill, 2000), 6.

52. Conway, *Choices at the Heart of Technology*, 97.

53. Virilio, *Information Bomb*, 42, 104.

54. Wayne Arnold, "Rapid Spread of PCs Threatens Hierarchy of Society across Asia," *Wall Street Journal Interactive Edition*, 22 September 1998, n.p. [cited 23 September 1998]. Online: http://interactive.wsj.com/articles/SB906398289670183500.htm.

55. Brown and Duguid, *Social Life of Information*, 13–14.

56. Talbott, "The Trouble."

57. Tocqueville, *Democracy in America*, 279.

58. Ibid.

59. I am indebted here to Jean Bethke Elshtain's fine book, *Who Are We? Critical Reflections and Hopeful Possibilities*. Although she makes a case for the limitations of the market, where "*everything* is up for sale" and where we lose our sense of what it truly means to love one another, one can make the same case against the technologizing of culture and society. Elshtain, *Who Are We?* 63. Without such diversity, the cyber-world becomes what Virilio calls a form of "cybernetic colonialism," the "ultimate exemplar of monopoly" (Virilio, *Information Bomb*, 134).

60. Archbishop Charles J. Chaput, "Information Superhighway Must Not Bypass Humanity," n.p. [cited 26 October 2001]. Online: http://www.archden.org/archbishop/docs/internet.htm.

61. Kierkegaard, *Provocations*, 360–61.

62. Talbott, *Future Does Not Compute;* Borgmann, *Holding On to Reality;* and Virilio, *Information Bomb*.

63. Archbishop Charles J. Chaput, "These Things Shape the Soul" (speech delivered before the Senate Committee on Commerce, Science, and Transportation, 4 May 1999), n.p. [cited 26 October 2001]. Online: http://www.archden.org/archbishop/docs/media_vio lence.htm.

64. Berry, *Unsettling of America*, 174, 179.

65. Gross, *Past in Ruins*, 123.

66. Alfonso Gumucio-Dagron, "Is the Internet a Form of Electronic Apartheid?" *Media Development* 48, no. 1 (2001): 3.

67. Robert S. Fortner, "Excommunication in the Information Society," *Critical Studies in Mass Communication* 12, no. 2 (1995): 133–54.

68. David Gelernter, *Machine Beauty: Elegance and the Heart of Technology* (New York: Basic Books, 1998).

69. Mumford, *Transformations of Man*, 119.

70. Quoted in Kevin Maney, "Life Is an Experiment for British Tech Wiz," *USA Today*, 13 March 1997, p. 5B.

71. Peter Cochrane (petercochrane@conceptlabs.net), email to author, 25 October 2001.

72. Quoted in Richard Price, *Augustine* (Loguori: Trimumph, 1996), 28.

73. Colin E. Gunton, *The One, The Three, and the Many: God, Creation, and the Culture of Modernity: The Bampton Lectures 1992* (Cambridge: Cambridge University Press, 1993), 184.

74. Ibid.

75. Ibid.

76. Greenleaf, *Servant Leadership*, 142.

Chapter 7

1. Kundera, *Book of Laughter and Forgetting*, 11.

2. The *Chicago Tribune*, for instance, editorialized at the dawn of the twentieth century that Americans should expect "a century of humanity [bringing] a keener realization of the brotherhood of man" (Lawrence L. Knutson, "Folks in 1899 Said 20th Century Would Be Peaceful," *Grand Rapids [Mich.] Press*, 5 July 1999, p. D4).

3. Michael Dertouzos, *What Will Be: How the New World of Information Will Change Our Lives* (San Francisco: HarperSanFrancisco, 1997), 32.

4. Conway, *Choices at the Heart of Technology*, 16.

5. Willson, "Community in the Abstract," 145. See also Edward M. Hallowell, "Connectedness," in Edward M. Hallowell and Michael G. Thompson, *Finding the Heart of the Child: Essays on Children, Families, and Schools* (Washington, D.C.: National Association of Independent Schools, 1997).

6. See Kenneth L. Smith and Ira G. Zepp Jr., "Martin Luther King's Vision of the Beloved Community," *Christian Century*, 3 April 1964, 361–63.

7. Hope Lewis, "Exploring the Dark Side of Telecommuting," *Computerworld*, 12 May 1997, 37.

8. David Prescovitz, "The Company Where Everybody's a Temp," *New York Times Magazine*, 11 June 2000, 94.

9. Nicholas Negroponte, "Being Rural," *Wired*, June 1999, 14. Cited 21 June 2001. Online: http://www.wired.com/wired/archive/7.06/mustread.html?pg=14.

10. Thornton May, quoted in William M. Buckeley, "Corporate Seers," a panel discussion, *Wall Street Journal*, 16 November 1998, p. R37.

11. William J. Mitchell, *E-topia: "Urban Life, Jim—But Not as We Know It"* (Cambridge: MIT Press, 2000), 7.

12. D'Souza, *Virtue of Prosperity*, 8.

13. Dertouzos, *What Will Be*, 282.

14. Quoted in Oliveira, "Global Algorithm 1.7." Virilio also argues that we are experiencing a "global de-localization" (Virilio, *The Information Bomb*, 10).

15. Ivan Illich, *H2O and the Waters of Forgetfulness* (London: Marion Boyars, 1986), 10.

16. Quoted in "Ivan Illich with Jerry Brown," We the People, KPFA Radio, originally aired 22 March 1996, n.p. [cited 13 April 2001]. Online: http://www.wtp.org/archives/pages/ivan_illich_jerry.html.

17. Ibid.

18. Felix Stalder, "The Logic of Networks: Social Landscapes vis-à-vis the Space of Flows," review of *The Rise of the Network Society, The Information Age: Economy, Society, and Culture*, vol. 1, and *The Power of Identity, The Information Age: Economy, Society, and*

Culture, vol. 2, by Manuel Castells, *CTHEORY*, n.p. [cited 7 April 2001]. Online: http://www.ctheory.com/review/r046.html.

19. Roszak, *Cult of Information*, 62.

20. Ian Spandau, quoted in *The Industry Standard*, 29 March 1999, 10.

21. Gross, *Past in Ruins*, 27.

22. Carey, "The Chicago School," 27.

23. Tocqueville, *Democracy in America*, 403.

24. John Dewey, *The Public and Its Problems* (Athens, Ohio: Shallow Press, 1954), 218.

25. Eugene H. Peterson, *Traveling Light: Modern Meditations on St. Paul's Letter of Freedom* (Colorado Springs: Helmers & Howard, 1988), 130.

26. Frederick Buechner comments that through Jesus' parable of the Good Samaritan, neighbors are defined as "anybody who needs you" (Buechner, *Wishful Thinking*, 78).

27. Berry, *What Are People For?* 8.

28. Quoted in Bertman, *Hyperculture*, 108.

29. Robert Putnam, a professor at Harvard, quoted in "Valley Residents Network."

30. Ibid.

31. Mumford, *Transformations of Man*, 146.

32. Michele Hershberger, *A Christian View of Hospitality: Expecting Surprises* (Scottdale, Pa.: Herald Press, 1999).

33. Quoted in "Ivan Illich with Jerry Brown."

34. Putnam, *Bowling Alone*, 172.

35. James W. Carey, "Salvation by Machines," in *James Carey*, 301.

36. Stoll, *High-Tech Heretic*, 25.

37. Greenleaf, *Servant Leadership*, 39

38. Stephen Doheny-Farina, preface to *The Wired Neighborhood* (New Haven: Yale University Press, 1996), xi.

39. Greenleaf, *Servant Leadership*, 38.

40. Ford, *Shape of Living*, 95.

41. Jonathan G. S. Koppel, "No 'There' There," *The Atlantic Online*, August 2000, n.p. [cited 23 March 2001]. Online: http://www.theatlantic.com/issues/2000/08/koppell.htm.

42. Ibid.

43. Tocqueville, *Democracy in America*, 487.

44. Elshtain, *Who Are We?* 132. This kind of gradual shift in the language of community has reached many social institutions, including churches. See Hewitt, "Can There Be?"

45. Don Steinberg, "The Man with the E-Commerce Answer," *smartbusinessmag.com*, February 2001, 101.

46. Ibid., 102.

47. Ibid.

48. Stoll, *High-Tech Heretic*, 193.

49. Sarah Schafer, "E-mail Fosters Misunderstandings at the Office," *Washington Post*, 31 October 2001, p. E01. Cited 3 November 2000. Online: http://washingtonpost.com/ac2/wp-dyn/A43099-2000Oct30.

50. Cecily Berry, *The Actor and the Text* (New York: Applause Books, 1992), 10.

51. Christians, "Justice and the Global Media," 86.

52. Alasdair MacIntyre writes that "conversation, understood widely enough, is the form of human transaction in general. Conversational behavior is not a special sort or aspect of human behavior, even though the forms of language-using and of human life are such that the deeds of others speak for them as much as do their words. For that is possible only because they are the deeds of those who have words" (MacIntyre, *After Virtue*, 211).

53. Walter J. Ong, *The Presence of the Word: Some Prolegomena for Cultural and Religious History* (New Haven: Yale University Press, 1967), 115.

54. Ibid., 125.

55. Ibid.

56. Ibid., 126.

57. Stoll, *High-Tech Heretic*, 92–93.

58. For a further discussion of the necessary relationship between the created and Creator, see Houston, *I Believe in the Creator*, 130–31.

59. The only advantage of email firings, admits one management consultant, is that it "gives management an opportunity to duck and dodge angry employees" (Stephanie Armour, "E-mail Lets Companies Deliver Bad News from Afar," *USA Today*, 20 February 2001, p. 6A).

60. Ellen Ullman, "Elegance and Entropy: Ellen Ullman Talks about What Makes Programmers Tick," interview by Scott Rosenberg, n.p. [cited 25 March 2001]. Online: http://www.salon.com/21st/feature/1997/10/09interview.html.

61. Houston, *I Believe in the Creator*, 310.

62. David Lyon also addresses these two themes in *Jesus in Disneyland: Religion in Postmodern Times* (Cambridge: Polity Press, 2000), 133–35.

63. Ong, *Presence of the Word*, 315.

64. Berry, *What Are People For?* 157.

65. John L. Locke, *The De-Voicing of Society: Why We Don't Talk to Each Other Anymore* (New York: Simon & Schuster, 1998). Also see Wurman, *Information Anxiety*, 89.

66. Michael Heim, *The Metaphysics of Virtual Reality* (New York: Oxford University Press, 1993), 100.

67. Edward M. Hallowell, "What Do You Want for Your Children?" in *Finding the Heart*, 175.

68. Margaret MacLean, *Time and Bits: Managing Digital Continuity* (Los Angeles: Getty Trust Publishing, 2000).

69. Havel, *Art of the Impossible*, 127.

70. Shapiro, *Control Revolution*, 9, 10–11.

71. Gross, *Past in Ruins*, 106.

72. Putnam, *Bowling Alone*, 176.

73. C. A. Bowers, "The Paradox of Technology: What's Gained and Lost?" *Thought and Action* 14, no.1 (spring 1998): 52–53.

74. Roemer, *Telling Stories*, 357.

75. Ed Krol, "An Early Chronicler of the Internet Reflects on a Decade of Growth," interview by Stephen C. Miller, *New York Times*, 9 December 1999, p. D14.

76. Francis Fukuyama, "The Great Disruption: Human Nature and the Reconstitution of Social Order," *The Atlantic Monthly*, May 1999, 59.

77. Amy Jo Kim, quoted in Mark Glaser, "Take Your Site beyond Content: Construct a Society on the Web," *New Media*, 3 March 1997, 37.

78. Paul Holt, "E-commerce's Toy Story," *Communications News*, July 1998, 35.

79. Jeff Shuman, letter to the editor, *Business 2.0*, 1 May 2001, 20.

80. Quoted in Thomas J. Peters, *The Tom Peters Seminar: Crazy Times Call for Crazy Organizations* (New York: Vintage Books, 1994), 257.

81. Lawrence Lessig argues that without public regulation, the technical structure of the Internet will one day be a platform for little more than effective commerce. Perhaps he is correct, but it is also possible that the technological nature of cyberspace is intrinsically individualistic and instrumental (Lawrence Lessig, *Code and Other Laws of Cyberspace* [New York: Basic Books, 2000]).

82. Bill Gates, interviewed in "After the Media Class," *New Perspectives Quarterly* 12 (spring 1995): 51.

83. Diane Brady, "Why Service Stinks," *Business Week,* 23 October 2000, 118–28.

84. Already some Web shoppers are getting weary of online companies' attempts to control their cyber-habits. See Erika Morphy, "Report: Web Shoppers Desensitized to Marketing," *E-Commerce Times,* 10 October 2001. Cited 12 October 2001. Online: http://www.ecommercetimes.com/perl/story/14052.html.

85. Peter L. Berger, *The Heretical Imperative* (New York: Doubleday, 1979).

86. Rifkin, *Age of Access,* 97.

87. Lesslie Newbigin, *Truth to Tell: The Gospel as Public Truth* (Grand Rapids: Eerdmans, 1991), 76.

88. Solzhenitsyn, *A World Split Apart,* 59.

89. Sunstein, *republic.com,* 201. For a sense of the existing range of cyber-special interests, see David Bell and Barbara M. Kennedy, eds., *The Cybercultures Reader* (London: Routledge, 2000).

90. Peterson, *Subversive Spirituality,* 179.

91. Ibid., 178.

92. Berry, *What Are People For?* 155.

93. Chaput, "Deus ex Machina," 20.

94. A study conducted at the UCLA Center for Communication Policy, for instance, concluded that Internet use enhances rather than detracts from social life. But the study merely asked respondents to report the quantity of their online communication with friends, family, colleagues, and the like. It did not address the quality of these relationships—their depth and richness. Moreover, the data indicated that Internet users report greater life dissatisfaction, interaction anxiety, powerlessness, and loneliness (Harlan Lebo, *The UCLA Internet Report: Surveying the Digital Future* [Los Angeles: UC Regents, 2000]).

95. Martin E. Marty, *By Way of Response* (Nashville: Abingdon, 1981), 72.

96. Paul Tournier, *The Meaning of Persons* (New York: Harper & Row, 1973), 131.

97. Elshtain, *Who Are We?* 128.

Chapter 8

1. James Stevenson, *New Yorker,* 31 January 2000, 58.

2. In response to *The Fifth Generation,* a book that advocated technicism as the means of bringing about a great new world of intellectuals, James W. Carey writes, "It is not merely the arrogance of such an argument that is offensive; the book as a whole contains no telos, no end in view, no sense of what this technology is supposed to achieve beyond mere survival. What is this new world the computer will bring about? What is so desirable about it? What aspects of a valuable way of life will it preserve? What aspects will it extinguish? Alas, on this subject the technologists are silent, even the claims made on behalf of high technology and computers are silent" (James W. Carey, "Salvation by Machines: Can Technology Save Education?" in *James Carey,* 296).

3. Quoted in Coles, *Secular Mind,* 6.

4. Virilio, *Information Bomb,* 38.

5. Wolff, *Burn Rate,* 134.

6. Birkerts, *Gutenberg Elegies,* 21.

7. Steiner, *Real Presences,* 24.

8. Kierkegaard, *Provocations,* 312.

9. Borgmann, *Holding On to Reality,* 208.

10. Ellul, *Presence of the Kingdom,* 83.

11. Solzhenitsyn, *A World Split Apart,* 25.

12. Percy, *Message in the Bottle*, 25.

13. Berry, *What Are People For?* 172.

14. Ivan Illich, *In the Vineyard of the Text: A Commentary to Hugh's Didascaliocon* (Chicago: University of Chicago Press, 1993), 118.

15. "Free Ride on Internet Could Come to Screeching Halt," *Manatee (Fla.) Herald Tribune*, 18 March 2001, p. 6A.

16. Quoted in Dor Jones Yang, "New Tolls on the Info Highway," *U.S. News & World Report*, 9 April 2001, 44.

17. Paul Virilio, "Speed and Information: Cyberspace Alarm!" *CTHEORY*, n.p. [cited 7 April 2001]. Online: http://www.ctheory.com/article/a030.html.

18. Winner, *Whale and the Reactor*, 29.

19. Wolfe, "Digibabble," 218.

20. Borgmann, *Holding On to Reality*, 215

21. Wills, *Saint Augustine*, 25.

22. Quoted in Chaput, "Deus ex Machina," 19.

23. Berry, *What Are People For?* 175.

24. Ibid.

25. Louise Wilson, "Cyberwar, God, and Television: Interview with Paul Virilio," *CTHEORY*, 21 October 1994, n.p. [cited 7 April 2001]. Online: http://www.ctheory.com/article/a020.html/.

26. Eugene H. Peterson, *Under the Unpredictable Plant: An Exploration in Vocational Holiness* (Grand Rapids: Eerdmans, 1992), 144.

27. Carl Mitcham, *Thinking through Technology: The Path between Engineering and Philosophy* (Chicago: University of Chicago Press, 1994), 129.

28. Thomas Frank reveals in *One Market, Under God* how the rhetoric of the New Economy became faith. Frank argues that the New Economy is described as a bubble and synonymous with "faith" and "cosmos." When the bubble bursts, it is not just a loss of profit, it is a "loss of faith." Quoted in Molly Ivins, "Profits Aren't Everything," *Manatee (Fla.) Herald Tribune*, 16 March 2001, p. 11A.

29. Havel, *Letters to Olga*, 375.

30. Valovic, *Digital Mythologies*, 210.

31. "Without religious commitment," claims George Gilder, "new ideas cannot take flight and flourish, new technology cannot be projected into untilled markets, and new systems cannot be built" (George Gilder, "The Faith of a Futurist," *Wall Street Journal Interactive Edition*, 1 January 2000, n.p. [cited 31 December 1999]. Online: http://interactive.wsj.com/archive/retrieve.cgi?id=SB44523888324958741.djm). Gilder fails to point out that without religious commitment, technology could also unravel the moral fabric of our lives.

32. Paul F. Camenisch concludes that "one of the major conditions for such resistance and redirection is the existence of a community which perceives in technology significant disvalue, and whose shared values provide it with a place to stand as it tries to limit or redirect technology" (Paul F. Camenisch, "Medical Technologies and Communities of Value," in *Technological Change*, 128–29).

33. Mumford, *Transformations of Man*, 112.

34. Certainly consumer capitalism and media technologies have weakened tradition. These ideas begin with a remark by Carl Hovland in Carey, "The Chicago School," 26.

35. Winner says that it is the "tendency of large, centralized, hierarchically arranged sociotechnical entities to crowd out and eliminate the varieties of human activity" (Winner, *Whale and the Reactor*, 48). Today, information technology threatens to co-opt all noninstrumental and nontechnical human pursuits, including religion.

36. Gross, *Past in Ruins*, 88.

37. Quoted in Der Derian, "Future War."

38. John Huey, "Waking Up to the New Economy," *Fortune,* 27 June 1994, 36.

39. Lewis, *Abolition of Man,* 68.

40. Ellul, *Presence of the Kingdom,* 87.

41. Peterson, *Under the Predictable Plant,* 112.

42. Houston, *I Believe in the Creator,* 161.

43. Ibid.

44. Thomas W. Cooper, "Plain Speaking in a World of Suspect Communication Technologies," *Media Development* 48, no. 1 (2001): 26–29.

45. Berry, *Unsettling of America,* 212. Rheingold rightly discovers that the Amish are not anti-technological. They want to make sure that their technological practices will make them good persons who live in good communities (Howard Rheingold, "Look Who's Talking," *Wired,* January 1999, 128–31, 160–63). Also see Jamie Sharp, "The Amish: Technology Practice and Technological Change," n.p. [cited 24 May 2001]. Online: http://www.loyola.edu/dept/philosophy/techne/sharp.html.

46. "Living a Tradition," *Smithsonian Journeys,* April 2001. Cited 9 April 2001. Online: http://www.smithsonianmag.si.edu/journeys/01/apr01/9feature_full_page_6.html.

47. Isaac C. Rottenberg suggests that the postmodern age is not post-religious or post-pagan. Instead, it seeks to follow new, humanly devised gods and paganisms, including a "neo-pagan glorification of the less-than-rational impulses of the human heart" (Isaac C. Rottenberg, "The Body of Christ and the Embodiment of Christianity," *Perspectives,* May 2001, 12).

48. Quoted in Walter Isaacson, "In Search of the Real Bill Gates," *Time,* 13 January 1997, 51.

49. Alistair I. McFadyen, *The Call to Personhood: A Christian Theory of the Individual in Social Relationships* (Cambridge: Cambridge University Press, 1990), 63.

50. Eugene H. Peterson, *The Wisdom of Each Other: A Conversation between Spiritual Friends* (Grand Rapids: Zondervan, 1998), 43.

51. Ford, *The Shape of Living,* 62.

52. Suzanne G. Farnham, Joseph P. Gill, R. Taylor McLean, and Susan M. Ward, *Hearts: Discerning Call in Community* (Harrisburg, Pa.: Morehouse Publishing, 1991), 17.

53. Berry, *Unsettling of America,* 222.

54. Krieger, *Entrepreneurial Vocations,* xiv.

55. Ibid.

56. Ramachandra, *Gods That Fail,* 128.

57. "Ivan Illich with Jerry Brown."

58. Ibid.

59. Lewis, "The Inner Ring," 65.

60. Martin Buber, *I and Thou,* trans. Walter Kaufmann (New York: Charles Scribner's Sons, 1970).

61. "Ivan Illich with Jerry Brown."

62. Marva J. Dawn, *Keeping the Sabbath Wholly: Ceasing, Resting, Embracing, Feasting* (Grand Rapids: Eerdmans, 1989), 123.

63. Ibid.

64. Houston, *Heart's Desire,* 94.

65. Ibid.

66. Brittanica.com notes that he died sometime before 431; the exact year is not known. "Palladius," *Brittanica.com,* n.p. [cited 21 September 2001]. Online: http://www.britannica.com/eb/article?eu=59577&tocid=0&query=palladius.

67. Quoted in Houston, *Heart's Desire,* 191.

68. Ibid., 198.

69. Richard J. Mouw, *When the Kings Come Marching In: Isaiah and the New Jerusalem* (Grand Rapids: Eerdmans, 1983).

70. Bellah and his colleagues write, "Communities . . . have a history—in an important sense they are constituted by their past" (Robert Bellah, Richard Madsen, William M. Sullivan, Ann Swidler, and Steven M. Tipton, *Habits of the Heart: Individualism and Commitment in American Life* [Berkeley: University of California Press, 1996], 153).

71. MacIntyre, *After Virtue*, 221.

72. Ibid., 261.

73. Bellah et al., *Habits of the Heart*.

74. Tocqueville, *Democracy in America*, 489.

75. Ibid., 502.

76. "Dumped Dot-Commers Start Out All Over Again," *USA Today*, 15 March 2001, p. A1.

77. Joseph Sittler, *The Ecology of Faith* (Philadelphia: Muhlenberg Press, 1961), 24.

78. Emil Brunner, *The Divine Imperative: A Study in Christian Ethics* (Philadelphia: Westminster Press, 1949), 249.

79. Borgmann writes that the sheer abundance and disposable nature of information in this age causes the information itself to lose its bearing on reality (Borgmann, *Holding On to Reality*, 211).

80. Illich, *In the Vineyard of the Text*, 23.

81. Havel writes about *The Mountain Hotel* in Havel, *Letters to Olga*, 171.

82. Ibid., 55.

83. Solzhenitsyn, *A World Split Apart*, 61.

84. Václav Havel, *Disturbing the Peace: A Conversation with Karel Hvížďala*, trans. Paul Wilson (New York: Vintage Books, 1990), 111.

85. John Lukacs, *Confessions of an Original Sinner* (South Bend, Ind.: St. Augustine's Press, 2000), 193.

Select Bibliography

Bass, Dorothy C. *Receiving the Day: Christian Practices for Opening the Gift of Time.* San Francisco: Jossey-Bass, 2001.

Bellah, Robert, Richard Madsen, William M. Sullivan, Ann Swidler, and Steven M. Tipton. *Habits of the Heart: Individualism and Commitment in American Life.* Berkeley: University of California Press, 1996.

Beniger, James R. *The Control Revolution: Technological and Economic Origins of the Information Society.* Cambridge: Harvard University Press, 1990.

Berry, Wendell. *The Unsettling of America: Culture and Agriculture.* San Francisco: Sierra Club Books, 1977.

Bertman, Stephen. *Cultural Amnesia: America's Future and the Crisis of Memory.* Westport, Conn.: Praeger, 2000.

———. *Hyperculture: The Human Cost of Speed.* Westport, Conn.: Praeger, 1998.

Birkerts, Sven. *The Gutenberg Elegies: The Fate of Reading in an Electronic Age.* New York: Fawcett Columbine, 1994.

Boorstin, Daniel J. *The Americans: The Democratic Experience.* New York: Vintage Books, 1973.

Borgmann, Albert. *Holding On to Reality: The Nature of Information at the Turn of the Millennium.* Chicago: University of Chicago Press, 1999.

———. *Technology and the Character of Contemporary Life: A Philosophical Inquiry.* Chicago: University of Chicago Press, 1984.

Borsook, Paulina. *Cyberselfish: A Critical Romp through the Terribly Libertarian Culture of High Tech.* New York: PublicAffairs LLC, 2000.

Bowers, C. A. *Educating for an Ecologically Sustainable Culture: Rethinking Moral Education, Creativity, Intelligence, and Other Modern Orthodoxies.* New York: State University of New York Press, 1995.

———. *Let Them Eat Data: How Computers Affect Education, Cultural Diversity, and the Prospects of Ecological Sustainability.* Athens, Ga.: University of Georgia Press, 2000.

241

Brockman, John. *Digerati: Encounters with the Cyber Elite*. San Francisco: HardWired, 1996.

Bronson, Po. *The Nudist on the Late Shift: And Other True Tales of Silicon Valley*. New York: Broadway Books, 1999.

Brown, John Seely, and Paul Duguid. *The Social Life of Information*. Boston: Harvard Business School Press, 2000.

Brown, Robert McAfee. *Creative Dislocation: The Movement of Grace*. Nashville: Abingdon, 1980.

Burke, Kenneth. *The Rhetoric of Religion: Studies in Logology*. Berkeley: University of California Press, 1970.

Carey, James W. *Communication as Culture: Essays on Media and Society*. Boston: Unwin Hyman, 1989.

———. *James Carey: A Critical Reader*. Edited by Eve Stryker Munson and Catherine A. Warren. Minneapolis: University of Minnesota Press, 1997.

Castells, Manuel. *The Rise of the Network Society*. Malden, Mass.: Blackwell Publishers, 1996.

Coles, Robert. *The Secular Mind*. Princeton, N.J.: Princeton University Press, 1999.

Conway, Ruth. *Choices at the Heart of Technology: A Christian Perspective*. Harrisburg, Pa.: Trinity Press, 1999.

Coupland, Douglas. *Microserfs*. New York: Regan Books, 1996.

Davis, Erik. *Techgnosis: Myth, Magic + Mysticism in the Age of Information*. New York: Harmony Books, 1998.

Dawn, Marva J. *Keeping the Sabbath Wholly: Ceasing, Resting, Embracing, Feasting*. Grand Rapids: Eerdmans, 1989.

Dewey, John. *The Public and Its Problems*. Athens, Ohio: Shallow Press, 1954.

D'Souza, Dinesh. *The Virtue of Prosperity: Finding Values in an Age of Techno-Affluence*. New York: The Free Press, 2000.

Ellul, Jacques. *The Presence of the Kingdom*. 2d ed. Colorado Springs: Helmers & Howard, 1989.

Elshtain, Jean Bethke. *Who Are We? Critical Reflections and Hopeful Possibilities*. Grand Rapids: Eerdmans, 2000.

Ford, David F. *The Shape of Living: Spiritual Directions for Everyday Life*. Grand Rapids: Baker, 1997.

Gaillardetz, Richard R. *Transforming Our Days: Spirituality, Community, and Liturgy in a Technological Culture*. New York: The Crossroad Publishing Company, 2000.

Gay, Craig M. *The Way of the (Modern) World: Or, Why It's Tempting to Live as If God Doesn't Exist.* Grand Rapids: Eerdmans, 1998.

Gelernter, David Hillel. *Machine Beauty: Elegance and the Heart of Technology.* New York: Basic Books, 1998.

Gergen, Kenneth J. *The Saturated Self: Dilemmas of Identity in Contemporary Life.* New York: Basic Books, 1991.

Gilder, George. *Telecosm: How Infinite Bandwidth Will Revolutionize Our World.* New York: The Free Press, 2000.

Groothuis, Douglas. *The Soul in Cyberspace.* Grand Rapids: Baker, 1997.

Gross, David. *Lost Time: On Remembering and Forgetting in Late Modern Culture.* Boston: University of Massachusetts Press, 2000.

―――. *The Past in Ruins: Tradition and the Critique of Modernity.* Amherst, Mass.: University of Massachusetts Press, 1992.

Gunton, Colin E. *The One, The Three, and the Many: God, Creation, and the Culture of Modernity: The Bampton Lectures 1992.* Cambridge: Cambridge University Press, 1993.

Hamelink, Cees J. *The Ethics of Cyberspace.* London: Sage Publications, 2000.

Handy, Charles. *The Age of Unreason.* Boston: Harvard Business School Press, 1989.

Havel, Václav. *The Art of the Impossible: Politics as Morality in Practice, Speeches, and Writings, 1990–1996.* Translated by Paul Wilson. New York: Fromm International, 1998.

―――. *Letters to Olga: June 1979–September 1982.* Translated by Paul Wilson. New York: Henry Holt and Company, 1989.

―――. *Open Letters: Selected Writings 1965–1990.* Edited by Paul Wilson. New York: Vintage Books, 1992.

Heim, Michael. *The Metaphysics of Virtual Reality.* New York: Oxford University Press, 1993.

Hershberger, Michele. *A Christian View of Hospitality: Expecting Surprises.* Scottdale, Pa.: Herald Press, 1999.

Holeton, Richard. *Composing Cyberspace: Identity, Community, and Knowledge in the Electronic Age.* Boston: McGraw Hill, 1998.

Houston, James M. *The Heart's Desire: Satisfying the Hunger of the Soul.* Colorado Springs: NavPress, 1996.

―――. *I Believe in the Creator.* Grand Rapids: Eerdmans, 1980.

Illich, Ivan. *Tools for Conviviality.* Edited by Ruth Nanda Anshen. New York: Harper & Row, 1973.

————. *In the Vineyard of the Text: A Commentary to Hugh's Didascalio-con.* Chicago: University of Chicago Press, 1993.

Innis, Harold A. *The Bias of Communication.* Toronto: University of Toronto Press, 1981.

————. *Empire and Communications.* Revised by Mary Q. Innis. Toronto: University of Toronto Press, 1972.

Kerckhove, Derrick de. *The Skin of Culture: Investigating the New Electronic Reality.* Toronto: Somerville House Publishing, 1995.

Kierkegaard, Søren. *Provocations: Spiritual Writings of Kierkegaard.* Edited by Charles E. Moore. Farmington, Pa.: The Plough Publishing House, 1999.

Klapp, Orin E. *Essays on the Quality of Life in the Information Society.* New York: Greenwood Press, 1986.

Krieger, Martin H. *Entrepreneurial Vocations: Learning from the Callings of Augustine, Moses, Mothers, Antigone, Oedipus, and Prospero.* Atlanta: Scholars Press, 1996.

Kroker, Arthur, and Michael A. Weinstein. *Data Trash: The Theory of the Virtual Class.* New York: St. Martin's Press, 1994.

Lanham, Richard A. *The Electronic Word: Democracy, Technology, and the Arts.* Chicago: University of Chicago Press, 1993.

Lessig, Lawrence. *Code and Other Laws of Cyberspace.* New York: Basic Books, 2000.

Levy, Stephen. *Hackers: Heroes of the Computer Revolution.* New York: Doubleday, 1984.

Lewis, C. S. *The Abolition of Man.* Nashville: Broadman & Holman, 1996.

Lochhead, David. *Shifting Realities: Information Technology and the Church.* Geneva: WCC Publications, 1997.

Locke, John L. *The De-Voicing of Society: Why We Don't Talk to Each Other Anymore.* New York: Simon & Schuster, 1998.

Lyon, David. *Jesus in Disneyland: Religion in Postmodern Times.* Cambridge: Polity Press, 2000.

MacIntyre, Alasdair. *After Virtue: A Study in Moral Theory.* Notre Dame: University of Notre Dame Press, 1984.

Madrick, Jeffrey. *The End of Affluence: The Causes and Consequences of America's Economic Dilemma.* New York: Random House, 1997.

McFadyen, Alistair I. *The Call to Personhood: A Christian Theory of the Individual in Social Relationships.* Cambridge: Cambridge University Press, 1990.

Mitcham, Carl, and Jim Grote, eds. *Theology and Technology: Essays in Christian Analysis and Exegesis*. Lanham, Md.: University Press of America, 1984.

———. *Thinking through Technology: The Path between Engineering and Philosophy*. Chicago: University of Chicago Press, 1994.

Mumford, Lewis. *The Transformations of Man*. New York: Collier Books, 1962.

Nardi, Bonnie A., and Vicki L. O'Day. *Information Ecologies: Using Technology with Heart*. Cambridge: MIT Press, 2000.

Negroponte, Nicholas. *Being Digital*. New York: Vintage Books, 1995.

Noble, David F. *The Religion of Technology: The Divinity of Man and the Spirit of Invention*. New York: Knopf, 1997.

Ong, Walter J. *The Presence of the Word: Some Prolegomena for Cultural and Religious History*. New Haven: Yale University Press, 1967.

Park, Robert E. *The Crowd and the Public and Other Essays*. Edited by Henry Elsner Jr. Translated by Charlotte Elsner. Chicago: University of Chicago Press, 1972.

Pascal, Blaise. *Pensées: Thoughts on Religion and Other Subjects*. Edited by H. S. Thayer. Translated by William Finlayson Trotter. New York: Washington Square Press, 1965.

Pelikan, Jaroslav. *The Vindication of Tradition*. New Haven: Yale University Press, 1984.

Percy, Walker. *The Message in the Bottle: How Queer Man Is, How Queer Language Is, and What One Has to Do with the Other*. New York: Picador USA, 2000.

Perkins, Anthony B., and Michael C. Perkins. *The Internet Bubble: The Overvalued World of High-Tech Stocks—and What You Need to Know to Avoid the Coming Shakeout*. New York: HarperCollins, 2001.

Peterson, Eugene H. *Subversive Spirituality*. Grand Rapids: Eerdmans, 1997.

Postman, Neil. *Technopoly: The Surrender of Culture to Technology*. New York: Vintage Books, 1992.

Putnam, Robert D. *Bowling Alone: The Collapse and Revival of American Community*. New York: Simon & Schuster, 2000.

Ramachandra, Vinoth. *Science and Technology in Christian Perspective*. Singapore: Graduates' Christian Fellowship, 1991.

Rifkin, Jeremy. *The Age of Access: The New Culture of Hypercapitalism, Where All of Life Is a Paid-for Experience*. New York: Putnam, 2000.

Robins, Kevin, and Frank Webster. *Times of Technoculture: From the Information Society to the Virtual Life*. London: Routledge, 1999.

Roemer, Michael. *Telling Stories: Postmodernism and the Invalidation of Traditional Narrative.* Lanham, Md.: Lowman and Littlefield, 1995.

Roszak, Theodore. *The Cult of Information: A Neo-Luddite Treatise on High Tech, Artificial Intelligence, and the True Art of Thinking.* Berkeley: University of California Press, 1994.

Shapiro, Andrew L. *The Control Revolution: How the Internet Is Putting Individuals in Charge and Changing the World We Know.* New York: PublicAffairs, 1999.

Shenk, David. *Data Smog: Surviving the Information Glut.* San Francisco: HarperSanFrancisco, 1998.

Sittler, Joseph. *Evocations of Grace: Writings on Ecology, Theology, and Ethics.* Edited by Steven Bouma-Prediger and Peter Bakken. Grand Rapids: Eerdmans, 2000.

Solzhenitsyn, Aleksandr I. *A World Split Apart: Commencement Address Delivered at Harvard University.* New York: Harper & Row, 1978.

Steiner, George. *Real Presences.* Chicago: University of Chicago Press, 1989.

Stoll, Clifford. *High-Tech Heretic.* New York: Anchor Books, 1999.

———. *Silicon Snake Oil: Second Thoughts on the Information Superhighway.* New York: Doubleday, 1995.

Sunstein, Cass. *republic.com.* Princeton, N.J.: Princeton University Press, 2001.

Talbott, Stephen L. *The Future Does Not Compute: Transcending the Machines in Our Midst.* Sebastopol, Calif.: O'Reilly & Associates, 1995.

Tocqueville, Alexis de. *Democracy in America.* Edited and translated by Harvey C. Mansfield and Delba Winthrop. Chicago: University of Chicago Press, 2000.

Tournier, Paul. *The Meaning of Persons.* New York: Harper & Row, 1973.

Turkle, Sherry. *Life on the Screen.* New York: Simon & Schuster, 1997.

Ullman, Ellen. *Close to the Machine: Technophilia and Its Discontents.* San Francisco: City Lights, 1997.

Valovic, Thomas S. *Digital Mythologies: The Hidden Complexities of the Internet.* New Brunswick, N.J.: Rutgers University Press, 2000.

Veith, Gene Edward Jr., and Christopher L. Stamper, *Christians in a .com World: Getting Connected without Being Consumed.* Wheaton: Crossway Books, 2000.

Virilio, Paul. *The Information Bomb.* London: Verso, 2000.

Waal, Esther de. *A Life Giving Way: A Commentary on the Rule of St. Benedict.* Collegeville, Minn.: The Liturgical Press, 1995.

Wassermann, C., R. Kirby, and B. Rordorff, eds. *The Science and Technology of Information.* Geneva: Labor Et Fides, 1992.

Weiner, Norbert. *The Human Use of Human Beings: Cybernetics and Society.* Garden City, N.J.: Double Anchor Books, 1954.

Willard, Dallas. *The Divine Conspiracy: Rediscovering Our Hidden Life in God.* San Francisco: HarperSanFrancisco, 1966.

Willinsky, John. *Technologies for Knowing: A Proposal for the Human Sciences.* Boston: Beacon Press, 1999.

Winner, Langdon. *The Whale and the Reactor: A Search for Limits in an Age of High Technology.* Chicago: University of Chicago Press, 1986.

Wolff, Michael. *Burn Rate: How I Survived the Gold Rush Years on the Internet.* New York: Simon & Schuster, 1998.

Wolterstorff, Nicholas. *Divine Discourse.* Cambridge: Cambridge University Press, 1995.

Wurman, Richard Saul. *Information Anxiety.* New York: Doubleday, 1989.

Index